AF590043

Power over Darkness:

A Journey of Self-Discovery, Trauma and Healing

By

Dr. Victoria Borg

Published by Infinity Books USA, LLC

All rights reserved

© Dr Victoria Borg

Copyright March 2022, Infinity Books USA

ISBN: 978-1-7374425-2-3

The author and publisher made every effort to make sure that the information is correct. They do not take any responsibility for any liabilities incurred by the reader or consumer for this material.

Both the author and publisher cannot be held responsible for the strategies employed by the author. Seeking professional help is highly encouraged. No part of this book may be reproduced without the publisher's prior written consent.

For more information, email Dr.VictoriaBorg.au@gmail.com

Dedication

This book is dedicated to my traumatised and resilient inner child who became both the means and the end during this journey of self-discovery. She was the beacon that lit the dark pathway which led to reclaiming her innocence and freedom.

This book is also dedicated to you, the reader and your inner child who may want to hold hands with Little Victoria during vulnerable times – especially if some aspects of my past experiences resonate with you.

Acknowledgements

I would like to thank my husband, Rosario (known as Louie), for supporting me throughout this journey. His continuous support is greatly appreciated, especially during those critical times resulting from my medical condition. He is the wind beneath my wings. Special thanks are also extended to my two children, Michelle and Mark, for being there for me when I needed them and believing in my potential. My granddaughter Monique came into my life when I was going through the healing process. I am very grateful to her for allowing me to enter her world of play and beyond. My son-in-law Louis, my extended family and so many other people who reached out to me at various times in one way or another are highly acknowledged. I would also like to acknowledge the professional people who helped me along the way through therapy and counselling as well as my academic journey.

I would like to specifically thank Prof Ron Adams. He was one of my tutors at Western Institute in 1987 when I did some short courses as preparation for tertiary studies. From the very beginning I looked up to him as a role model. He always believed in my potential and was highly supportive during my academic journey and beyond.

Finally, I would like to thank my deceased parents, Ġuseppa and Mikieli Bajada, for the gift of life.

Contents

Chapter 1
Introduction

And the end of all exploring
Will be to arrive where we started
And know the place for the first time.

—T.S. Eliot (Four Quartets, Little Gidding)

I reached the point of needing to revisit my past, or more specifically, the beginning of my inner journey of self-discovery, in 1987. On 1 August 1987, I identified a highly distressed inner child that I had been carrying, hidden from my awareness, for over thirty years. I had blocked her from my consciousness altogether, although she had tried to communicate with me in a number of ways for many years. In hindsight, I was not ready to face her because she was carrying the baggage of psychological, sexual and physical pain, as well as various related traumas.

This is what I wrote in my diary when I wanted to capture that significant moment in my life, soon after I discovered her:

Saturday, 1 August 1987
8:00 a.m.

I'm sitting on my bed, reflecting upon the events that led to yesterday's insight. I tried to console myself and change that experience to my advantage, telling myself that this was why

I had so many psychiatric problems. But then I was afraid that coming into contact with little girls three-to-five years old would be a constant reminder of myself at that age. I tried to picture my daughter Michelle at that age. Then all of a sudden, it clicked for me. When she was about that age, my fears about her facial hair were intense. I developed that fear the first time I bathed her as a newborn. Her fine facial hair reminded me of my mother. So did the way I held her while I was washing her hair. That's when panic struck and the fear emerged, which haunted me day and night for many years. From then on, I started to look at her through the eyes of fear rather than love. As she grew older, she became my scapegoat. At times I wanted to hurt her emotionally, and I became hostile towards her.

As I was reflecting on how I have been treating Michelle, a fantasy I had for many years came to mind. In that fantasy, I used to see myself as a schoolteacher walking down the corridor of the school, holding a folder in my hands. As I approached the classroom, I saw a little girl sitting on the floor outside with her face down on her bent knees. She was greatly distressed. I would attend to her and did not see myself in the classroom. As that fantasy came to mind while I was sitting on the bed, I realised that the distressed little girl outside the classroom in my fantasy was ME! That's when I broke down crying. I cried and cried on my bed for quite some time. I felt this was a special moment in my life. **This is a moment of triumph!**

The genie was out of the bottle now, and there was no way that she could go back. Indeed, within hours I reached a point of no return and wanted to find out why this little girl was so distressed. I wanted to find the truth and the 'real self'. I had no idea of the rabbit hole that lay ahead of me, both in terms of the journey and the further painful insights I would subsequently have over the years. Within a few days, as I started slipping down into depression and acute panic attacks,

I knew I needed to undertake a journey of recovery and healing to face my demons and free myself from the bondage that had enslaved me for so many years. I needed to bring this distressed inner child out of her hiding place, allow her to communicate with me and let me know what had happened to her, embrace her and help her grow and shine. From the beginning, I had the determination to do it. I needed to convince and reassure my husband Louie, my two children, Michelle and Mark, and my eldest sister Mary that this was not an illness but a recovery – at least, that was how I described it at the time.

I embarked on an intensive self-analysis, which I recorded in my handwritten diary for about fifteen years. In this memoir I am focusing on the first five months or so. I will be taking the reader on a journey not only of psychological pain and suffering but also of vulnerability, strength and resilience, as well as insights into the chaotic inner world and mind of a highly mentally disturbed person as I navigated through this critical time. I will show the reader how I managed to disentangle the confusing threads of contradictory thoughts and emotions that kept criss-crossing and eventually brought order to my chaotic inner world. In doing so, I also identified various selves that had lives of their own. In spite of all that, I managed to keep a sense of wholeness.

Although I consider my case to be unique, I believe my story resonates with many people in one way or another. Feelings of loneliness, alienation, abandonment, betrayal, rejection, loss and fear are common to the human experience. However, many times such feelings become pathological and interfere with our lives. This is more likely to happen if there is a lack of support and resources, as well as a lack of understanding of the underlying issues. In many cases, unresolved traumas (including intergenerational traumas) are embedded in such experiences.

When I embarked on this journey of self-discovery, I had to attend to the needs of my children and my husband, including assuring them that this experience was not a sickness, even though it could have easily been classified as such if I had not known what was happening (at least at one level), and if I had not been willing to be open and receptive to the painful journey and the unknown. The fact that I used this inner journey constructively by embarking on an intensive study of myself provided me with another purpose for going down this horrendous yet highly promising path. It also gave me a sense of a future and hope that I would pull through it.

This journey started with a lot of strength as well as vulnerability. Indeed, within a short period of time, I identified a self that had many positive traits. Some weeks after I discovered the distressed inner child, I even went through a period of about nine days of 'elation' when I experienced inner freedom and joie de vivre – something I had never experienced before. However, when it was over and I started slipping into the throes of depression, I could not feel that strength, and many times I felt I was losing not only the battle against mental illness but also the war. In addition, there was a self that was weak and vulnerable to my inner forces, and it required considerable inner work to help her get strong. That self, which had a life of its own, needed a lot of nurturing along the way.

Vitorja Sultana

Ġuseppe Sultana

Ġuseppe and Karmena Bajada

Ġuseppa and Mikieli Bajada

Chapter 2

The Maltese Islands: Growing up in the 1950's and 1960's

To gain an understanding of some of the complexities of my inner world, including my weaknesses and strengths, it is important to provide an overview of the personal, cultural and social background of my childhood and highlight some aspects of it.

I was born in 1952 in the village of Xagħra, on the island of Gozo, which is part of the Maltese archipelago. My parents, Ġuseppa and Mikieli, had been married for some years when I was born and already had three children – two daughters and a son (born in 1949, 1950 and 1951 respectively). Eventually I would have two younger brothers. The youngest died at birth. My youngest brother was born in 1954. My older sister Carmen died in 1961 when she was eleven years old. We lived off the land, as my father did not have a regular paid job, and there was no social or financial support or benefits – except that twice a year we were entitled to some 'Care' through which we could get butter, cheese and flour that had been donated by the American government. We used to sell some dry cheese and few dozen eggs twice a week. My mother also managed to earn a few shillings by hand washing clothes for a couple of families. Occasionally my father worked in a quarry for some weeks. We also had some money which my father saved when he was working in Australia before he got married.

My mother was a traditional Maltese housewife with minimal education. She could read and write in Maltese just enough to get by. Her father had died from natural causes when she was only fourteen years old. I remember my mother reminiscing about his death. Whenever she spoke of it, I could see that there was still a lot of unresolved grief. Although my grandmother lived until I was about fourteen years old, I hardly know anything about her family, including my grandfather. According to one of the neighbours, my maternal grandfather, Ġuseppe, never called my grandmother, Vitorja, by her name! To me, that says a lot about interpersonal relationships and connectedness (or lack of it). It also explains, at least in part, why my mother was such a hostile person, especially when we were growing up.

My father was born and raised in the same neighbourhood as my mother. He was illiterate. He migrated to Australia and stayed in Sydney, returning to Malta before the outbreak of World War II. He never spoke about his experiences in Australia, except for mentioning Paramatta. He had a photo taken at a studio during his stay in Australia. We kept this photo in a showcase in the bedroom upstairs. He married my mother in 1946.

His father, Ġuseppe, died in 1947, soon after my sister Mary was born. His mother, my grandmother, Karmena, was about ninety-three years old when she died. Although we lived in the same house, I do not remember much about her. Like my maternal grandmother, my father and his mother hardly spoke about the family history, and we never bothered to ask questions. I know she had some sisters still living in the house where she grew up, on the other side of the village. I remember visiting them when I was little. I do not remember whom I went with. One of her sisters used to come to our house for a visit occasionally.

Knowing what I do now, it is not surprising that the family history, both maternal and paternal, was such a taboo. Incest, children 'sold' for sexual abuse, promiscuity, satanic practices and infanticide were happening in the neighbourhood. And my family, especially on my father's side, was not exempt from it. This came as quite a shock to me when I found it out later in life through my journey of self-discovery.

Malta had a strong culture of secrecy. As gossip and the code of honour and shame were characteristic of traditional Maltese culture, any deviance from cultural values, attitudes and beliefs had to be strongly protected *li taqa' fil-ilsien in-nies* (in case one becomes the subject of gossip). It is also possible that certain deviances were so common that at one level they became another norm, and people would not talk about them: *għax kulħadd għandu xi jxomm* (everyone has something to smell). So, it was like 'No one knows but everybody knows.'

When I was growing up, the village of Xagħra, like most other villages, was still highly traditional and rural. Some houses, including ours, did not have electricity or tap water. Kerosene lamps and lanterns were quite common. Public water taps were scattered around the streets for people to use for drinking and cooking. Many people had a well in the house. In one of the streets in my neighbourhood, there was a well for nearby members of the community. Many people were full-time peasants. Unless you had a profession or worked with the government, there were hardly any job opportunities besides working in a quarry or building houses. Many families (including mine) lived off the land, especially if the husband did not have a paid job, making sure that they had certain vegetables, such as potatoes, onions and garlic lasted for a whole year. Having animals, such as sheep, cows, rabbits and a donkey as well as poultry was quite common for such families. Homemade cheese, tomato paste, sun dried tomatoes, marinated olives, pickled onions and capers, homemade wine and dried figs were found in every household living off the land. It's also important to point out it was quite common for women to work in the fields, including housewives, spinsters and widows.

Agricultural tools were still traditional. Ploughing using a donkey or horse, digging, sowing and harvesting using tools that dated from centuries past were common. Thrashing machines were used to thrash the wheat and separate the grain from the stalks and husks. Water from wells in the fields was used for irrigation. It was not uncommon for farmers to share a well with others. Windmills were sometimes used to pump out the water from the wells. In certain areas, water from an underground spring, known as *mina*, was also used for irrigation by nearby members of the community.

The Maltese archipelago is a number of small islands strategically located in the Mediterranean Sea. Malta and Gozo are the main islands of habitation. Malta is twenty-seven kilometres long and fourteen and a half kilometres wide and currently is the home to some 400,000 plus people. Malta is eighty kilometres south of Sicily and 284 kilometres north of Tunisia on the north coast of Africa. This location has made Malta important in any shipping and trade on the Mediterranean Sea for centuries.

The history of Malta, which dates back to about 5200 BC, in the prehistoric times, was (and still is) an integral part of our life. The Neolithic Temples, including the *Ġgantija Temples* in our village were a constant reminder of that era.

Throughout the centuries were many historical events that influenced and shaped the Maltese as a people. Malta was ruled by the Phoenicians, Carthaginians, Romans, Byzantines, Normans, Spaniards, Arabs and Kingdom of Sicily before it was given to the Knights of St John. It was under the protection of the Knights that Malta faced her greatest challenge. The Great Siege of Malta in 1565 against the Turks was pivotal for not just Malta, but all Christendom. Suliman the Magnificent, ruler of the Ottoman Empire, and grandson to Sultan Mehmed II, who had conquered Byzantium, wanted the Maltese archipelago in order to control all shipping in the eastern Mediterranean, and much of Europe. The Knights Hospitaller, the Order of St John, had been expelled from Rhodes by Suliman many years before and were given the Maltese Islands as their home base. These two enemies battled from May to September. The Knights were led by their Grand Master De La Vallette who had been on Rhodes when Suliman expelled them. It was a great battle of wits, strategy, grit, determination and faith: Christianity versus Islam.

Malta and the Knights finally won the battle, changing forever the balance of Christian and Muslim worlds. If Suliman had won, the door to all Europe would have been opened and conquest would have followed easily. The Knights ruled Malta until they began to be abusive, and the Maltese sought to get out from under the yoke of their oppression. It was at this time they invited the French under Napoleon Bonaparte to rule. This occupation was short lived, as Bonaparte and his soldiers looted the islands to help fund his wars. The British were invited to help them rid the islands of the French. Malta remained a British protectorate until the 1970's when independence was granted. Plans for independence from the British were in the works for many years, however at the outbreak of WWII everything was put on hold. Hitler had his eye on Malta, again as the gateway in all shipping and control of the Mediterranean Sea. Malta became the most bombed place on earth as the Italians and Nazis bombarded the island for two long years hoping to bring her to her knees. Hitler failed. The British left Malta formally in September 1979, and Malta began home rule.

When I was growing up, Malta was still a traditional and patriarchal society. Traditional values, attitudes and beliefs grounded in Catholicism were strongly upheld. Religion based on the teachings of the Catholic Church dates as far back as 60 A D when St Paul was shipwrecked on the island on his way to Rome. This event is documented in the Bible. With the coming of the Order of the Knights of St John to Malta in 1530 and their stay till 1798, the Catholic Church was highly consolidated. The iron hand of the Spanish Inquisition also left a horrendous imprint upon Malta and its people. Indeed, even during the 1950's and 1960's, fear tactics were still predominant. Many churches and chapels were built on the Maltese islands over the years, as well as niches with various statues of God, Our Lady and the Saints on the facades of houses.

The Catholic Church continued to predominate even after the Knights of St John left Malta with the occupation of the French during the Napoleonic Wars in 1798. Its dominance was further perpetuated during the British colonisation of the island in 1800. In the 1950's and 1960's it maintained a strong hold on its people and dominated all aspects of life. Strict adherence to religious values, attitudes and beliefs was considered the norm. Any attempt to deviate from the church and its teachings was inconceivable. Coercive techniques, such as the fear of God, condemnation and the fire of hell were common. These were reinforced through holy pictures and paintings depicting the fire of hell and purgatory. The notion of the devil as the embodiment of all evil was prevalent. The devil was believed to manifest itself in subtle and sometimes not-so-subtle ways, ranging from having 'bad thoughts' to any other evil acts that went against the Ten Commandments and the teachings of the church. Statues and paintings of the Archangel Michael in his suit of armour, with a shield in one hand and a sword stabbing the devil at his feet, were also common.

To understand the extent of the notion of evil, its association with the devil and its influence on individual members of the community (including myself), it is important to look at the history of paganism in Malta, which dates back many centuries. Indeed, there are many artifacts related to witchcraft and pagan relics at the Inquisitor's Palace at Birgu. These were confiscated by the Church. The evil eye, *seħta* (curse) and *it-tbaħħir* (a smoking ritual) were deeply embedded in Maltese culture. For this ritual, people would burn a small part of olive branch with a handful of salt in an old saucepan and go around each room while holding the smoking olive branch and saying specific prayers to ward off the evil spirits. *It- tbaħħir* was no longer commonly practiced when I was growing up. However, I vaguely remember my maternal grandmother, Vitorja, practicing it. One member of her extended family had the nickname *Tas-Seħta* (those who curse). As children, older people used to threaten us with *Jiġu tas-setta għalik* (people that belong to a sect will come for you). The sect in question was the Freemasons, who came to Malta through British colonisation and the subsequent settlement.

When the concept of the devil was introduced by the Catholic Church, the idea of an evil spirit was thereby perpetuated through the devil. When I was growing up, a religious society known as The Society of Christian Doctrine (M.U.S.E.U.M) started to establish itself in our village. The notion of the devil was at the core of its teachings, together with the incarnate Jesus. Indeed, the words *Verbum Dei Caro Factum Est* (Word of God Made Flesh) were on the badge worn by the members. These words were supposed to 'keep the devil away' – or so we were told! The female members of this society used to wear long black clothes, black stockings and black shoes. They also wore the black *għonella* (a traditional form of women's headdress and shawl or hooded cloak). They had an austere demeanour.

The great devotion that people had towards God, Our Lady and the Saints was apparent and entrenched in their lives. I remember taking part in pilgrimages to the sanctuary dedicated to Our Lady of *Ta' Pinu* at the village of Għarb and another church dedicated to the *Madonna tal-Karmnu* (Our Lady of *Karmnu*) on the outskirts of the village. Although Our Lady is perceived as one deity, there were (and still are) numerous Our Ladies – Our Lady of Victories, Our Lady of *Ta' Pinu*, Our Lady of the Rosary, Our Lady of the Tears (*Il-Madonna tad-Dmugħ*), Our Lady of the Way (*Il-Madonna tat-Trieq*), Our Lady of Loreto (*Il-Madonna ta' Loreto*), Our Lady of Sorrows (*Id-Duluri*), etc. Each one was highly specific and had a unique place in people's hearts, minds and souls.

Intertwined with devotion was a great sense of spirituality that dates back to the Neolithic Age (3600–2500 BC). The abovementioned temples at Ġgantija are a testament to that. These are enormous megalithic structures of two adjacent temples, one older than the other. Archaeologists believe that they were probably used for the worship of the Earth Mother goddess by a fertility cult. One of the temples faces southeast. A large stone block with a recess at this temple's entrance suggests that a purification process took place before entering. The altars inside this temple indicate that animals, most likely goats, sheep and pigs, were sacrificed.

I remember going to the fields adjacent to these temples and being impressed with the enormity of the stones. The old lady who owned some of those fields used to say that a giant had carried those stones. The word Ġgantija in Maltese means giantess. At the time, I did not know their significance, because they were not looked after by the authorities. It was when I was at primary school that I started to get some idea of what they were all about. Once I did, I became attracted to them.

As the primary agent for socialisation, the Maltese family generated, perpetuated and transmitted values, morals and beliefs that were traditional and consistent with those of the Catholic Church. Babies were baptised within days of birth. Indeed, the mother did not attend the baptism because she would still be recuperating. It was also common for the baby to be presented to Our Lady. In Gozo, the presentation was usually to Our Lady of *Ta' Pinu*.

Growing up, children were constantly reminded of a chastising God and his watchful eye, ready to punish them with the fire of hell at every undesirable, unacceptable or naughty act. The adage *Il-Bambin jiġi jaħarqek bin-nar* (Jesus will come and burn you with the fire) was colloquial among parents and adults in the community. The preparation for the Sacraments of First Holy Communion and Confirmation was quite intense at preschools, which were usually run by the nuns. The introduction to stories from the Bible, Jesus, God and his love, sin, offending God, absolution from sins through the Sacrament of Confession and repentance were all part of the preparation for these sacraments, which were received at six years of age.

Going to church to hear mass every day and going for confession at least once a week was the norm. So was the daily recitation of the Rosary and other prayers. These focused mostly on protection (both spiritual and non-spiritual) and intercession through Our Lady and the Saints with regard to specific prayers, such as for the sick, mercy, repentance and the repose of the souls of the dead. Children were encouraged to attend catechism classes at least once a week, in addition to daily religious instruction at school. Like the adults, many children, including myself, wore a brown scapular with the image of Our Lady holding baby Jesus or the miraculous medals under their outer clothing for spiritual protection.

Another institution that had a great influence on me was school and the education system. Back in the 1950's local nuns ran the preschools. Usually, children attended classes for about two years. As mentioned above, a significant component of these classes was religious instructions and the preparation for the Sacraments of Holy Communion and Confirmation. There was also an introduction to English language and counting. Students started primary school at five years of age. Boys and girls attended different schools. There was a strong focus on reading, writing and arithmetic. Religion played a significant role in education, with daily prayers, religious teachings and attending mass once a month as a school. The Maltese language was also taught at school. Since Malta was under British rule, most textbooks were in English. In those days secondary education was not compulsory. Students who wanted to further their studies were required to sit for an entrance examination. Secondary school went up to Form V leading to a General Certificate of Education from Oxford University or London University, with the exceptions for Maltese and Religion. The certificates for the latter subjects were issued from the University of Malta. Students who wanted to further their education were required to attend Form V1 and get certificates in some subjects at Advanced Level.

Chapter 3

Overview of My Life in Australia

In April 1972, a month after I got married, I migrated to Australia with Louie, who had been living there since migrating with his family in 1951. We came by ship. The voyage took thirty-four days.

We lived with my mother-in-law, Maria, and her two sons in North Sunshine, where many Maltese migrants had settled after World War II. For me, it was like a second home. There were many Maltese people living in the area, including the priests who ran St Bernadette's Church and the nuns just around the corner from our house. Louie's family warmly embraced me. Most of his married siblings lived in the same neighbourhood.

A few weeks after arriving in Australia, I found out that I was pregnant. This was a surprise, as I was intending to further my studies, and I felt disappointed. Unfortunately, this was compounded by my husband's verbal and emotional abuse, which took place behind closed doors. Louie was an ex-serviceman who had been on the front line during the Vietnam War. We got married within nine months of his discharge from the army.

Soon after our daughter Michelle was born, I became obsessed with a particular fear, namely that her fine facial hair would develop into a beard, and she would look like a monster. As much as I loved her, part of me was finding it difficult to bond with her. Indeed, it was only during the night that I managed to spend some time gazing comfortably at her as she slept peacefully in the bassinet. She was so cute. She looked like Shirley Temple, with curly hair and rosy cheeks.

When Michelle was fifteen months old, I became pregnant with Mark – once again a surprise. This was difficult for me to come to terms with. When he was six months old, I decided to go to work and ended up working in a clothing factory as a plain machinist.

In 1975 we moved to our newly built house in St Albans – the beginning of quite another chapter of my life. I soldiered on as a traditional housewife and mother. Louie was working two jobs – one full-time and one part-time – as I was no longer in a position to go to work once Michelle started school.

After Michelle did her First Holy Communion in 1981, I started experiencing bouts of depression and anxiety attacks. I went to my doctor, and I confided to him the fear that had haunted me for so many years, which I had thus far kept to myself. I showed him a photo of Michelle, and he assured me that I had nothing to fear. She looked quite normal to him. I told Louie about that fear, and he was relieved because he thought there was something more serious that I had been keeping from him.

My situation got worse, and I ended up spending six weeks in a mental hospital. This was a difficult time not only for me but also for the family. Michelle and Mark stayed with my sister Mary and her family. Once, when my sister brought them over to the hospital to visit me, I was in such a bad state, overridden by guilt and a sense of not being worthy to be their mother, that I told them not to call me Mum anymore! As soon as they left, I regretted what I had said. I waited till they got home and then rang them up to apologise. It is still heartbreaking to think about, even after all these years!

Before I was discharged, I was given the opportunity to see a psychologist on a weekly basis. However, I did not want to commit to this, as I was not confident in using public transport to get to my sessions. Also, at the time I did not know what psychotherapy was all about, or how I would benefit from of it. No one explained it to me, and I did not bother to ask.

When Michelle was about ten years old, she developed a phobia of spiders. She was referred to the Child Psychiatry Unit at a local hospital, and we had a family interview with Dr. Garcia. After a brief family history, he suggested that I undergo therapy with him, while Michelle would see another therapist. I agreed. Again, I had no idea what therapy was about, or how it was going to help. I saw Dr Garcia once a week. Later, I found out he was a psychoanalyst. For more than four years, I felt that I did not achieve anything from this therapy in terms of insights.

The year 1987 was a significant year for me. Indeed, it is the year that made me. It is when I started questioning my direction in life. As a married woman with a husband and two children, I strongly felt that there was still a vacuum within me, and I was far from satisfied with life. As I questioned my direction in life, it became clear to me that I wanted to extend my horizons and go beyond the roles of the traditional wife and mother.

This time coincided with the opening of the Western Institute at the suburb where I live. With great hesitation, I attended a meeting for prospective mature students returning to study at the tertiary level. I enrolled in three courses – Preparation for

Tertiary Studies, Speaking Up and Childhood across Culture.

Halfway through these courses, I had an insight into my psychological problems, namely that I am a victim of incest. This set me on an unprecedented, painful inner journey of self-discovery. Within a few days of this insight, I had a strong urge to use this experience constructively and started a diary. This ended up being more than just a diary. It was also an intensive study of my chaotic inner world. I became highly analytical of what I was experiencing, and I made a conscious decision to study the mechanisms of the mind and the realm of negative emotions of someone experiencing mental illness.

While I was still doing the abovementioned courses, I started experiencing a strong inner conflict. Although I wanted to go forward and return to study at the tertiary level, another part of me wanted to go backwards and explore where I was coming from. As mentioned in the Introduction, I had what I called at the beginning of this journey a 'fantasy'. I can now confidently say that it was a *premonition*, as I successfully completed my tertiary studies, including my Doctorate of Philosophy, and I was also a tutor and lecturer at the same institution for many years. I had that premonition for some years, and it came to the forefront before I started these courses. Within days after the insight that I am a victim of incest, I realised who that little girl was. It was in fact my inner child, who needed to be heard, as she had quite a story to tell. She also needed a lot of nurturing along the way.

Across St Albans Road where I used to get this fantasy, there was a railway running parallel to the road. A few metres away from the railway line was some vacant land. This is the land on which the Western Institute, which later became Victoria University, was built in 1987.

After successfully completing the short courses and applying for the Bachelor of Arts, I was offered a place to start my degree in 1988. However, because of the deplorable state I was in, I was not able to accept. Deferring my tertiary studies was extremely disappointing and heartbreaking. However, in spite of my deferment, I continued with the intensive study of myself, feeling strongly that something unique was going to come out of it, which would add to the body of knowledge about mental illness and beyond. As I experienced acute depression and intense panic attacks, I also tried to convince my general practitioner and my psychoanalyst that this was *not* an illness but a process I needed to go through for my recovery.

I had a history of mental illness. It started when I was about fifteen years of age and still living in Malta. I had a psychological breakdown and could not cope with my studies or everyday life. I became highly scrupulous; in other words, extremely conscientious about my actions and thoughts, because no matter how trivial they were, to me they were a 'sin'. For example, if I saw or used a lipstick and associated it with a dog's penis, I would be overridden with a guilty conscience and have to confess it. The general practitioner identified this as a sign of mental illness. My mother, like so many other people, thought that my illness was because I spent a lot of time studying, as I was a highly ambitious student at secondary school. Luckily, that breakdown did not last for long, and I was able to continue with my life.

After that, I managed to get through life reasonably well. However, in hindsight I would say that I experienced chronic depression until 1981, when I had an acute psychological breakdown and was in a psychiatric hospital for six weeks.

After discharge, I was able to soldier on and continue with my life, even weaning myself from medication, and I ended up relying completely on my inner resources for some years. In 1987, when I arrived at a crossroads and wanted to extend my boundaries, I certainly rocked the boat. As mentioned above, this coincided with my insight that I was a victim of incest and the subsequent discovery of a highly traumatised inner little girl that I had blocked from my consciousness for so many years.

In 1988 I was offered a place at Western Institute. As I was not in a position to start my degree, I ended up deferring for two years. In 1990 I started my Bachelor of Arts at Western Institute on a part-time basis. This was quite challenging for me, not only because I was still on the painful journey of self-discovery but also because I was the first person in my family to go beyond primary school. I came from Malta, a highly traditional country. I had to break that glass ceiling to move beyond my traditional roles.

Psychology was one of my major subjects as an undergraduate. In spite of the continuous personal challenges that I faced due to my inner journey of self-discovery, I did well and ended up with First Class Honours Degree. I applied for the highly competitive Postgraduate Award. I ended up winning that award, through which I did my doctorate degree while working as a sessional tutor. My thesis was about the life satisfaction of adolescents across cultures.

In 2000, while still working on my doctoral thesis, I slipped into acute depression and needed to take some time off. For about two months, I could not only not get any relief but also experienced full-blown anxiety attacks. Many times I felt that I was not only losing the battle against mental illness but also the war. Eventually I admitted myself to Sunshine Psychiatric Hospital. As a last resort, I agreed to have electroconvulsive therapy (ECT). I had reached the point where I was ready to do anything to elevate my acute state of depression. This was very hard for me to undergo, especially the last treatment. Apparently, I cried a lot during the treatment, while I was under general anaesthetic. I was told so by one of the nurses who attended to me. She added, 'You must have had lots of trauma in your childhood.'

A week after I finished the ECT, I was discharged from hospital. I was still quite frail, both physically and psychologically. Soon after I was discharged, I discovered that the ECT had affected my memory. As my leave of absence from my academic commitment was nearing an end, I started to work on my thesis, only to find that my reading and concentration skills were at a very low ebb. At first it startled me. However, with a strong determination to keep going, I gradually retaught myself academic skills, including reading skills. I began this process a week after my discharge from hospital. It was a tough road, but eventually I started to pick up again. I even went to work at the university, which once again helped me to regain my confidence. I finally earned my Doctorate of Philosophy in 2005.

As an academic, I was passionate about my work. I committed myself wholeheartedly to the students and to Victoria University, which had played a significant role in broadening my horizons. However, I could see that there was still a vacuum in my life. Many times I tried to start writing, both academic and non-academic books. But I did not get far, as various parts of myself came to the forefront – all wanting to have a voice. I was also not ready to revisit my inner journey of self-discovery, as it was too painful for me.

In 2010 I started a painstaking process to give myself a voice and fight for justice. As an academic I was subjected to bullying, both horizontally and vertically. I went through the internal procedures to deal with it. This was a tough process, through which I was subjected to further bullying, especially through the writing of the report I received by one of the investigators. This was highly traumatic for me. At the same time, it spurred me to keep going. I believed that if, as an academic, I was not heard and even suppressed, what chance did students have if they lodged complaints? I was determined to fight for justice, even though I suspected I would lose my job as a result. Indeed, in 2013 the university terminated my employment without providing any reason – even though I was a prospective employee.

Although I was not surprised by this, it was still a big blow for me and affected me at a deep personal level. I was highly traumatised, both by the process and by the way my academic journey came to an end. The institution that had a duty of care towards me turned against me. I experienced feelings of betrayal and abandonment and went through quite a grieving process. I felt that the university had breached the Fair Work Act in a number of ways. As I was determined to exercise my workplace rights, I started a case with the Federal Court in 2014. I represented myself, since I could not afford legal help. The hearing took place in 2015 and lasted for five days.

As I was in the witness box, I felt enormous inner strength. I was composed and handled the experience extremely well. My inner child was very much in the forefront, and I took her with me into the court room – the same inner child that had been frightened to speak up for so many years was really shining. I was wearing a gold ring on the little finger on my left hand – the ring that I had as a child. The day following my experience in the witness box, I noticed that it had cut open with the energy that came out of me, but it stayed on my finger until I noticed it!

Although I did not win the case, I felt proud of myself. As I said in the witness box, 'Having had the opportunity to give myself a voice, I already feel I am a winner – irrespective of the outcome.' The court case will always be another significant achievement in my life. I provided a precedent for others to take on such academic institutions and fight for justice.

In 2016 I reached another crossroads, as I started questioning my direction in life once again. By that time, I was no longer an academic. The election for the local government was coming up, and after lots of soul-searching, I realised that the time had come for me to give back to the community. I wanted to represent the community and bring its voice to the chamber where important decisions are made. I became a candidate and was elected, thereby opening another chapter of my life.

This was a highly satisfying role. However, I could see that I was still avoiding revisiting my experiences and journey of self-discovery through the volumes of diaries that I started in 1987. I had always wanted to write a book about it, but I kept it on the back burner for all these years. I dreaded the idea of going back to the diaries.

Towards the end of 2020, I did more soul-searching, as once again I reached a crossroads and started questioning my direction in life. This was a difficult and challenging time for me, as I spent a lot of time introspecting and chipping off further layers of the image of myself that I was still carving, while lying helplessly in bed for hours on end. I even had to deal with my own mortality. Indeed, for about two months I had a strong feeling that I was going to die by suicide. It was a critical time for me. However, I had an understanding of what was happening. The suicide I was facing was *not* in relation to a physical death, but rather a virtual/psychological one. In other words, I needed to 'die' in order to rise again from the ashes with a renewed spirit.

By February 2021 I could clearly see where I was heading and the path that I needed to take to find the seat of my soul – the centre of my being. This is the place where the traumatised little girl had resided while being protected from the inner dark forces that turned against her. She had not been in a position to face and deal with them for so many years. That protective place was also a hiding place. She was hiding from her own self. Although she wanted to stay in hiding, she also wanted to come out and reveal herself. As such, she became both the end and the means of this self-discovery.

This prospective pathway was and is the convergence of the respective pathways of my inner child and adult selves and the telling of their story through the written word. Through this journey I will be sharing with the reader the invaluable knowledge I gained along the way, the battles I had to fight, the subsequent pain and suffering I had to endure and last but not least the courage, strength and resilience I demonstrated to get where I am today.

In my inner journey I had to go through extremely dangerous terrain. Many times, I was bombarded by the inner dark forces from all angles. Such terrain included the crossing of a desert, during which I had to fight all elements, feeling terribly exhausted. I came out of the desert some years ago. Far away, I could see a beautiful castle that was very much within reach. Although the path ahead appeared to be smooth, I could not walk towards it, mostly because I was far too exhausted to do so. I was still not ready to go down that path, even though the beautiful castle looked promising. I could not bear the thought of accessing the diary entries that I started in 1987 and revisiting this period of my life to write about it.

As the diary entries included in this memoir indicate, one of the challenges I faced during my inner journey of self-discovery was the fragmented self and the different 'personalities' I had to deal with along the way. One of the selves was my traumatised inner child, who had a voice and needed to be heard.

Although now there is a fine line between my inner child and the adult self, I am mindful that I will be walking down this path together with my inner child as we head towards this enchanting castle. Although there are times when I still feel hesitant about it, I have the will and determination to walk down this path, and I look at it as an adventure with a sense of excitement, while being open and receptive to any wonderful places I may encounter along the way.

I believe that although the path ahead of me may seem smooth, there is still a demon I need to fight along the way. There are still hidden pitfalls that can be quite dangerous. To some degree, this pit is the abyss that I found myself in so many times while battling mental illness. In the past, while in the abyss, I felt I was losing not only the battle against mental illness but also the war. Not only that, when eventually I came out of the abyss, I would find myself at 'ground zero' – with lots of destruction around me. Picking myself up and continuing with my life was tough, to say the least. Many times I felt I was walking on hot ashes. But as time went on, I managed to build stepping-stones that enabled me to soldier on.

Knowing myself as well as I do, if I fall into this pit now, it takes me a few days to get out of it, whereas it used to take me months. I do not need to experience the fear of losing my mind and losing the war against mental illness – a fear that haunted me so much along the way. And that is quite encouraging. Moreover, whenever I stumble and fall, I now have more skills to pick myself up, dust off my clothes and continue with this leg of my journey.

My inner child will take centre stage in writing my personal story. This is an opportunity to give her a voice and empower her with the power of the pen. Most importantly, she can now tell her story from a secure space where she is responsive rather than reactive. It is also a space where she is experiencing unconditional love and does not have to fear anything – including speaking up, shame, guilt, rejection and abandonment. She has now completed a full circle from the time I discovered her in 1987 till the time I started writing this book in 2020. So has the adult self. We are more or less on the same wavelength and have come to where we started – much stronger, with a better understanding of what happened in the past and highly compassionate towards the people that hurt her.

As part of this journey, I will be sharing some of my diary entries, which I handwrote in 1987 and 1988. I will be omitting certain parts that are highly detailed with regard to the intensive study of myself. I will also include the times of the entries as recorded in the diaries. Among other things, this indicates how unstable and unpredictable I was. The names of the people mentioned are not their real names – except those of my immediate family, Ron Adams, Mary, Freddie, Charles, Alex, Irene, Craig, Samantha, Ms Farrugia, Ms Natalina Sultana, Ms Carmen Rapa and Ġuseppa ta' Lażru. In conclusion, I will draw together a number of themes and expand on them using the knowledge that I gained as I continued with my inner journey for about a decade, introspecting and writing volumes of diaries and love letters to my inner child and my deceased parents.

Little Victoria

Chapter 4

The Blue Pimpernel

I had never written a diary before. I started this one in 1987, when I had an insight into my mental health-related problems. Indeed, within twenty-four hours I got the urge to start writing this diary. And almost immediately, I could see that it would play a critical role in my inner journey of self-discovery and beyond.

Thursday, 30 July 1987
4:00 p.m.

Earlier today, one of my sisters-in-law had an intimate conversation with me about her experiences as a child, as we sat in the car outside my house after returning from a shopping trip. She told me how she ended up a victim of incest after migrating to Australia when she was fourteen years old. It was not the first time she has told me about it. I was quite familiar with her personal story. However, this time it kept going through my mind, even after I went inside the house. While I was unpacking the groceries in the kitchen, something clicked as if a light bulb went on. I was feeling poised and calm. A question went through my mind: Am I a victim of incest? As soon as I asked myself that question, all hell broke loose. My heart rate escalated, my head started going fuzzy and I kept saying 'Oh my God' as I sat in a chair, holding on to the kitchen table. At the same time, another part of me felt composed and calm – as if that self had known all along. I felt like two selves in one body!

The self that felt like she knew faded away, and I was left to pick up the pieces. The sand at the bottom of a glass bottle full of water had been shaken. The genie was out of the bottle. There was no turning back. I soon realised that I was a victim of incest.

Friday, 31 July 1987
2:30 a.m.

I had a conversation with Louie, explaining to him the factors that led me to that conclusion – the fantasy that I had about a penis as a child – the penis was detachable and was stored in this hole in a wall, next to the heap of manure that my father used to keep to dry up after cleaning the barns. The roaming chickens used to lay eggs in that hole, and I would go and collect them. I also had a vivid dream that I was milking the venom out of snakes, which frightened me so much. Indeed, I have always had a phobia of snakes, even though the snakes in Malta were not poisonous.

11:00 a.m.

I had a conversation with my sister on the phone, giving her an account of what had happened – my insight into being a victim of incest and how I had started to connect some dots. I also spoke about my father's neurosis and his obsessive fear about a specific wall collapsing. This wall overlooked the backyard of one of our neighbours. I mentioned how sleazy my father had been. He used to make comments about this particular girl who lived in the neighbourhood – that she was his girlfriend. Even my sister remembered that.

2:00 p.m.

In spite of the state of shock I'm in, I feel like I'm being born again.

5:00 p.m.
I made an appointment with my psychoanalyst.

Saturday, 1 August 1987
8:00 a.m.

I'm sitting on my bed, reflecting upon the events that led to yesterday's insight. I tried to console myself and change that experience to my advantage, telling myself that this was why I had so many psychiatric problems. But then I was afraid that coming into contact with little girls three-to-five years old would be a constant reminder of myself at that age. I tried to picture my daughter Michelle at that age. Then, all of a sudden, it clicked for me. When she was about that age, my fears about her facial hair were intense. I developed that fear the first time I bathed her as a newborn. Her fine facial hair reminded me of my mother. So did the way I held her while I was washing her hair. That's when panic struck and the fear emerged, which haunted me day and night for many years. From then on, I started to look at her through the eyes of fear rather than love. As she grew older, she became my scapegoat. At times I wanted to hurt her emotionally, and I became hostile towards her.

As I was reflecting on how I have been treating Michelle, a fantasy I had for many years came to mind. In that fantasy, I used to see myself as a schoolteacher walking down the corridor of the school, holding a folder in my hands. As I approached the classroom, I saw a little girl sitting on the floor outside with her face down on her bent knees. She was greatly distressed. I would attend to her and did not see myself in the classroom. As that fantasy came to mind while I was sitting on the bed, I realised that the distressed little girl outside the classroom in my fantasy was ME! That's when I broke down crying. I cried and cried on my bed for quite some time. I felt this was a special moment in my life. **This is a moment of triumph!**

3:00 p.m.

Rang up my psychoanalyst at home.

11:00 p.m.

Had an intimate conversation with Louie – him lying down in bed and me sitting beside him – giving him an account of my day's findings.

Sunday, 2 August 1987
10:30 a.m.

The sun is shining as if even nature wants to celebrate my freedom. I feel like I have broken the chain of bondage that kept me in captivity for all these years, depriving me of peace within myself – peace I have been yearning to find for so long.

That little broken-hearted girl I discovered yesterday gave me her final stamp of approval, which justified my conclusion that by the age of five I was already a very distressed little girl, who felt so alienated from everyone around her. She fell in love with the beauty of nature that surrounded her – nature, the only thing that gave me reciprocal love by making me feel so contented, with the exception of 'harmless' snakes, which seemed to follow me wherever I went.

Monday, 3 August 1987
12:20 a.m.

Just woke up after having a nightmare. I dreamt that I was a little girl going to the fields on the way to Ramla Bay. I was chased by a slave who had a lethal weapon – a *minġel* – in his hands. I started running, and another slave joined in the chase. I ended up in a field where there were plenty of slaves at work. One of them was friendly. He talked to me in Maltese, so the others wouldn't understand him. He asked me who had the lethal weapon. I secretly pointed out to him who had it. He grabbed it from him and cut off the tie that bound my hands. I was free.

I'm crying again. I just realised what happened. When the first slave started chasing me, I was already running away from someone. It could have been my father, who was working in another field (*il-pergla*).

It was when I was free again that I woke up from the nightmare – petrified. As soon as I remembered the dream, I fished for the photo of me at age six or seven that I kept under the pillow and held it tightly against my chest, trying to comfort the little girl and protect her.

Yesterday afternoon I was already feeling down. When I was in church for the 7:00 p.m. mass, I had a panic attack. After the gospel I left church and walked to my mother-in-law's house. I stayed in the backyard by myself, crying whole-heartedly.

At one stage I was cupping my hands over my ears, trying to yell out 'No, no!' Then I decided to go in. I locked myself inside the toilet and cried my heart out. I kept saying, 'It's true! It's true! But why?...Why?' to my sister, who came in to comfort me. It's 1:00 a.m.

8:23 a.m.

Mark left for school. I assured him that I will be all right. I explained to him that no matter how painful it is, this is my only way to recovery. He felt better when I told him that. He begged me to ring him up if I needed him, and he assured me he would come straightaway.

8:27 a.m.

Michelle is still asleep, and I can't wait till 9:00 a.m. I want to ring up the psychoanalyst to give him an account of these last twenty-four hours.

I also need to ring up Mr Collins, the principal of St Albans South Primary School, to tell him that I won't be able to help out the Grade three unit with their maths activities, for two reasons – first, I don't feel well, and second, I'm scared of another panic attack in the classroom.

In spite of this ordeal, I feel good writing about my thoughts and fears. I feel I have a split personality at the moment – a frightened little girl from whom another personality is emerging: a strong, courageous person who has great promise for the future and is not vindictive – she doesn't feel vindictive towards her father, because she is sure that he must have been mentally disturbed to do such a thing (sexually molesting me).

8:58 a.m.

Three different personalities in me:

The old self – inhibited, frightened, indifferent and doubtful

The frightened little girl who keeps insisting 'It's true! It's true!'

Part of the still-emerging me – a promising one.

Tuesday 4 August 1987
2:30 p.m.

I just had lunch. I was starving and as I was eating, I kept thinking of that little girl as if I wanted her to have lunch with me, I'm realizing now that as the hours and days go by, I'm getting close to her, so close that I want to take her wherever I go. I'm even showing her off to other people – my tutor Ron Adams, and Stephanie, one of the other students. I want to make another copy of that photo, but at the moment I can't – first, in case it gets lost, and second, I don't want to separate myself from her, not even temporarily. I feel that she has now become part of me.

As I was explaining to Mark last night about the three different personalities I have at the moment, he came up with a good concept of the old me. He referred to it as a 'transmission block'. I was impressed by that expression because after all, it's the old me who stands in the way of the little girl, who is trying to reach out to the new me.

By writing about it, I feel that I'm keeping in touch with her.

3:05 p.m.

I slipped into 'anger depression', which was triggered by a cheque for $102 that I received unexpectedly and was supposed to make me happy. Instead, I feel panicky – it must have reminded me of my father. In spite of this deplorable state, I'm trying to determine which personality I'm identifying with at the moment. I can see that the little girl is angry, and on the other hand is interrelating with the new personality that is still emerging. This makes me feel good, and I regard this bout of depression as an opportunity for the two personalities to interact.

Wednesday, 5 August 1987
5:40 p.m.

I just finished my essay for Preparation for Tertiary Studies (one of the subjects I'm doing at the Western Institute) and quickly had tea because I have a lesson at 6:30 p.m. I haven't had much time to write since yesterday because I had a lot of studying to do.

This morning I had a session with the psychoanalyst. I showed him the photo for the first time. During the session a few personal things regarding my sexuality were brought up. I felt uncomfortable talking about them, but I feel I handled it pretty well.

These last couple of nights, I have been disturbed in my sleep. I've been getting up at about 2:30 a.m. in a state of shock. The first thing I did was to reach out for the photo I have been keeping under the pillow. Apparently, I have been dreaming about the little girl standing up in the middle of the field known as *Għajn Xejba* – down the cliff across the road from our house.

Before I go to sleep, I look forward to dreaming about her – she might throw some light on the 'dark' past – a past that I need to get in touch with.

Thursday, 6 August 1987
8:21 a.m.

Louie just took Mark to school, and he is going to get a few things from the market. He took a day off from work because of the state I'm in. Last night after I returned from school, I felt both mentally and emotionally frozen. Then I was panicky because of the fear of losing my mind.

At 10:30 p.m. I rang up my psychologist at home. He asked me to relax and explained that I was feeling this way because of the different personalities I have been experiencing lately. Although I'm still not sure what is happening to me, it seems inevitable, and I feel that this is my *only* way to recovery.

I'm finding it difficult to convince Louie of that, and he is so heartbroken to see me this way. I kept assuring him that I will be all right, and this is my only way to recovery – no medication can help me. He needs emotional support, and I'm trying to get in touch with my sister to come over.

9:00 a.m.

I'm cold and shivering.

10:50 a.m.

I assured Louie that this is not a sickness but a recovery.

10:51 a.m.

Superego taking over. This is the voice that keeps saying, 'You have to do this, and you have to do that.' Otherwise, I would feel guilty.

11:58 a.m.

I'm now realising who is behind the superego.

The moment has come to free myself from guilt, which has been choking me for all these years. He (my father) is the one to free me – to release me and set me free again.

12:08 p.m.

I want my freedom! I want my freedom!
Please help me, God.
I have been persecuted all these years with fear, shame, guilt, inner conflict and last but not least, by my inner slave master.

12:13 p.m.

I feel triumphant! I have won my freedom – I'm being born again – *not yet!*
Superego taking over again.

1:01 p.m.

What an emotional conflict!
I'm being choked again . . .
But in spite of this, I feel closer to freedom. I'm pleading with my father to release me from this guilt – I feel the power is in his hands.

I don't seem to be thinking any longer of the little girl. She led me to my father. It's now between me and him. This is a big moment in my life. That's why I want to write about it. One day the whole world will know about it – inner conflict.

I'm proud of the little girl – so courageous and *so innocent* (conflict). You are the one (my saviour – conflict). Yes, you are the one! You are my saviour! (conflict). She is the one that led me to my freedom.

1:40 p.m.

I'm cold and shivering.

5:35 p.m.

I had the session with the psychoanalyst. It went well. Even Louie and my sister came in. During the session I realised that every time there is a need to challenge someone regarding incest, I end up being the little girl again, who stands up for herself as if she is ready to challenge anyone.

She *is* the beacon that lights the path that leads me to meet my father.

5:51 p.m.

Once I convince myself that I'm a victim of incest, I don't need to convince anyone else.

6:07 p.m.

Michelle is angry at the moment. She feels irritable because she thinks she is fat. I realise that she is angry at me, but instead of directing her anger at me, she is unconsciously directing it at herself. I explained that to her, and I assured her that I understand and am ready to tolerate it – this is one trait of the real me: understanding.

8:15 p.m.

This is another special moment in my life. For the first time, I reached out to my baby Michelle. I hugged her and kissed her as if I'd found her again. In spite of my fears, deep down I have always loved her. When she got lost at Highpoint Shopping Centre at age three, I hugged her and kissed her because I thought I had lost her forever.

8:55 p.m.

I just took one of Michelle's photos from her album. This photo is special to me. I don't know exactly why. In this photo, Michelle looks exceptionally cute, and at the same time, the sad expression on her face reminds me of the other little girl, who is also cute and inhibited.

Oh Michelle, you have no idea how much I **love** you – I love you – I feel like holding you close to my heart. I will take you with me wherever I go, together with the other special little girl, because you have so many things in common. I will be showing you off to everybody because you are so special to me.

Friday, 7 August 1987
7:32 a.m.

Michelle has just left for school. Last night I couldn't sleep. I had a lot of thinking to do. Now that I have settled my business with Michelle, I feel I'm ready to have a break from the family. I need to slip back into the past. I can't do that in my home environment. I need to go away somewhere, away from everyone and everything that reminds me of the present. The best person to be with is my psychoanalyst – he is my past and the moment I am with him, I will automatically regress to the past. I still don't know what arrangements need to be made.

I woke Louie up at night and told him about my plan. He was upset when I told him I need to go away. He misunderstood me completely. I tried to explain to him, and he still insisted that going away is not necessary. On top of that he got angry, but that's understandable. Since he misunderstood me, he got hurt. I didn't get angry at him – I couldn't. I assured him of my love for him and the rest of the family. I owe it mostly to them to gain my recovery, or more accurately, to be born again. I've never felt so close to Louie as I did last night, and I meant it. There is no shred of doubt what a strong and courageous person I am – two features that the little girl and I have in common.

At about 5:30 this morning, I woke Louie up and again pleaded with him to let me go away. I needed not only his approval but also his blessing, because that way my mind will be at rest. I'm sure that Michelle and Mark will understand, once they see that Louie has accepted it.

I'm hoping to go somewhere in the country, surrounded by the beauty of nature, which is a constant reminder of the cherished love that *only* nature would offer to the little girl.

9:45 a.m.

I have come close to a decision regarding the name of that little girl. Since I met her, I've been thinking of calling her 'the blue pimpernel', my favourite flower, which she used to touch, caress and handle so cautiously, making sure that no harm befell it because like her, it was so fragile. After picking it up from among the rocks and weeds that were trying to strangle it, she would hold and cup her hands around it, to protect it from any breeze that would destroy it.

9:58 a.m.

Now I feel that the 'blue pimpernel' is no longer so fragile – she is becoming stronger and stronger as the hours go by. She is close to victory over the power of darkness. The Christian name her parents gave her on 20 October 1952 was an appropriate one. That name was VICTORIA.

12:26 p.m.

I just got home. I had a session with the psychologist. To be honest, I feel disappointed because I was looking forward to going away with him. The little girl feels broken-hearted. Her hopes are dashed – she is disappointed.

On top of that, she feels trodden down with guilt. Apparently, she tried to get her father's sexual attention. **GUILT** – I don't think anybody knows how destructive it can be. But why should I feel so guilty? Even if it was me who made the first move, wasn't it my father's responsibility to put an end to it? If that's the case, he is mostly to blame.

Then another question crops up. Why did I try to get my father's attention? I strongly believe that's a simple question. Something must have gone wrong in the early stages of my development. I must have not been properly nurtured by my mother, who had some psychological problems herself. Unfortunately, she was a hostile person. I say 'unfortunately' because she must have been a victim of hostility herself. From the little information I have, I believe her father was responsible for that. One of the neighbours once said to me that he never called my grandmother by her first name! He died when my mother was about sixteen years old.

On top of that, life was not meant to be easy for her. Relentless everyday pressures added to her burden. Both of my parents were trying to make ends meet. We were not financially secure. Far from it. My father did not have a paid job, and there was no financial help from the government. We lived off the land, which meant that minor disasters like draughts, floods, or the death of a sheep would hit us hard.

If that wasn't enough for my parents, there was another misfortune in the family. My second eldest sister, Carmen, became ill when she was eleven months old and developed paralysis in her left hand. This must have been a big blow to the family. Carmen ended up being both physically and mentally handicapped. Thus, she needed extra attention from my mother.

Then my brother Laurry, who was one year younger than Carmen, became the family scapegoat. He was a healthy, intelligent and creative boy, whose life became so unbearable that he tried to get attention through negative behaviour.

I was next in line. It is clearly evident that by the age of five, I was a terribly unhappy child, at times alienated from everyone around me. I was also a victim of my mother's hostility. I used to dread having her wash my hair. She would hold me tight under her left arm, facing upwards. With the other hand, she scrubbed my hair. Water used to splash over my face. I would scream, and the more I screamed and kicked, the more she held me tight with my head under the water.

That trauma was still inside me, so much so that it was triggered when I bathed Michelle for the first time in Western General Hospital, about four or five days after she was born.

This fear had been disguised by another fear – the fear of facial hair on the cute little face of a sweet baby girl. As I held baby Michelle to bathe her for the first time, I noticed she had fine blonde facial her, which reminded me of my mother. I was quickly overcome by the fear that Michelle's facial hair would grow out of control, and she would end up looking like a monster. I bottled up this fear inside me for eight and a half years. Not even Louie knew. I was too embarrassed to talk about it. Michelle's babyhood was marred for me because that fear haunted me day and night. Most of the time, I looked at Michelle through the eyes of fear rather than love.

Unfortunately, Michelle became a victim of my hostility, and I took my anger out on her. She became like Victoria, the other little girl, emotionally disturbed and insecure, not cherished and nurtured enough by her mother.

But these two little girls had one positive thing in common. In spite of the mental instability of their mothers, both mothers cared – there is no doubt about that.

When I was little, my mother would always try to cure my minor ailments. She would get me some fresh camomile from the fields to make tea to settle my upset stomach. When I suffered from constipation, she would make me a hot lemon drink, with plenty of sugar to kill the bitter taste. That hot lemon drink certainly kept me busy all day, hardly giving me enough time to find a secluded place in the paddock, which was attached to the house. We were not lucky enough to get a proper dunny. She also took me to Frenċ ta' l-Għarb, who was considered to have mystical power, because I used to get sores on my leg and dry patches on my face. He would give me a bottle of herbal medicine 'to clean my blood', because according to him I had lots of frights. How right he was!

5:17 p.m.

At this point I decided to stick to events of today. At about 3:00 p.m. I had an intimate talk with Louie about my sexuality in adolescence. We certainly had a few laughs, and Louie was so pleased to see me laughing again. Then I explained to him what was happening. I quickly grabbed a pen and a paper and drew a graph for him. I showed him the point of intersection of the two axes. I told him that yesterday at 12:13 p.m., when I felt I had been born again, I reached that point. This is what happened. For these last three and a half years since I started psychoanalysis, I was still below the negative axis of the graph. I've been aiming at that point of intersection. Now I feel I finally reached that point, which is the point in my life. In spite of the ups and downs I might have, I still belong above the y-axis. This makes a lot of sense to Louie too.

I also explained to Louie why I was hooked so much on the pacifier. I kept taking (sucking on) the pacifier till the age of seven. I couldn't go anywhere without it. Even at the preschool. I would keep it around my neck, hidden under the uniform, and every time I went to the toilet, I would take it out from its hiding place and have a suck at it. To me, this activity indicates that I wasn't properly nurtured and was emotionally insecure.

Chapter 5

The Old Self vs. the New

Saturday, 8 August 1987
12:33 p.m.

I feel down again, a little panicky too. I have just been to St Albans Library and borrowed the book, *Sybil*. When I got hold of the book, I had a sinking feeling in my stomach, and my heart started pounding. Louie was waiting for me outside the library. When he saw the book in my hand, his tone indicated concern. He was concerned about me reading that book, so much so that he suggested I read some other books that have to do with my further studies (i.e. the Bachelor of Arts). I assured him I'll be all right reading that book. If it upsets me, it means that it has triggered a signal in me, which might lead me to the unknown.

On the way home I opened the book in the car, flipped a few pages, and the first word that struck me was **Vicky**. My heart started pounding faster and faster. I wanted to know who Vicky was – I couldn't wait to read the book to find out. At this stage I only knew that Vicky was a nickname for Victoria, one of Sybil's multi-personalities. I kept thinking of what I told my psychologist yesterday (Friday) afternoon.

To be honest, I don't know much about Sybil. I watched the film about her two years ago. I don't remember the whole story. All I know is that when she was young, she spent a long period of time in an institution because of her psychiatric problems, which resulted from her mother's treatment of her.

I know she spent a lot of time with her psychologist. When she was in some kind of rehabilitation centre, she tried to learn office skills, which she found hard to do. At this stage Sybil, although not fully recovered, was well on her way to recovery. Then, when it was time to leave the institution, one nurse told her that she would return as a patient.

I remember seeing Sybil lying down on the lawn in a park with her psychologist. At that moment Sybil started meeting her 'friends' one by one.

Another incident in Sybil's life stuck in my mind. It was the speech she delivered on her graduation. I remember clearly the look that Sybil and that same fat nurse exchanged, while the former was saying that someone had thought she would never make it.

One Saturday afternoon in June, Michelle was upset by what my neighbour said. She told her that I will get mentally sick if I go back to study. Michelle came into the kitchen and started crying. I tried to comfort her because apparently, she was scared that I might get sick again. Then I reminded her of the story of Sybil, how she recovered from her illness and especially how she proved the nurse wrong. At that moment I identified with Sybil after her recovery, and I told Michelle that.

I knew that I myself was on the way to recovery, and I didn't need to prove anything to anyone. But the thought went through my mind that one day, I *will* prove my neighbour wrong.

Last Saturday, I identified myself with Sybil's mother. I cried my heart out on my bed when I recollected those frightening moments when I used to sit next to Michelle at the kitchen table, supposedly helping her with her homework, and was so hard on her. Last Saturday is when I realised what had happened. Michelle, at the age of six or seven, must have reminded me of Victoria and the other little girl, who herself was so badly hurt emotionally and physically that she wanted to hurt someone else the same way. And unfortunately, my daughter Michelle happened to be my victim (while I'm writing this part I feel like crying, because that little girl Michelle was hurt so badly). The only consolation I have is that if I wasn't hurt myself, I never would have done it. I did explain that both to Louie and Michelle.

Then yesterday (Friday) afternoon during the session with my psychologist, I told him that one day the whole world would know about my life story. 'I'm another Sybil,' I said. 'The only difference is that I'm not sure if Sybil wrote her life story herself.' (While I'm writing this, I have a sharp pain in the lower abdomen – a psychosomatic symptom, I suppose.)

I never realised how close I was to the truth – that I am another Sybil, even though I knew that Sybil's afflictions were different than mine. And then to find out that Vicky was a nickname for Victoria – one of Sybil's personalities – I could not believe the coincidence. Since migrating to Australia, I have become known as Vicky. In Malta I was known as *Vitorja* or *Vitorina.*

After all, it was only yesterday that I christened the little girl and called her Victoria, even though that was my proper Christian name. So now the more I'm getting to know Sybil, the more I'm identifying with her. The time is 2:07 p.m.

I can't wait to read her story.

4:00 p.m.

Those sharp pains in the abdomen were period pain – I just started menstruating. This was only a three-week cycle, not four weeks as usual.

Anyway, as I was getting tea ready, something clicked for me. Back home, there was this schoolteacher, who was not only my teacher when I was in primary school but also a close friend, despite our age difference. I must have identified with her as my mother. That explains something to me.

Last Friday I told my psychologist about a personal problem I have during intercourse with my husband. I found it extremely embarrassing to talk about. But now, since it makes a lot of sense to me, I don't find it so embarrassing. This is what I told him.

Every time I have intercourse with my husband, I think of that friend of mine. I imagine her watching me making love to my husband. I want to make her feel jealous. I don't know why, because when I went to Malta for a holiday eight years ago, there were rumours that she had had an affair with a married man who was twenty years younger.

If I identify with her as my mother during intercourse, I would say that justifies my conclusion, not only that I was a victim of incest but also that I did enjoy 'having an affair' with my father, and I wanted to make my mother jealous. I must have been angry at my mother, even at such a young age. What could she have done for me to be so angry with her? The simple answer – I must have blamed her for not nurturing me enough.

While I'm writing this, I feel sorry for my mother. As I already pointed out, she herself had psychological problems, and the pressures of life added to her burden, which apparently was too heavy for her to carry.

7:37 p.m.

I just finished cleaning up the kitchen. I couldn't wait to come to bed and continue writing. The more I write, the more I want to write. I can't believe it. It was only three weeks ago that the idea of writing an essay frightened me. But when I wrote my first short essay for the Preparation for Tertiary Studies course, I felt not only better but also confident.

Returning to my studies was not easy for me, especially after seventeen years of intellectual lethargy. During that period, I felt that I stopped growing intellectually due to the chronic depression that shrouded me, day in and day out. I could not continue with my studies – I could not even pick up a magazine and read it. I hardly followed the news on television. In other words, I was living in darkness.

Every now and then I did try to peep out of my shell. When Michelle and Mark were in primary school, I joined the school council. This took a lot of courage, considering the fact that I'd had a complete psychological breakdown only a year before. During my involvement at the school, I must have displayed some potential because the school principal used to speak highly of me. In fact, when I got in touch with him at the end of July, he sent me a letter of reference in which he wrote that I made 'an excellent and valuable contribution', and he recommended me very highly to return to study as a mature student.

But no matter how much I contributed to that school, I felt I didn't contribute enough. I wish I could have done more. But then again, considering the condition I was in, I do give myself a lot of credit.

Not only that, the first ten years of my marriage were shaky, not only from my own psychological problems but also because Louie was himself suffering from chronic depression, among other things. In 1969 he had been conscripted to join the Australian army and went to fight in Vietnam. I'm sure this was one of the major factors that contributed to his chronic depression. I was also subjected to a lot of verbal and emotional abuse.

Louie and I were then constructing one trap after another. But in spite of that, I had a ray of hope. It's true that many times I felt like breaking up the marriage. The only thing that stopped me was the kids. I certainly had my pitfalls during that time. But somehow, I could always manage to see dimly the light at the end of a tunnel – a tunnel not only long but also difficult, sometimes almost impossible to get through. There were times when I had to cut through barbed wire; at other times I felt I was going through a swamp and tried desperately to hang on to something to keep me from drowning. I hung on to every bit of twig or straw I came across, and then as the years went by, I started hanging on to branches, which happened to be much stronger than the twigs, thus making me feel more secure. I finally managed to fight my way through the swamp and land on solid ground, exhausted but relieved.

Now that I was on more solid ground, I could continue with my journey, cautiously though, lest I step on any hidden mines that covered my path. It took me about fourteen years to reach that point.

I had to watch out not only for the mines but also for snakes, which followed me wherever I went. There were times when the tunnel was so winding that it got dark – I couldn't see the dim light at the other end. I even got tangled with cobwebs, which together with the fear that haunted me, nearly suffocated me. It took me five years to get through that part of the tunnel.

These last twelve months, the ground in the tunnel has been much smoother. I did stumble every now and then. But every time I stumbled, I managed to get up quickly, dust off my clothes and continue with my journey. The tunnel was no longer so winding, and I could now see the light.

I was running to the other end of the tunnel when all of a sudden, I slipped in another swamp – not as big as the first one – but certainly just as dangerous. **That was on 30 July 1987, when I stumbled on the unexpected – the insight that I am a victim of incest.**

It shocked me so much that in spite of the evidence, I'm still finding it hard to convince myself. It's true that when I first had the insight, I also experienced another part of myself that *knew* I was a victim of incest, and I soon came to the conclusion that it was true. However, I am now dealing with the new self that is finding it hard to believe – but at the same time is open-minded.

When I started going to the Western Institute three weeks ago, I felt like a snail halfway out from under the shell. Every now and then I shrivelled in a bit and then out again – but not completely out.

Now I feel I'm no longer a snail but a chick ready to hatch. Yesterday that chick that can't wait to come out managed to crack the shell. It's still in there. Apparently, it's not ready to come out yet (9:09 p.m.).

9:32 p.m.

I just went over what I have written over these last twelve hours. I'm feeling down again. It is clearly depicted in my handwriting.

Sunday, 9 August 1987
2:44 a.m.

Just finished writing an emotional letter to my mother (she lives in Malta). I just couldn't go to sleep.

At about 1:30 a.m. I had this sudden urge to write to her and tell her the good news –that I intend to continue with my studies. Above all, I sincerely thanked her for what she did for me. When I was at school, even though we were poor, she would always buy some fresh ham to make my lunch or the best apples to take to school.

'Yes Mum, I sincerely meant it when I thanked you in the letter. In spite of your psychological problems, you are the best mum in the world, and I'm proud to have you as my mum.'

As for my father, I feel the same way. 'You did have your problems, and deep down you did care for us too. I also want to thank you sincerely for all your hard work and for your concern, which was reflected in your worries and anxieties. The fear of not being able to make ends meet is a proof of that. Now that I understand the reason behind your actions, I don't have any grudges against you' (3:00 a.m.).

Victoria has just introduced me to my father. I am proud of you, Victoria. I admire you for your courage, humility, compassion and last but not least your innocence. You have certainly accomplished your mission.

You are my saviour! You are triumphant! While I was writing this last paragraph, I kept looking at the photo, and I had tears running down my cheeks

9:41 a.m.

I just got up. I can't believe what I wrote last night, especially Mum's letter. As I got up, I was back to the old self again – doubtful and indifferent. I started looking at Victoria on the photo of my identity card, and then I started changing into the new me again. I realised then what my mission is.

Before I came to Australia, I felt a premonition that I was going to embark on a mission. I had no idea what it was. I told the psychologist about it a few times. Now I realise that my mission is to 'preach the gospel' of psychology, which is much needed among the Maltese people, both in Malta and Australia. Unfortunately, they don't know much about mental illness, and there is a lot of stigma attached to it. At one time I was one of them.

I had never realised how beneficial psychotherapy can be until a while ago. As I was on the way to recovery, I started reaping the benefit of it. *And it was only twelve days ago that I decided to embark on an intensive self-analysis* with the help of my psychologist, whom I have been seeing these last four years. It started when Michelle, who developed a phobia about spiders, was referred to the Child Psychiatry Unit. As a result of the initial assessment, Dr Garcia suggested that I also undergo psychotherapy. He could see there was a problem, considering that I'd had a breakdown in 1980 and was hospitalised for acute depression for six weeks.

My self-analysis in August included exploring my sexuality, an area I was always so sensitive about. I felt there had to be a reason behind my sexual problems, and I was sure that once I discovered those reasons, it wouldn't be so embarrassing anymore. That's when I felt the need to explore my sexuality.

8:16 p.m.

I feel panicky again – frightened like a little girl. I don't know why, but writing about it makes me feel better, as if I find consolation in writing. We've just been to church. I didn't panic, but I must say the hymns for that mass reminded me of a funeral mass in Malta. I've already started feeling depressed.

After mass, we went over my mother-in-law's place. I had a nice conversation with her. She certainly enjoyed my company. I promised to bake her a cake tomorrow because I know she likes it, and I really want to do something for her. When we came back home, I felt more panicky. I kept thinking of the emotional letter I wrote to Mum yesterday. I don't feel ready to post it yet. I don't know why – I feel confused. There is something in that letter bothering me.

Early this morning while I was writing it, I felt I was ready to tell her the good news – that I'm going to university to continue my studies. I know how happy she would be to hear that. That's why I can't wait to tell her. What's bothering me then? Could it be me doing the Bachelor of Arts (BA)? I do have this strong urge to write. But even if I become a writer, what's wrong with doing the BA?

At the moment I'm doing three short courses at Western Institute, and I feel I'm doing well with my preparations to return to study. I'm sure I would perform much better if only I had a clearer mind. This split of personalities, together with the bouts of depression I've been having lately, does interfere with my concentration.

This afternoon I have been reading a handout on gender differences. The way I put it in point form was quite good. When I get these acute bouts of depression, I get a strong urge to write – I have to drop everything and start writing. I warn Louie and the kids not to interrupt me; if they do happen to interrupt me, I get irritable at them for disturbing me.

Writing seems to be a strong trait in my new personality.

I don't think I will be posting that letter to my mother. I'll have to write her another one. I feel disappointed, because I was looking forward to telling her about returning to my studies. What if I don't do the BA? Wouldn't the family be disappointed in me?

I feel confused. It seems that writing my autobiography is my first priority.

Monday, 10 August 1987
6:45 a.m.

I woke up at six o'clock. I felt in a state of shock. One thing that struck me last night was my indifference – I was emotionally frozen. I realised that when I am in that state, I'm frozen not only emotionally but also mentally. It frightens me because it's going to interfere with my studies. After that frozen state I become panicky and depressed. I know that anger and hostility lie behind depression. In other words, this is one way to discharge my anger.

Could there be another way? I wonder how long this anger depression will last.

Before Louie left for work this morning, I explained to him what's happening and assured him that I'll be all right.

Tuesday, 11 August 1987
2:45 p.m.

I haven't written anything in the diary since yesterday

morning. I don't know why. It could be because I was busy with my studies. But I don't think that's the real reason.

Somehow, these last twenty-four hours I have hardly been in touch with Victoria. I'm not sure whether that's a good sign or not. I must admit that since I discovered her, I have been in constant touch with her. That did frighten me up to a certain point. I was afraid that I would become obsessed with her. She has a lot of courage, and I do feel safe with her.

But now there is a big gap between us. The events of these last twelve days seem like a nightmare to me. When I reflect on them, I can't believe what happened to me.

That's probably why I have been avoiding Victoria. Does this mean that personality has vanished, and the new one has emerged or is taking over? If that's the case, the new personality is still fragile, in fact even dazed, in spite of its strong healthy points.

This morning, I handed in my essay 'Returning to Study as a Mature Age Student' to be published in the newsletter at the Institute, and I just received a phone call from the P.R.O. telling me how impressed she was with it, so much so that she wants it to be the main article of the newsletter.

Also, the comments I've been getting regarding my essays from the tutors are very encouraging indeed.

Wednesday, 12 August 1987
12:00 p.m.

I had a session with my psychologist this morning. I told him how Victoria seems to be fading away. I questioned whether this eruption was inevitable. I thought about the lava that came out of it, which consisted of anger, hostility, jealousy, fear and guilt.

Yes, guilt was one of the major factors that fuelled that eruption. Why was it that I always felt guilty regarding confession? No matter how much I said in confession when I was growing up, it was never enough. What was I *really* guilty of? To me, this supports my belief that I was the one who chased my father. Indirectly it shows that I am a victim of incest. This is the core of this whole mess.

There is no doubt about my anger against the teaching of the Catholic Church in Malta. Why was I so much against it? Is it because it interfered with my sexual drives when I was growing up? I wouldn't be surprised. We were consistently taught to remove any 'bad thoughts' (i.e. sexual thoughts) from our minds, because they were considered a sin!

Now the question of guilt comes up. Why was I so guilty and inhibited? I just answered this question in one of the above paragraphs.

If I can prove that I wasn't properly nurtured, that would explain why I wanted excessive attention from my father. I do know that I sucked on my pacifier till I was six or seven years old, whereas my other siblings didn't. To me that's sufficient proof that something went wrong during my early development.

10:30 p.m.

Feeling down again. During the Childhood across Culture class, I felt panicky. The word 'anthropologist' must have triggered something. I remember bringing up a point regarding women anthropologists in another class three weeks ago. Then I thought of Michelle and Mark being at home by themselves. I suppose I must have felt guilty. Before I left for the Institute, I was angry at Mark. He has been so sensitive lately. I have tried to be understanding with him because there must be a reason behind it. I'm afraid I couldn't take it anymore and got angry at him. But by the time I was about to leave, he apologised, and we were on good terms again.

Anger, guilt and constriction seem to trigger my panic attacks. I'm looking forward to going to sleep. I might have a dream that will lead me to the unknown.

Thursday, 13 August 1987
9:26 p.m.

Today I took an important step regarding studying. I went to Footscray TAFE Library for the first time, at my own initiative too. We have to do an essay, and I wanted to do some research there. I felt strange walking around such a college. But I must admit that I was proud of myself. It took a lot of courage, considering my mental state at the moment, to take that first step. It was certainly worth it!

These last few days I've noticed that my self-esteem has escalated dramatically. It's clearly depicted in my writing.

I also feel that I've now mastered something – I don't know what it is. All I know is I can look down on people (in a positive way). I don't feel trodden down by anyone, no matter how hard they try to hurt me emotionally. They themselves must also have been hurt.

Friday, 14 August 1987
(Somehow, I did not record the time!)

This morning I felt I was ready to post Mum's letter. As I was having breakfast, I watched the news. There was this nine-year-old British boy who just passed in maths at Advanced Level. When I saw the slip of paper (his results) in his hands, it reminded me of the days when I received my GCE (General Certificate of Education) from Oxford

University – what a happy moment it was for me. I was in the seventh heaven of delight. That boy rekindled in me the feelings I had when I read my results. To be honest, I felt jealous of that boy for passing the GCE at such a young age. But then I admired him, for he is a special boy. However, at that moment I felt I was a special girl too. In fact, I was special in another way. Unlike that boy, who apparently comes from an intellectual family (his father was his tutor), I had to fight all the way to achieve that high standard of education at a secondary school level. I come practically from 'nowhere' – a poor family. My father could not even read or write, and my mother could read and write Maltese only enough to get by.

I gained recognition at secondary school and was highly regarded and respected by the community at large – including teachers and students, young and old.

Yes, this morning I was ready to break the news that I am returning to study, not only to my mother but also to my old friends – people within the education department who always encouraged me to continue with my studies when I was at primary school. I felt that I owe it not only to myself and to my mum but also to those special people.

I did the right thing by posting the letter to my mother this morning and breaking the news that I'm resuming my studies.

Sunday, 16 August 1987
11:22 a.m.

Yesterday I didn't write anything in the diary, not because I didn't think of it but because I didn't have time. At the moment I'm writing an essay about Maltese migrants in Australia, and I'm quite interested in it. I came up with a good structure, and the more I think about it, the more I'm getting ideas from my observations and recollections of these last fifteen years in Australia.

This morning, while Michelle and I were making pizzas together in the kitchen, I had a good talk with her about her abrupt attitude towards her family. Last night when we got out of church, Michelle ran into this boy her age, whom she had met once before on an excursion. They seem to fancy each other. Mark knew about it, and as we were outside the church, he whispered in my ear, 'That's the unlucky boy Michelle fancies.' That remark really hit me.

As I have already pointed out, I am concerned about Michelle's attitude. She does use a different attitude towards her family – namely her father, her brother and myself. With her friends she is not as abrupt, and her tone is different. However, occasionally she does clash with her teachers. She seems to stand up for herself pretty well. The problem is she doesn't do it in an acceptable way, especially at home. That worries me a lot.

This morning I told Michelle that I don't want to see her falling in the same trap as her uncle. She quickly retaliated, 'Oh no, I'm not going to be like him. I don't even want to know him.' I said to her, 'But I'm afraid if you do not improve your attitude, you will end up like him.'

Then I went on to explain to her that the reason behind her negative attitude is either that she is still hurt emotionally from her past relationship with me, or that the attitude has now become a habit, and she is not aware of it. 'If it's hostility that will subside in time, but if it's a habit, we have to work at it,' I said. 'Otherwise, you will be living in hell like your uncle.'

I feel that I'm the one who can help her, through patience, tolerance and perseverance. To me, the combination of these three factors is the key to success. In Michelle's case I feel I can do it, and I'm determined to do it. Please help me, God! All I need is cooperation from the rest of the family.

I explained all this to her while we were in the kitchen this morning. I told her that once her attitude improves, the people around her will feel better. She herself will be happier, and she will enjoy life to the fullest.

I have already noticed a great deal of improvement in her. These last few weeks I can see that her hostility is subsiding gradually, thus making room for affection, which she has already started showing in relation to nature, like flowers and animals, and above all in relation to her dad, Mark and myself.

This morning I felt it was time for me to talk to her about the improvement in her attitude. When the opportunity arose, I just couldn't let it slip away. In spite of her objections, I kept talking to her while she was helping me put the toppings on the pizzas. I didn't frame it in a negative way. I made it clear to her that she is improving, which is a healthy sign. The only problem is that when she is abrupt, she needs to control it, lest it become a habit and affect her later in life. I feel optimistic about the whole situation. Time, patience, perseverance and tolerance will eradicate this.

Monday, 17 August 1987
11:45 a.m.

These last twenty-four hours I've been thinking a lot about the essay on Maltese migrants in Australia. Yesterday afternoon I started writing the good copy, and before I started, I realised that this was going to be more than an essay, because I have so much to write about. The more I think about it, the more ideas I get – I'm even surprised at the sequence of ideas. It's coming to me so naturally – it's all depicted in my writing. I'm sure this is a healthy sign.

At the moment I'm waiting for a phone call from the Phillip Institute. About six weeks ago, I heard this Maltese lady being interviewed on 3 EA (a community radio station), and she said that she is teaching Maltese there. She pointed out that there are some students preparing themselves for HSC in the Maltese language. By the end of the interview, I found out that she had been one of my teachers at St Mary Grammar School in Malta twenty years ago! She was Miss Pauline Vella, now Mrs. Spiteri.

Since I started writing the essay (now it seems it's going to be a mini thesis, not an essay), I've become interested in doing Maltese as a major for the Bachelor of Arts. That's why I got in touch with Phillip Institute – to inquire about the structure of the course.

Tuesday, 18 August 1987
9:51 p.m.

I've just been looking through the book *The Maltese in Australia* by Barry York. When my tutor told me about it this morning, I was eager to look at it. But once I got hold of it, panic struck, especially when I saw this couple's name in the acknowledgments. I had been thinking of interviewing them myself – they settled on the other side of the city. I suppose I felt angry because someone else had beaten me to it. But when I flipped through the book, I realised it was completely different than what I'm doing.

This afternoon, I rang up Channel 7 and asked them to send me a copy of the interview with Barry York that aired recently. I want to watch it with the class on Tuesday.

Yesterday evening I rang up Mrs. Pauline Spiteri, my ex-teacher from twenty years ago, and she was so pleased to hear from me. We ended up chatting for an hour.

Wednesday, 19 August 1987
10:30 a.m.

I've just had a session with my psychologist. I'm in a state of shock. Have I stumbled on another family scandal? I told my psychologist about a recurring dream. In this dream I see a sturdy, fancy coffin. I don't know who is inside. I see it being drawn on a cart, as if it's a pompous funeral. And beside this coffin, I see a lady standing motionless. This woman happens to be the daughter-in-law of one of the neighbours back home.

During the session I also spoke about a fear involving a coffin. I can relate this fear to my father's death. (As I started writing this sentence, I got the pain in my left leg again – one of my psychosomatic symptoms – and as I got into the house, I got the hunger pains again.) Two coffins: one in a fear and one in a dream. Who could the dead person be? Is it the same person? If it is one person in both coffins, who would that person be? The one in the fear I would say is my father, who passed away in 1980. But what is he doing in the other coffin? Or rather that woman, why is she in the dream? In other words, why is she involved with my father's death? And why is it a pompous funeral? The woman in the dream is stunned and motionless.

I don't want to jump to another conclusion – but I'm afraid I'm thinking of the possibility that I witnessed my father having sex with this woman. Somehow, I feel close to revealing another family skeleton. I'm stunned, dazed and confused (my left arm feels weak again). I want to talk to Louie about it, but I'm afraid of his reaction. He might think I'm jumping to conclusions. I'm stunned.

Did I witness something when I was little? I'm thinking of Victoria again. I haven't been thinking of her lately. My head is buzzing. What can Victoria tell me? Is she leading me to another unknown path?

This is so painful to me. I can't talk it over with anyone except my psychologist. Only he and Victoria seem to know what's happening.

All I know at this stage is that this entire mess, including my psychological problems, is interfering with my studies, or rather my ambition. Yes, I have discovered that I have an ambition to embark on something that nobody has never embarked on before. Maybe that's why I felt threatened when I discovered that book yesterday.

I'm feeling down again. In spite of this mess, I have courage and hope to continue, both with my studies and exploring the unknown through my inner journey of self-discovery. Revealing these scandals is the only way to recovery.

I just left a message for my psychologist to ring me back. I'm cold and shivering again. I've been invaded by these recollections from my early childhood. *These recollections share a common theme: promiscuity.*

What a mess!

Amongst these invading thoughts, I had doubts and fears that led me to a fantasy I had as a child, regarding incest within a particular family in the neighbourhood. Why that family? I know that the father was the one who raped my auntie – according to the people in the neighbourhood. But was I aware then (when I was so little and had this fantasy) of that scandal? I doubt it. So back to that question again. Why that particular family? This question took me back when I was four years old. I can vaguely remember going to play in a paddock that belonged to that family. Was I sexually assaulted there? I'm frozen.

Another episode of my life is being unfolded. I have come to two more possible insights:

> That my father and that woman had an affair.
> That I was sexually assaulted *also* by an outsider, the same man who raped my auntie.

But why was I a victim of incest and rape? Did I actually look for trouble? I have a feeling that I did. When I was about ten years old, I clearly remember wanting to be sexually involved with this man who was waiting in a dark corner for his girlfriend down the street, a few metres away from our house.

Once again, why did I chase men as a little girl? Why did I yearn for their attention so much? Why was I so vulnerable to incest and other sexual abuse?

2:37 p.m.

After reflecting upon the above question, I have come up with an answer. At first, I thought the reason was that I wasn't properly nurtured. But now I strongly believe that I must have witnessed my father having an affair with someone, which upset me a lot. Therefore, I looked for other men to identify with as my father.

I also believe that I was a victim of incest before I witnessed the affair. That is why I was so disappointed in my father. That may also explain why I was jealous of other women (and want to make another woman jealous during intercourse as an adult).

It must have left a deep wound in me – a wound I still carry as an unresolved trauma.

While I'm writing all this, I feel emotionally frozen. It's probably a side effect of the shock. In spite of this deplorable state I'm in, I still feel that I'm going to be all right.

2:56 p.m.

I'm entering into the unknown.

4:16 p.m.

I'm crying in my room. Michelle is angry, and Louie is both angry and upset. When I told him that I'm a victim of rape, he got angry at me and went out. I had tea ready for him, but he wouldn't eat. In spite of the state I was in, I felt strong enough to fight it by myself, and I didn't need to convince him or anyone else. At that moment I felt angry at my psychologist. When he rang me up at 3:00 p.m., he sounded abrupt, even though he was concerned about me. After I assured him I'd be all right, he sounded as if I was expecting too much from him. I got the impression that the reason I called him was because I wanted to see him again before Friday. I know he has other commitments, but somehow, I couldn't wait to tell him about my insights.

Mark has just come into my room to check on me. I started crying while he stood beside me on the bed. Both Louie and Michelle deserted me, and I was by myself. It broke my heart. They were not there when I needed them. Only Mark was there. I know that both Louie and Michelle care about me. But what a way to show it!

Yes, I don't need to convince anyone. I am strong enough to face it by myself.

Earlier when I was getting tea ready, I felt angry at my father for the first time. I'm feeling sorry for myself. I have been hurt so much that nobody can hurt me anymore – nobody, no way.

As I was walking to my room, I got this pain on the left side of the groin.

5:01 p.m.

I'm cold and shivering. Nobody can change my conclusion. Nobody can convince me otherwise. Deep down I know it's the truth.

I feel victorious over the power of darkness.

There is a lot of anger inside me. But that's understandable. At the moment I hate my native land. I hate the people who hurt me when I was so little. I realise how much promiscuity existed in our neighbourhood so many years ago.

10:23 p.m.

Just had a slight panic attack. I was thinking about my mother. She might receive the letter today. I thought of the reaction of the people there, especially my favourite teacher who lived down the road.

That's when panic struck. I have convinced myself of my past experiences, and I don't need to convince anyone else. I was thinking of writing it down in my diary, but somehow, I couldn't. Panic struck. I had a fear/wish[1] of not having the

---

1 According to psychoanalytic theory, where there is a fear, there is a wish.

urge to write. That was followed by depression (anger). Then I had the urge to write.

Having analysed this fear, I feel better. This makes a lot of sense to me.

I realise now, though I feel reluctant to write it, that all these years I have been trying to block the first five years of my life. My memory is scant. I remember turning up at my maternal grandmother's house when I ran away from home at about three years old. Another time I vaguely remember tearing up a rag doll! I went to buy a dummy from the grocer down the road and it was getting dark; playing in the paddock; crying to go and sleep over at my auntie's place as we walked together after visiting my grandmother; spending a day at her place after she shifted to a new house; staying with my blind uncle, and my father came to pick me up. He put me in a sack and carried me over his back. He took a shortcut through the meadows. I must have been about three years old.

I also remember my father giving me a piece of bread sprinkled with sugar. It was during the day, and I was standing at the entrance of the house. I remember my paternal grandmother holding the broom, humming a tune while removing the cobwebs, and I stood there close to her, looking up at the sky light.

I remember the carnival at night in our village, when people used to disguise themselves, hiding their faces behind masks and walking around in the streets wearing odd clothes.

Thursday, 20 August 1987
7:20 a.m.

I've been up since six o'clock. I slept right through and didn't have any dreams. I was looking forward to going to sleep, in case I had a dream that might throw some light on the unknown.

This morning I have been thinking of the events of these last twenty hours. I kept talking to myself. I felt convinced of my insights. I was full of sympathy for myself. I cried as I remembered how alienated I felt yesterday.

Mark was the only one who believed me, even though I didn't give him much information regarding being sexually abused.

I didn't tell the kids that I witnessed my father having sex with someone else. I wouldn't be surprised if when I went to

tell my mother, she became angry with me. That's probably why she took her anger out on me when she used to wash my hair.

I'm still in a state of shock. Somehow, I feel reluctant to write. Maybe it's one way to express my anger. I probably feel angry for writing about all of this. I must hate the new me, because this is one way to face the truth – by writing about it. This makes some sense to me; that's understandable. These revelations are new to me.

I can now see that the old me and the new me are clashing. I seem to have left the little girl behind. It's now a struggle between the above two personalities. Although it is confusing, this is a healthy sign. I realise what a strong person I am. I don't know where that strength comes from. All I need now is time and understanding from the people around me.

I know this must be painful for them. I'm sure one day they will understand. I can't hate them (Louis and Michelle) for not believing me, even though it hurts me. I'm sure of their concern about me. They must be hurt themselves. Perhaps even frightened. One day they will understand.

Both my left arm and my left leg have been aching since yesterday. Psychosomatic symptoms, I suppose.

9:24 a.m.

I feel vindictive. I want to take revenge. I feel that when I was little, I was ridiculed, the laughingstock of part of the neighbourhood. I wish I could go back to face those people. I would certainly make their faces go red. I'm thinking of a way to speak up.

When I was at secondary school and reached the summit through my outstanding academic achievements, I was considered a heroine among the community in my village. When I decided to give up my career to get married, I felt I had made a fool of myself. I couldn't face the people around me – the sooner I left Malta, the better. I left Malta one month after I got married. Before I left, I purged the house of everything that belonged to me. *I remember clearly that I did not want to leave any traces of me in the house, as if I had never lived there.* Now I understand why and what I was running away from.

The new me wants revenge. She wants to speak up. She is victorious over the power of darkness. She has been hurt a lot. At the moment she is vindictive. But nobody can hurt her anymore – nobody. She has full control over herself. She has strength and courage. She not only had to handle her own problems, but she also had to handle her husband Louie (an ex-serviceman), her daughter Michelle (who happened to be her scapegoat) and Mark falling into the same trap as Michelle.

WESTERN INSTITUTE
STUDENT CARD

Name BORG, V

Number 871371

School C & GS

While I'm writing this, I'm looking at the photo that was taken two weeks ago at the Western Institute for my student identity card. In that photo I can see the new me. There is a warm, natural smile, beauty coming from within and reflected in her face.

I can see power, strength, courage, determination, understanding and caring for people who like her, have been hurt.

I feel like carrying her wherever I go. She has courage. She is leading me to the future. Like the little girl, she is a leader. *Victoria led me to regress to my early childhood, and the new Victoria will lead me to the future.*

After reading what I just wrote, I feel cold and am shivering.

8:00 p.m.

Anger – revenge – defensive – ready to challenge anyone – my last resort, facing my mother. I'll do it if it comes to that.

Chapter 6

Meeting the Real Self

Friday, 21 August 1987
6:38 p.m.

While I was having tea, I was thinking of writing in the diary – then panic struck. I feel puzzled. Is the old me angry at the new me for trying to find the truth by writing about it? Or is the old me doubtful as usual? The little girl and the new me seem convinced about my insights. *But somehow there seems to be an opponent among them – it's standing in their way.*

Having written that, I can now relate what happened during the session today. I told the psychologist the reasons that led me to those two conclusions yesterday and gave him an account of these last twenty-four hours. What's behind that conflict – doubt, anger?

Last night I vaguely remember having a dream. I was back home. Someone had died. The old woman next door came to fix up the corpse. My mother and I were waiting for the caretakers to come and take it. My eldest sister was following the small procession, which was supposed to lead the funeral. The caretakers went past our house, but they didn't come in. They went to pick up someone else. My mother and I exchanged a look. In the meantime, the dead body began to stink. It stunk so bad that everybody closed their windows.

I don't know why I feel reluctant to write about yesterday's events. But I'm going to write about them anyway. When

Louie came home from work at 8:00 p.m., I had tea ready for him. When he walked in, I could see he was angry at me. That broke my heart. I went into my room and turned into that little girl – like her I felt alienated; nobody wanted to believe her. When she was little, she felt nobody wanted to listen to her when she dobbed her father in. Last night that little girl wanted to convince the people around her. And through that scenario that involved the whole family, she did. I felt that Louie wasn't convinced. I couldn't face him; in fact, I didn't want to reach out to him. I can see that the new personality took over last night. How am I going to get rid of the old one – the one that is doubtful and panicky? How can I exterminate her forever, so I can continue with my life and have a fresh start?

Sunday, 23 August 1987
11:30 a.m.

I didn't write anything in the diary yesterday, not because I didn't have anything to write – on the contrary, I had a lot to write about. But I was reluctant to write.

I can clearly see now that the old me, the one who is doubtful, is clashing with the new emerging me, the one who wants to record all these happenings as evidence of the past that she has been blocking all these years.

The psychosomatic symptoms I have been experiencing these past few days give me a clue of what happened when I was so little. By Wednesday night, the pain in my left leg got worse. Then I had sharp pains in the left groin. Thursday morning, I had a small sty in my lower right eyelid – not as bad as the ones I used to get when I was a child. I remember pretty well the horrible and painful sties I used to get. I would also get sores on my legs with pus in them. They were painful too. I still have some scars on my legs. People used to say it was because I ‘had frights’. I remember my mother taking me to this man who was believed to have spiritual powers, and he used to give me this horrible herbal medicine to drink to cure my sores.

When I got up this morning, I noticed a sort of pimple with pus in it on my right thigh. I have not had such a pimple there since my childhood.

Then, yesterday evening when I was about to start working on the essay on feminism in Australia, panic struck. I felt restricted – I was panicky because for Preparation for Tertiary Studies, we have to do an essay to be admitted to the Western Institute next year. That feeling of having to do something / restriction / having no choice triggered something. Then I got this sharp pain at the back of my head. It felt as if someone had inflicted an injury on me. I still have that pain today.

Yesterday I also realised the psychological harm caused by the pressure Louie put on me during the first ten years of our marriage. I must have a lot of fear bottled up inside me. Before I went shopping yesterday, Louie asked me to get him something from the hardware section at Coles. I didn’t remember this until I had walked out of the store. Then I had a shocking feeling. It rekindled in me the fear I used to have when he would tell me to do something, and it sounded more like a threat than an order.

There is no doubt about the psychological damage he inflicted on me. I told Louie that in the afternoon, and I explained it to him in an acceptable way. I didn’t want to make him feel guilty, but I needed to let him know how I felt. First, by telling him I would get rid of my hostility, thus making room for affection. Second, I wanted to make him aware of that damage, so he would change his attitude towards me and the kids. Louie was very understanding, and it made me realise what a remarkable woman I am – a woman who is playing so many different roles – roles that I have learned through introspection and logical thinking.

I can see now how much benefit I'm reaping through all this mess. It's making me become aware of my healthy points.

I just went to give a chocolate to Samantha, the seven-year-old girl who lives next door. She is learning how to ride a bike. I wanted to give one to Michelle, too, because she is my little girl.

Tuesday, 25 August 1987
2:00 p.m.

During the Childhood across Culture class this morning, Ron Adams asked us to write what we want to be remembered with when we die, and this is what I wrote:

Loving, caring mother
One who won over the 'power of darkness'

I felt nervous reading it out loud, but I handled it pretty well. I said loving and caring mother. I was thinking of Michelle being my scapegoat. But deep down I did care about her. When she was psychologically disturbed, I stayed with her and comforted her for so many hours.

Wednesday, 26 August 1987
10:30 p.m.

Yesterday afternoon I rang up the Maltese Consul General to arrange an appointment to see him. But he answered the phone, and I had a conversation with him. I wanted to know first of all if anybody has done any anthropology about the Maltese migrants in Australia, and second, whether financial help would be available if I embarked on such a study. He didn't even know what the word 'anthropology' meant, and when I tried to explain it to him, he cut me short. He was extremely arrogant and told me he is not a detective or Sherlock Holmes. He is just a consul. That really upset me. But I'm proud of myself because I handled him pretty well.

I told my psychoanalyst all about it. I also told him that I wanted to challenge him regarding facts and assumptions. Somehow, we disagree about my being sexually abused, either because we are misunderstanding each other, or he is doing it on purpose. I intend to discuss this further next Friday – my last session for this year.

I would like to point out that yesterday, when I was talking to my sister on the phone about my mother, I experienced the fear of losing my mind. Luckily it didn't last long. We were talking about money that my mother had put aside for her funeral. That night I had an acute panic attack. I was worried that if I lost my mind, Louie would not be able to handle our money.

Sunday, 30 August 1987
1:00 p.m.

Last Friday I had my last session with my psychologist for this year – he is going on long service leave and will be back on 4 January. At first, I wasn't sure how I was going to handle that session. I was feeling a bit down on Thursday, and when I'm like that I tend to rely on him.

Wednesday night I rang up my sister, and she told me she had received a letter from my mother. Besides telling her about the money she had put aside for her funeral, she also said that she invited a missionary from India and two of her cousins (one of them is a nun) over and cooked a three-course meal for them. Apparently, they enjoyed each other's company. I admire my mum – she does have a nice personality. Unfortunately, as we were growing up hostility stood in the way, and she didn't develop her real personality. I told my sister that, and I also told her that my mother knew of my father's sexual activities and kept it all to herself. I would say that was the main factor that contributed to her hostility. My sister replied, '*Kollox jista' jkun*' (anything is possible).

That night I had a dream. I was going to have a session with my psychoanalyst, and somehow, I was naked in a bathtub. As I saw him coming towards me on my right, I was embarrassed, and I said to myself, 'Do I have to be naked for this session?' I tried to cover my pubic hair. Through my embarrassment, I turned my head to the left and fell asleep.

Still dreaming, I had another session. This time I was fully clothed, but I looked peculiar indeed. I was wearing my new pyjamas, and over them I was wearing Louie's dressing gown. I had my moccasins on, and strangely, I wore a veil over my head. On top of that, I smelt bad. I felt embarrassed by the way I was dressed and that awful smell. During the end of the session, Michelle appeared on the scene. My psychoanalyst was talking to her, and I was embarrassed about it because I felt she was not attractive enough. She had this hood on her head, and somehow, she was a bit old for it.

Monday, 31 August 1987
2:30 p.m.

I have just received a letter from my mother. I'm extremely disappointed with it. I was looking forward to hearing from her because I thought my last letter would make her happy. But it didn't. That's exactly what she said in the letter. She is worried for me. She thinks that by returning to study I'll get sick again, just like when I was at secondary school and had a psychological breakdown at about fifteen years old. She doesn't understand that studying is not the reason for my psychological problems.

According to my mother, 'It's better to eat a simple piece of bread than a banquet with a turkey.' She doesn't know the real reason I want to go back to study. I feel like an orphan again. Yes, I'm afraid I can't talk to my mother. It's just as well I have Louie and the kids behind me. Otherwise, I'd be lost.

9:30 p.m.

Just finished writing a letter to my mother, and I am pleased with the way I wrote it. I explained myself pretty well. I know that my mum meant well, and she had her reasons for being concerned about me.

Last night after I came home from the Institute, I was still upset about the letter, and I ended up writing an essay about it, which I called 'A Personal Crisis'.

I was so pleased with that essay that I wanted to show it to Ron Adams (one of my tutors at the Institute). He was so impressed with it that he photocopied it. I told him that I don't want to burden anybody with my problems – I don't want sympathy – all I want is understanding. If my mother can't understand me, I'm sure that people like my tutor would understand me.

I believe that these last sixteen years or so have taught me so much that I have mastered something I could never have learned through books.

Today for the Childhood across Culture class, I took some *pudina* (traditional Maltese cake) and fresh cheese that I made the Maltese way. I also took my knitted jacket and the *magħżel* (spindle for the wool). My mother spun the wool that she sheared from her sheep, and I knitted the jacket. Everybody was so impressed with them.

I just realised that I have mastered something else – whenever I have a panic attack, *I can analyse myself*, which is extremely important.

Friday, 4 September 1987
10:00 p.m.

This evening I attended the first meeting of the Maltese Education Council at the Maltese Centre in Parkville. I found the meeting very interesting, and I also met some important people within the Maltese community, among them two Maltese authors: Hugh Azzopardi and John Cassar.

Michelle is at the bush survival camp. I've been thinking about her because it's her first night sleeping in the bush. I can imagine how cold it is out there, but at least it's not raining. They might be having a good time.

Now I seem to have come to a decision regarding my studies. I'm interested in anthropology, and I want to get a degree in sociology. I've been told that multiculturalism will be introduced at Western Institute during the second year. That would fit in with what I'm doing.

Sunday, 6 September 1987
4:00 p.m.

Michelle came back from the bush survival camp at Cumberland River. Although exhausted, she was pleased that she went. She got an award certificate, which said that Michelle overcame all obstacles with a smile. That certificate means a lot to me. It indirectly says a lot of things, and through it I can see that I am now reaping the benefit of my hard work with Michelle regarding improvement in her personality. Good on you Michelle, and above all good on you Victoria – keep up the good work!

This morning my sister rang me up to tell me that last night she rang up my mother. Mary sounded upset because she is concerned about my mother. Somehow, I couldn't cry, but I felt understanding.

This afternoon I rang up Prof Alfred Briffa at home. These last forty-eight hours, I have been thinking about the decline of the Maltese language in Australia. I strongly believe that the roots of this problem originate in Malta, where the English language is emphasized and highly regarded. Indeed, Maltese is considered 'the language of the kitchen'. Alfred agrees with me wholeheartedly, and he was glad I shared my opinion with him.

Tuesday, 8 September 1987
(Somehow, I didn't record the time!)

What a special day for me! Today is one of our National Days, (There are five National Days in Malta.) – Victory Day. I've never felt so patriotic.

Today, for our last class for Childhood across Culture, I took some *pastizzi* (pasties) and two *qassatat tal-ful* (traditional Maltese pies). Ron got some coffee from the staff, and we all had a great time. He enjoyed the *qassatat* too. That was quite a thrill for me. Then I showed some slides of Malta and Gozo. It certainly was an appropriate day for it.

This afternoon I rang up Telecom to complain about the excessive number of registered calls I've been getting. I feel I handled the Telecom officer pretty well. After that I rang up Consumer Affairs and explained my problem to them. Later on, I wrote them a letter, of which I intend to keep a photocopy. I have a feeling that this is going to emerge as an important case. If I'm not satisfied with the investigation, I intend to get in touch with the media.

Thursday, 10 September 1987
1:00 p.m.

I've just come back from shopping with my sister-in-law Irene and have been listening to the Maltese radio program while having lunch. Lately there has been a lot of patriotism inside me. I don't know why – these last fifteen years that I've been in Australia, I've tried to leave my patriotism behind. I was only fooling myself – it was a facade. I noticed my patriotism when my family and I went to the Commonwealth building in the city to apply for our Australian citizenship. I felt like a traitor. Psychologically, I'm not ready to give up my Maltese citizenship.

My self-esteem at the moment is quite high – so high that no matter where society places me according to my status, as an individual I feel that I am right up the top, where nobody can walk over me. However, I respect anybody no matter where society places them, whether at the top or the bottom.

I am a Maltese citizen, an individual with a high self-esteem who is ready to stand up for her rights – no privileges or favours.

Speaking of rights, this morning I posted the letter to the Commonwealth Ombudsman to lodge my complaint about my phone bill. I am proud of that letter.

My sister rang me up this afternoon. She is concerned about an eighteen-year-old girl who is having a nervous breakdown. I feel I need to help that girl – she needs emotional support from someone who can understand her. I was in the same situation myself. I know how painful it is, and when you are in that deplorable state you need all the support and encouragement you can get. I know that studying is not the real cause of her psychological problems. The fear behind her studies is disguising some other fear. I need to talk to that girl. I'm sure I might be of some help. If only I can help her! This is painful not only for her but also for her family.

Saturday, 12 September 1987

(Somehow, I did not record the time. Also, the following entry was originally in Maltese. This is the first time that I wrote the diary in Maltese!)

Today I went to the Maltese Community Centre at Parkville for the official opening of the Maltese Cultural Week. The Maltese High Commissioner, the Hon. Victor Gauci, was also at this event. I was ready to make a speech about the crisis of the Maltese language in Australia. But unfortunately, Prof Alfred Briffa said that it was not appropriate for this event. However, he encouraged me to publish it in *The Maltese Herald.* Even my friend Mary Cauchi was impressed with what I wrote and said I expressed myself well.

During the cocktail party I introduced myself to Victor Darmanin, a radio broadcaster, and told him how much I agree with what he said about how the Maltese National Day has taken a political slant. I also told him how I feel about the main contributing factors to the continuing decline of the Maltese language in Australia.

I don't know what happened to me, but these last two weeks I have had a strong rekindling of patriotism towards Malta and the Maltese culture. *Nothing is frightening me – whatever I feel, I say.* Indeed, that's what I did this evening with Victor Darmanin and his wife. They did not agree with me about the crisis and the contributing factors with regard to the Maltese language in Australia. After the discussion I felt concerned about speaking up, even though I made them laugh when I said that Victor is with me in the kitchen during his radio program. Mary told me afterwards how much she admired the way I argued and supported my position.

Monday, 14 September 1987
10:30 a.m.

I've just posted out some letters, including one to my brother Laurry, who lives in Sydney. I told him that next year I'm going to start tertiary studies. I felt that I should be the one to tell him, before he finds out about it from someone else. He was always proud of me when I was at school, even though he never told me so. I also felt that approaching him myself would mean a lot to him. Unfortunately, nobody in the family has reached out to him since he was a kid. He was considered the black sheep. That's why he ended up a delinquent child.

I also posted out an article that I want to be published in *The Maltese Herald*. I have a copy of the article, and I feel proud of myself.

And finally, I passed on a letter to June Gleeson, the Deputy Director of the Western Institute. I kept two copies of that letter – one for myself and one to pass on to the Maltese Education Committee.

Saturday, 19 September 1987
11:00 a.m.

Yesterday I had an intimate chat with my sister-in-law Mary (Laurry's wife). She came from Sydney, and she is staying here till Tuesday. I explained to her about my mother's hostility and how Laurry was the scapegoat of the family – important factors contributing to my brother's psychological problems. Mary was quite interested in what I told her. I also told her about his childhood – how creative and imaginative he was, why he ended up the black sheep of the family and how insecure we were. Our parents were parents in theory, not in practice. Then I explained why my mother was a hostile person – she herself was a victim of hostility, and God knows what else.

While I was explaining all this to Mary, I could see how moved she was, especially when I was telling her that my parents never showed any affection towards him. It all made sense.

Tuesday, 22 September 1987
7:00 a.m.

Yesterday I received a letter from my mother. As I started reading it aloud to my sister and sister-in-law, I was happy because now she understands about me going back to my studies. But then I stumbled on something unexpected. She said she is losing her eyesight in one eye, and the optometrist told her that it could be more from diabetes than from the cataract. That news devastated us. My mum said she can still read and write. I am going to write to her straightaway. This morning Michelle went to the airport with my sister to accompany Mary because she is going back to Sydney.

Thursday, 24 September 1987
10:00 p.m.

Yesterday at the library I came across the book *Dibs In Search of Self* by Virginia M. Axline. Since I started it, I have become so interested in it that I can't wait to read it all. It's a remarkable story of a five-year-old boy who was emotionally deprived, and consequently his real personality could not emerge. This boy reminds me of so many people within my family who have the same problem. I was one of them. Then there is my mother and my brother. This is what I have been trying to say to people around me these last couple of months and more recently to Mary, my sister-in-law.

Mary rang me up this afternoon because she hasn't told Laurry that our mother is losing her eyesight. She is frightened about how he will handle the news. She told me that apparently my letter has upset him, because when she asked him if he had received it, he didn't seem too keen to say 'yes' and acted rather strangely. He didn't even keep the letter in the place he usually keeps his letters, as if he wanted to hide it.

What upset him in that letter? It is either the fact that I want to seek advice from a psychiatrist regarding returning to study, or else my attempt to reach out to him and show him I care has emotionally moved him. My brother is so emotionally hurt and deprived, and I wish I could help him. How I wish that my recovery would be one day be responsible for his recovery – I can do it. I have no power to change others, but the change in me would be powerful and have a ripple effect. I want to help him, but how? I want to reach out to him, but he doesn't seem ready to respond to my help.

Friday, 25 September 1987
7:00 p.m.

When I opened *The Maltese Herald* at the newsagent this morning, I saw my article in it. I was so excited that I felt I was making a fuss over it. I looked around me at the market to see if I could see someone I knew to share my news with, holding the newspaper against my chest as if it were something precious. I suppose I have every reason to be proud of it.

Louie just read it, and he did say that it is good. To be honest, the more I read it the better it sounds. It only took me about half an hour to write it.

This afternoon I handed in another article to be published in the local newspaper through the Western Institute. Both Sophie and Donna (staff members) were pleased with it, and they suggested I have my picture taken. Somehow, the thought of that publicity frightened me – again, as if people 'were making a fuss over nothing'. It seemed like I was bragging or showing off, and people would laugh at me. I also felt as if now that I have had some publicity, people's expectations of me would be high, and I would be obliged to fulfil those expectations. That frightened me.

This morning I felt quite the opposite. I felt that I am already an achiever, even though I haven't achieved anything yet in terms of certificates or diplomas.

Monday, 28 September 1987
12:00 p.m.

These last three days I have been recollecting some highlights of my early childhood, and I ended up writing three essays: '*Il-Landa tal-Kunserva*' (The Tomato Paste Tin), '*In-Narċiss*' (The narcissus) and '*The Wied ta' Għajn Xejba*' (The valley at Għajn Xejba). Writing these essays rekindled in me the happiness I experienced in the early years of my life – that is, from five years of age onwards.

Why did I enjoy nature so much? Is it because in nature I found love – love that I couldn't get from my parents?

I've almost finished reading the book about Dibs. Like that five-year-old boy, I was emotionally deprived. No wonder I felt so insecure. What a loss! That's probably why I turned to nature. In nature I found love, peace, pleasure, even fun. I always wanted to express these feelings. I envied the British poet Wordsworth because he could express himself so well in his poems. I tried to express my feelings through painting, but I didn't succeed. And now I'm discovering that I possess a talent that is helping me give vent to these emotions – writing prose.

I was never aware of this talent before. I'm sure it was always there, but somehow it couldn't emerge because of my emotional problems. Now that I'm free of hostility, I have found peace within myself – that peace I have been yearning for all these years.

Dibs and I have so many things in common. Like him, I learned by observing the beauty of nature that was around me. I was limited in expressing my feelings. There was so much emotional hurt inside me. Dibs was not hurt as much as I was. He was not a victim of incest and other sexual abuse like I was. No wonder I had so many psychological problems.

Undoubtedly Dibs was a special boy, who at such a young age managed to find his real self. But he got professional help at the age of five – I managed to find such help only four years ago, when I started undergoing psychoanalysis.

I feel like I'm a special person too – very special indeed. Finding my real self was not easy and trying to 'make up' for the harm that befell my immediate family was/is even harder.

But through this turmoil I discovered my inner strength, which would not have happened otherwise.

Chapter 7

Depression and Fear

Friday, 1 October 1987
(Somehow, I did not record the time)

These last three days I have been feeling depressed. I have been trying to figure out what's behind my depression. I know I slipped into depression when Sophie (a staff member at the Western Institute) suggested I have my photo taken for the press release. I was also thinking of getting my driving licence before Christmas. October seems to be the time when my depression is at its worst. After all, that's when I had a psychological breakdown six years ago. This month seems to trigger something. Louie's birthday is on the fifth. The sixteenth is the anniversary of my father's death, and the nineteenth is my birthday. October was when I was going to start my teaching training in Malta. I was offered a place at the teaching college but didn't take it because I decided to get married and come to Australia. I suppose the fact that I had to give up my academic career has something to do with it.

The essays I've been writing about my childhood might have triggered something too. Through them I have been reliving those happy days of my life – at least the happy side of it, because I could see myself being so lonely too, trying to be in touch with nature, in which I found a degree of peace, serenity, friendship and love. These last few days I have been feeling sorry for myself. I've also been thinking of my psychoanalyst, as if I'm depending on him.

Saturday, 2 October 1987
10:00 p.m.

I am in an acute state of depression. It frightens me. I thought I would never slip into such a state again. I was wrong – it can still happen. Is this the October vicious cycle? I feel so down that I think this depression will never dissipate. How frightening it is! I even feel suicidal.

What a sharp contrast between the way I'm feeling now and the way I felt recently, when I was experiencing so much energy and inner peace. Now I can't seem to enjoy anything. I can't see myself returning to study. I feel pessimistic even about Michelle. I keep thinking of my psychoanalyst, who is away on long service leave.

Yesterday my depression lifted a bit when I received two letters, one from Victor Darmanin and the other from Dr Bob Montgomery. I read the letters a few times. In a way it does make me feel good. How good I felt when I wrote to Dr Montgomery, who had a segment on the radio! And now? I am in great emotional pain. I seem to have turned against God. I feel like swearing. There must be lot of anger and hostility inside me at the moment. But why? Or rather, what triggered it?

Monday, 5 October 1987
(No time recorded)

It's Louie's birthday!

The acute state of depression I've been in this last week or so frightens me. I seem to have lost interest in almost everything – reading, writing, listening to music, etc. Even the way I feel – I don't seem close to the family – at one stage I felt angry at Mark. Every time I look at the book *Dibs In Search of Self*, it sorts of put me off. Even the book *The Child, the Family and the Outside World* – I don't know why! I really enjoyed reading them. I suppose that's clear evidence that this depression has to do with my childhood. I feel so down. Will any good will come out of this? Does anybody within the medical profession understand *exactly* how it feels when you're in the throes of depression? I feel that you can't control depression – I've been trying so hard. And what a contrast with the way I have been before, when I experienced that state of elation. I don't want to lose that peace, serenity and contentment I experienced before. I felt so good!

Wednesday, 7 October 1987
2:00 p.m.

I'm still shrouded in acute depression. I feel so lazy – I want to lie down. I can hardly write in my diary. I'm sitting in the lounge, and as I looked at the books, I realised how acute this depression is. Some days ago, I couldn't wait to finish my chores, so I could catch up with my reading and writing. This state frightens me. Will I ever come out of it? There are times when I feel like giving up, and there are times when I feel some good will come out of it. I can't wait to come out of this depression. I felt so good before – I don't know how to express myself. I suppose it is depicted in my writing. This depression is also affecting the way I communicate with people. How destructive it can be!

Yesterday I had my first driving lesson with Barkley. I did very well; in fact, it lifted my depression a bit.

I can't stop wondering what's behind my depression. I've been thinking of incest again. I have been waking up at about 1:30 a.m. in a state of shock. This was the same time that I used to get up as a child. I remember my father giving me a piece of bread sprinkled with sugar at that hour of the night.

My parents slept in separate rooms. I used to sleep in the room where my mother and other siblings slept.

I've noticed that while I'm in this state of acute depression, I don't seem to have any affection towards anything or anybody – not even the dog or members of the family. That worries me a bit. Generally speaking, I don't seem to care about them. Is this a reflection of the little girl who was so emotionally hurt? I believe that the basis of psychological problems is emotions. When I was free of hostility and fear, my thinking was so logical. I found pleasure in every little thing. I enjoyed every moment of my life. And now? There are times when although I might not feel suicidal, I feel I would be better off dead.

And what about my feelings towards God? I used to see God in everyone and everything around me. Now I feel alienated from God. I don't feel close to him at all. He understands (I feel like crying). He knows what I'm going through. I'm sure he is not only walking beside me, but he is also carrying me. I have no strength to walk. I'm sure he understands. I don't need to ask him for forgiveness.

Thursday, 8 October 1987
10:00 p.m.

Still feeling depressed. Yesterday I started thinking again of the unknown. What could have happened to me during the first five years of my life that I don't remember? This morning I realised what triggered my depression. It's the essay I wrote about the *Wied ta' Għajn Xejb*a (valley in the neighbourhood), when I imagined myself as a toddler, sitting down in the field next to the valley while my mother was cutting grass for the sheep in the barn. I reflected upon myself at such a young age in relation to my mother; the idea that I was 'making it up' (i.e. being sexually abused by my father) as if I was not telling the truth triggered something. Could it be that I was afraid of lying, or is it that at such a young age I was *accused* of lying? Yes, that word *lying* seems to hold the key.

Let's assume that I was lying when I told my mother something regarding incest. Why would I lie about it? How could I make up such a lie? How am I going to convince myself?

Saturday, 10 October 1987
10:30 a.m.

I don't know why I'm writing this diary. My self-esteem is so low at the moment. I have just come home from shopping. My depression seems to be getting worse. I have just burst into tears, and Michelle put her arms around me and tried to comfort me. I was like a little girl. Speaking of little girls, what happened to Victoria? She seems to have vanished completely. She was so strong – in fact she was a leader.

Who am I now? Where is all the strength? I feel so helpless! Where is my recovery? I seem to have lost everything. What is behind my depression? The fear of facial hair seems to be coming back to me. Does that hold a clue? I don't even want to look at my face in the mirror. What am I afraid of?

What good, if any, will come out of this depression? It's so frightening! This is even worse than what I went through a couple of months ago. In spite of that ordeal, I felt so strong.

With this depression, I don't feel close to anybody. Poor Louie. It must be so heartbreaking to see me like this.

Monday, 12 October 1987
3:30 p.m.

This morning I rang up the Child Psychiatry Unit and made

an appointment to see Ms Jacob next Friday. When she spoke to me on the phone, my first reaction was disappointment. Somehow, she sounded abrupt to me. I hope that after meeting her I will feel close to her; otherwise, it's no use having therapy with her. I was thinking of Mrs Garcia today, how nice she sounded on the phone when I spoke to her recently. I feel so close to her, even though I've never met her.

Last night Brother Philip from Chisolm College rang me up to let me know about the Better Effective Parenting Course that he is starting soon. I told him about the acute state of depression I'm in and the possible reasons behind it. He was so understanding. He even told me to come and see him whenever I wanted to.

I'm going back to the Institute tonight for semester two. In one way I'm looking forward to it, but in another I'm not. This debilitating depression frightens me – it's certainly interfering with my concentration. I don't feel like reading or writing anything.

Tuesday, 13 October 1987
2:00 p.m.

I have just come from the Institute. I had my first class for Childhood across Cultures. I felt uncomfortable in class, which was disappointing. Not only could I not concentrate, but I couldn't communicate with Ron Adams after class. I told him about the acute state of depression I'm in at the moment.

This disappointment made me feel worse. I was hoping that my depression would lift. On the contrary, it seems to have gone from bad to worse. What am I going to do? I feel so broken-hearted. All of my hopes regarding returning to study are completely dashed.

I can't even express myself in writing. How frightening it is! Where is all the inner strength I had a few weeks ago? Depression seems to be more powerful than that strength. It seems to have completely extinguished the burning flame in me!

I have experienced both strength and flow of energy and depression. I want to study these two extreme states. When acute depression takes over, you are completely helpless. These two states have absolutely nothing in common. What more can I say except that I feel so negative? Nobody can understand this depression unless they experience it.

The sun is shining – spring is in the air. What a pity I can't enjoy it. Nature, which I enjoyed so much, can't alleviate my depression. I know I'm not thinking logically at the moment. It's depicted in my writing. After all, 'The way we think is the way we feel.'

Oh, help me, God!

Wednesday, 14 October 1987
7:40 a.m.

I'm so frightened of losing Michelle emotionally. She seems to feel rejected – I'm trying to reach out to her and assure her of my love for her. But there seems to be so much anger inside her towards me. I don't deserve this at all. I have tried so hard, no matter what. This is so painful to me – I can't afford to lose Michelle. I need her as much as she needs me.

5:00 p.m.

My depression lifted a bit – I do feel better. As my depression lifted, I felt reasonably angry at Michelle, which made me feel emotionally stronger. It seems to me to be justified anger. She told Mark that everybody in this house is against her, as if she doesn't belong in this family. I felt emotionally strong, and when I approached her, I asked her what I had been trying to do yesterday. I pointed out that I tried to reach out to her, and if she feels we don't want her to belong to the family, it's because she wants to believe that!

As I've already pointed out, this is justified anger – there is a reason behind it. I just picked up a beautiful lilac flower from the garden, the first one that blossomed, and put it in her room.

Please help me, God, to handle her the right way. This is not a matter of who is right or wrong. There has to be a reason behind her behaviour.

Thursday, 15 October 1987
4:30 p.m.

I'm on the verge of panic. This afternoon at the Institute I had an intimate talk with another student, Stephanie, who is doing two short courses with me and who also happens to be a client of Dr. Garcia. I felt threatened in two ways – academically and personally. What is behind this jealousy? If I witnessed my father making love to someone else when I was little, that must have been a great shock to me. I certainly have a great emotional problem!

I just told Louie how I feel about that woman. I hope he didn't misunderstand me – maybe I shouldn't have told him, because I know it's hard for him to understand transference (a psychoanalytical construct) and unresolved traumas.

Since I have been analysing myself lately, I've noticed a few things regarding my emotions. This morning, for example, I was listening to Derryn Hinch on the radio, and just before he learned the outcome of his appeal regarding the current court case, I was hoping he would be jailed. What a contrast! When the case was first brought up by Derryn, I applauded him and believed he was definitely doing the right thing by naming child molesters.

Saturday, 17 October 1987
9:00 a.m.

I'm sitting in the car at Queenscliffe. Louie brought Mark fishing because we have been promising him for so long, and we didn't want to disappoint him anymore. I really enjoyed the hour and a half trip. As I kept introspecting and analysing myself, it became clear what's behind my depression. There seems to be not only anger but also *a great sense of loss*. I seem to have lost my father a long time ago, long before he died in 1980. That's why I don't seem to have grieved over his death.

Lately, I have identified with Brother Philip as my father. Emotionally I felt close to him. I even had a dream about him the same night I went to see him. In the dream I experienced a good and comfortable feeling – so good that there are times I want to rekindle it by recollecting the dream. After I rang him up yesterday to tell him I will be seeing my new temporary psychologist, depression hit me again – I felt that I have lost him. Emotionally I was in a real mess.

As I'm sitting in the car, I just saw a man going past. I almost panicked with fear. But as he went past and I felt safe, I had a strong sexual impulse, which only lasted a few moments because I suppressed it – what a contradiction: fear and sexual desire!

These last couple of days, I could clearly see that I identified with Dr. Garcia as my father. When I met one of his clients, I felt threatened (and still do at times). I felt strongly jealous and a sense of loss (Dr. Garcia). With these emotions there is anger towards my therapist. That's when I wanted to turn to Brother Philip, because with him I didn't feel threatened.

What an inner drama! Loss – Jealousy – Threat.

These are the key words I'm working with at the moment.

I feel like a little girl in search of her father. She is trying to turn to someone (male) with whom she can feel secure. She wants affection and security. Why can't I identify with Louie? He is certainly showing me care and affection and a certain amount of security. What is he missing? I know that Dr. Garcia and Brother Philip better understand what is going on – Louie understands a little bit from what I explain to him. *With understanding comes security. Affection through physical contact is not enough.*

As I was questioning my intelligence at high school, panic struck. With this doubt of intelligence came the fear of competition – that other female patient came to mind. Could this academic competition disguise another fear? This competition is pressing the panic button – yes, this is *female competition.*

I'm dealing with a number of issues here. The question of intelligence, the issue of boundary, female competition – academically and personally.

One) Female client – double threat.

Two) Jasmine, a parent from St Albans South Primary School who is doing a Bachelor of Education, pressed my panic button. Since she lives in the neighbourhood and is doing the same course I was intending to do, I felt threatened – more specifically, my security was under threat as far as getting a job at St Albans South Primary School.

Now why did I look for security at that particular school? Is it because it is close to *home* – security around the home? Doesn't this come down to security at home as a child?

Jasmine seems to have threatened that security. She has also beaten me academically in terms of time. Why should it bother me so much? This is not a question of academic competition.

Coming up with these possible explanations makes me feel good. But unfortunately, this good feeling is interspersed with bouts of depression and fear.

I just realised that when I regress emotionally, I also regress intellectually. No wonder I can't follow what I'm reading or listening to. When this happens, I get frustrated and become panicky. Before I can continue with my return to study, I need to solve my emotional problems. Then I can keep growing intellectually.

My concentration span is so short! It's very self-centred. Through this self-analysis, I seem to have 'discovered' a number of theories. To me they are discoveries, because I am not familiar with theories about development. I haven't read much about this topic. Theories also remind me of theorems and riders based on theorems. I was so good at them at secondary school. Theories remind me of reasoning logically, which helps you come to a conclusion based on the data.

Mark came for a cuppa before, and he was so excited about the fish that he and Louie caught – Mark caught a flathead and a banjo shark, while Louie caught a monster of a squid. Mark looked so cute in his yellow raincoat and hood. I'm going to join them now. Good luck, Vicky!

4:00 p.m.

I want to ask my mother to send me my father's photo, taken when he was in his late thirties. I can't get angry at my father when I look at the photo that was taken when he was about sixty years old. In that photo he looks so fragile, I feel sorry for him when I look at him. I know how sick he was. Having said that, I need to allow my inner child to express her emotions, especially anger at him as a child molester.

Sunday, 18 October 1987
3:00 p.m.

These last couple of days I have embarked on an intensive self-analysis. There are moments when I feel good about it because it's helping me find the underlying causes of my depression, the disguises of the fears I'm experiencing and what's behind the fits of rage that are expressed when I get those frightening moments. It has become clear to me that in moments of rage I see God as my father and Our Lady as my mother and take my anger out on them. Last Saturday night, I felt so much despair that I kept saying, '*Alla, Madonna oqtluni*' (God, Our Lady kill me), and when I get angry at Michelle, I swear in Maltese using God's name: *F'ex ommok li Alla welled.*

I am being obsessed with this self-analysis – when I try to divert my attention, I keep coming back to it. It's clear that I have been and still am identifying with different people – sometimes differently with the same people at different times.

Monday, 19 October 1987
2:41 p.m.

Still waiting anxiously for a letter from my mother. From my self-analysis, all my emotions seem to be evolving around my insights.

These are the conclusions I have come up with:

1) Victim of incest - contradictory feelings about it. There are times when I'm angry at my father; there are times when I'm glad that it happened and disappointed when doubt arises – clearly indicates there is a sexual desire that needs to be fulfilled.

2) I must have witnessed my father having sex with my mother (perhaps even with someone else). This shocked me so much that I even envy other women – I feel threatened by them, and by what I witnessed as a child I felt that I had lost my father.

3) It is also possible that I saw my father being sexually involved with one of our male neighbours, and then I experienced feelings of excitement and relief because he found sexual pleasure with someone else and would leave me in peace.

4) I tried to express myself when I was little. But because I was so little, I couldn't express myself. Later on in life, I also expressed myself – however, it was my word against that of someone with authority.

5) I was accused of lying about being sexually abused.

6) I was punished for dobbing my father in. Indeed, I have some psychosomatic symptoms in my left wrist – burning pains caused by cigarette butts, which I feel from time to time. My father used to smoke a lot when I was little.

I was accused of being stupid – *ma' tafx x'qeda' tgħid* (she doesn't know what she is saying, implying that I was stupid and lying).

Emotions

1) Fear of my father – clearly depicted in the shocking feeling sometimes when I see Drago, my next-door neighbour. Fear that my father will be listening and seeing me doing something that I shouldn't, such as dobbing him and reaching out for help. This became evident last week when I went to the library at the Institute to do some research for my assignment. I was speaking to the librarian to get some help when my tutor, Jacob Smith, walked in. I turned to the librarian with a frightened look on my face and said to her shakily, 'My tutor is here.' And she replied reassuringly, 'It's OK. You are allowed to seek help from the librarian regarding your assignment.' I will never forget the surprised look on her face when she saw how frightened I must have appeared.

2) Sense of guilt regarding *incompetence* in bringing up my children – followed by anger at Mark, followed by depression.

3) Fear of being tested and proven wrong regarding intelligence (working sheet we had to do for Child Development).

4) Irritable feeling in class during the lesson on bibliography. I could not follow the example exactly. I felt I knew how to do it, and I did not need anybody else to tell me how to do it.

5) The inner voice seems to come out strongly when I'm questioning my IQ. There are moments when I realise how clever I am due to intuition. Then there are moments when there is evidence that I'm not. The inner voice tells me, 'You think you're clever, but you're not.' I've been thinking of an incident that involved my niece Rose when she was six years old. She told my sister-in-law that she would dob her in for smoking!

6) The times when I was angry at God, I identified with Him as my father. I could never get angry at my father (I'm experiencing a feeling of denial regarding incest while I'm writing this – feeling sorry for my father).

7) The superego was strong when I was on the way to have a session with Brother Philip.

When I think about how much I'm looking forward to the session with Ms Jacob, the thought 'How are you going to express yourself?' goes through my mind. A fear of not being able to express myself follows.

I'm also having problems listening to talkback radio and the news. I feel as if I don't want to know. As a result, I can't follow what's going on around me.

When I used to go for confession back in Malta as I was growing up and had to decide what 'sins' I was going to confess, the superego would try to find something extremely hard to confess due to embarrassment, and if I didn't confess it, I would feel guilty about it. The worst thing is that even if I confessed it, I still wouldn't be relieved of the psychological torture imposed by the superego through the intense sense of guilt. What a turmoil that inner world used to be and so vulnerable to the horrendous voice of the superego. It gives me the shivers just thinking about it. *What a psychological, mental and emotional torture!* And what is even worse, no matter what and how much I confessed, I would not get any relief from it. There was *always* something nagging to feel guilty about and need to confess.

Tuesday, 20 October 1987
1:45 p.m.

My Birthday!

After I returned from the Institute, I had a panic attack. There was a great sense of loss, which was preceded by fear of not expressing myself and fear of competition (at the moment it's taking the form of academic competition).

I need help – I need to regress into my childhood, because there seems to be a need to fulfil that paternal loss. That's what I have been doing recently when I get those panic attacks. I keep saying 'No! No!' as if I don't want to lose 'affection'.

I want to capture these moments of intense pain as proof of what I'm going through. I don't want to lose these moments; they are important to me. This is an essential process embedded in my recovery – no matter how painful it is!

Whenever I'm identifying with people, there is fear inside me, i.e. there is a self that is experiencing genuine fear – not fear as a result of mental fear. When I regress, I keep saying ‘No! No!’ At the moment this sense of loss is strong in me, more so than anger. I need to identify with someone as my father to make up for that loss. There is a great need for it.

During panic moments there are times when I experience *anger*, and there are times when I experience *loss*. It’s quite clear.

Chapter 8

Regression to Infancy

Wednesday, 21 October 1987
8:30 a.m.

I feel that my case is unique. Yesterday while I was going through that emotional ordeal, I wanted to record that moment because I felt that something is going to come out of it – something that nobody within the medical profession is yet aware of. Yes, my case needs to be studied. Something is going to come out of it. Just before, I strongly believed that I wanted to share my case with someone within the medical/mental health profession. But then I felt threatened because if I share it, then someone else is going to beat me. There is something going on here. I seem to want to keep it to myself because I want to be the founder of it. Maybe this is the mission that I talked about with Dr. Garcia.

When I felt threatened, I had a sinking feeling/sense of loss again. After that I didn't feel as strongly about sharing my experience because something is going to come out of it, as I had a few seconds prior to that sinking feeling.

Before, I strongly felt that just as Freud discovered the mechanics of the unconscious mind, I'm going to discover something else. Then an inner voice said, 'What do you think you are? You're stupid.'

2:30 p.m.

Somehow, I feel apprehensive about starting to write my diary in this new A3 spiral exercise book (up till now I have been writing it in a small 'jotter' notebook). I'm experiencing a sinking feeling. I'm scared of making mistakes in my handwriting. I want this diary to be special. That's probably why I'm so cautious of how to present it in terms of handwriting, grammar and neatness.

What am I experiencing now? Fear of expectations, because now I have told Ms Jacob about my feelings about being the founder or discoverer of something. This reminds me of another incident at the Western Institute. I wrote an article to be published in the local paper, entitled 'Returning to Study as a Mature Age Student'. The counsellor was very pleased with it, and she suggested that a picture of me be published with the article. That suggestion pressed the panic button. *I had a fear of expectations* – the same fear I'm experiencing now. Expectations – what do they remind me of? During the first few years of our marriage, a great deal of expectations were placed on me from Louie, especially when we were building our house.

Yes, I do have the fear of expectations. Perhaps that's why I'm so afraid of responsibilities. What does it trigger? My father was in a way an irresponsible man – partly because of his illness. This fear of responsibilities leads me to the fear of not being able to cope – one of the fears my father and I have in common.

At this point, panic struck. I was thinking of what Ms Jacob asked me during the session. She said, 'Do you regard me as a threat?' I said no (i.e. not sexually). But then I kept saying that at home this morning I had a fear of not being able to express myself because I have so much to tell her. I did identify with her to a certain extent.

Before I walked out of her office I told her, 'I'm going to be very *honest* with you regarding my emotions.' What I had in mind was 'open', not 'honest'. It must have been in my unconscious mind.

At the moment the fear of expectations is strong. I keep thinking of Dr. Garcia and his expectations of me regarding my future. That sinking feeling again . . . (pause)

The fear of expectations is strong right now. I'm frightened. This also reminds me of the way I felt after I wrote the letter to my mother in which I told her that I was returning to study. It was the fear of high expectations that stopped me from posting it.

High expectations frighten me.

At the moment I feel down – confused about analysing myself. I seem to be frightened to find out what my inner voice is telling me. I'm questioning that 'leadership' again – I feel doubtful about it – it's frightening me. Why do I have this doubt? It's like the old self again. The inner voice tried to tell me that I'm doing a wrong thing by analysing myself because I'm going to do it my way. The superego tells me that I'm wrong because I seem to be concentrating on incest.

The inner voice is telling me that I only want to be famous because I want to get attention from Dr. Garcia and that I'm trying to compete with Stephanie, the other prospective student who is also a client of Dr. Garcia's.

At the moment I'm thinking of the distinction between the superego and the inner voice. In my case there is certainly a distinction between them. I believe the inner voice (which is not imperative) is what I was told when I was little and is repressed in the unconscious (there is a doubt at the moment). *Doubt is a silent voice that creates conflict.* What creates doubts?

Doubt – this is one area I want to work on.

5:30 p.m.

During today's session, when I talked about the problem with Telecom, something inside me said, 'You see, no matter how sure you were, your strong feeling was wrong. So, this sense of "intuition" you have could be wrong (about being a victim of incest).'

I feel down. Could it be disappointment? When was I disappointed? If I was, why was I disappointed?

I wonder which Vicky I am at the moment. There is something I want to write in the diary, but I'm frightened. What am I frightened of? The old Vicky seems to be frightened of this new personality/self – the one who wants to write.

All I want to record is that there were times when I felt something strong inside me, which made me think that one day the people around me – my immediate family, my sister and her husband, my brothers, my psychoanalyst and even Sue, who works at the beauty salon, are going to be so proud of me because I'm going to be famous. I'm still hesitant to write about it because at the moment that feeling is not there, and therefore I feel like I'm lying, no matter how sure I was of what I felt and thought. I suppose this is the old self. That is why I have been trying to avoid the photo in the identity card. I was so proud of that Vicky/Victoria. To me she seemed so powerful, so much like a leader. Why am I avoiding her? Am I angry, jealous or frightened?

She has just tried to reach out to me with a gentle smile. She has so much courage; she is so gentle! She wants to hold my hand. She knows how fragile I am, just like little Victoria was reaching out to me during my ordeal in July/August. So is Victoria, the one in the photo. I hope she comes back.

9:25 p.m.

Just come from the Institute. SOMETHING HAPPENED IN CLASS – I REGRESSED INTO BABYHOOD.

I am emotionally and mentally frozen. Louie is concerned about me.

10:38 p.m.

I have just been crying for my mother like a little baby.

Thursday, 22 October 1987
7:00 a.m.

What a night it has been! I woke up before midnight. I felt panicky. I realised I needed professional help. I was thinking of going to a hospital in Maribyrnong where I will be under twenty-four-hour supervision. During that ordeal I had a lot of inner strength. I felt that this regression into babyhood was inevitable, and I am on the way to recovery no matter what happens. I kept saying to myself that I'll come out of it. Every time I thought of leaving Louie, Michelle and Mark, I burst into tears because I felt sorry for leaving them behind. But at the same time, I admired the inner strength I had. In my monologue I kept assuring them, 'I'll be back. I'll be all right.' I felt close to them. Yes, I was determined that if I regressed completely into babyhood, I would come out of it, not only for myself and my immediate family but also because there is a mission I need to accomplish. It is a mission – I'm not after fame or money, but *I want to do something for humanity* (I'm thinking of Dr. Elizabeth Kubler-Ross at the moment).

Then panic struck. I had a fear that I might turn up schizophrenic because I am so clever, and I would worry a lot about humanity, as I would be viewing the world differently. I prayed to God for help and said, 'May your will be done.' I was crying. Louie woke up. He wasn't angry, and I tried to explain to him what's going on. I told him that once he understands what's happening, it won't be so frightening. He held me close to him. I felt calm and relaxed. Then at about 2:00 a.m., I fell asleep.

I had two dreams. The first one was about some intruders in the house at night. Louie and I stayed calm. My brother Laurry had hired the intruders. He was even with them in the house. It seemed as if he was angry with me about something and wanted revenge. In the other dream, there was a little three-year-old girl. She was crying. Someone was putting her out of the window. She was rejected because she could not stop crying and go to sleep. I happened to be passing by, and when I saw her being thrown out of the window, I caught her in my arms and hugged her to comfort her. I went inside her house, where there were her parents and a number of little kids of similar ages. Holding the little girl in my arms, I turned to the parents and told them not to harm her, no matter what she did. I explained to them that when I was little, nobody cared about me. They looked at me in astonishment.

I now want to describe what happened in class last night. The first part of the lesson was an introduction to sociology lecture by Rob Clarke. He explained it well, but I found it hard to take notes. I understood what he was saying, but I could not register it in my mind. The second part of the lesson was an open discussion. I stayed motionless and speechless – all I could do was breathe and look. I could hear voices, but I couldn't follow what was being said. I picked out a few words but nothing else – not because it was difficult. That's when I realised that I'd regressed into babyhood. I felt like a baby emotionally – calm, just looking around, exchanging a smile every now and then. I didn't panic when I realised what was happening, because it explained why I couldn't follow what was being said. I regressed not only emotionally but also intellectually. What a beautiful experience this was!

Now I understand why I can't follow what I'm listening to on the radio or television. Even in conversations involving three people, I tend to switch off completely when the other two are talking and the conversation doesn't involve me. I have been regressing to babyhood, and I wasn't aware of it. When I stammer, I regress to infanthood. Yes, I have been regressing to different stages of my early life, and I wasn't aware of it.

9:19 a.m.

The superego has just been trying to make me feel guilty about the incest. Yesterday I told my psychologist that in my case there are two parts to incest – the part that frightened me and the part I enjoyed. As I was having breakfast, I was trying to remember the incidents when I regressed. Before, I used to think that the problem I have expressing myself has to do with the belief that when I was little, I tried to express myself as a protest against incest. At that point the superego tried to make me feel guilty, as if it wasn't true that I wanted to protest against incest. Therefore, I enjoyed it.

It seems that the superego doesn't want to be wrongly blamed.

11:00 a.m.

There are moments when something inside me tries to stop me from writing, as if this something feels threatened by my writing. What could it be? Is it the old self? I wouldn't be surprised. The old me seems to be frightened, jealous and even *angry at Vicky* – i.e. Vicky in the identity card photo. In fact, the former has been avoiding her. It was only yesterday afternoon that the two selves/personalities met temporarily.

Fear of not coping – Could it be possible that when I experience this fear, I regress into infanthood? After all, infants are not expected to cope with household chores.

What about the fear of not making ends meet? I inherited that from my father. I'm sure this is a disguise for another fear.

Then there is the fear of responsibility as a mother. My father didn't have this fear. I know there are times when I feel guilty regarding motherhood. I need to watch out for the circumstances and the other emotions that evolve around this fear.

I have already started questioning the difference between the superego and the inner voice. Let me take the question of my IQ as an example. Lately the inner voice has been telling me, 'You think you're clever, but you're not.' Then last night I had the fear of becoming schizophrenic because I was so clever.

I just realised that it is the old me who is behind the inner voice and that fear (of not being clever). In fact, just before I started writing this part I had a sinking feeling, and that same 'thing' tried to stop me from writing. There seems to be no doubt about it.

The old self is behind the inner voice when it comes to:

1) Writing/academic threats

2) The fear of becoming schizophrenic and losing touch with reality

3) High expectations

The question now is, what are the factors that moulded this 'old self'? (By the 'old self' I mean my personality – i.e. the negative side of it).

I just had a sinking feeling. Before, I was excited because I thought I had 'discovered' something in psychology. But when I realised that this old self is moulded by emotions and experiences from when I was little, I was disappointed. I could have discovered something, though, between the inner voice and the superego.

So far, the inner voice is a whole self and has a life of its own.

Is there any difference between the superego and the inner voice?

1:00 p.m.

I just went into the kitchen to prepare tea. I was cold and shivering. I was thinking that I must strip myself of the old self and get rid of her. I had that sense of loss and felt sorry for the old me. I was regressing into babyhood, when I started feeling cold and shivery. *That sense of loss is so strong in me that I don't even want to lose my old self.*

I have now regressed into babyhood. It's a good feeling. There is calmness inside me.

4:33 p.m.

I slipped into acute depression again. I'm breathing heavily. As for emotions, all I can say is DEPRESSION. My brain feels heavy, as if something is pressing on it. Even my ears seem to be blocked. What a painful state to be in. No words can describe it.

When Louie walked in, I could see stress and anxiety written all over his face. He looked pale too. He is concerned about me. While I'm writing, I feel like closing my eyes. They feel so heavy. I don't have the urge to write – I'm forcing myself. All that inner strength is gone. I'm pausing between one sentence and another. Perhaps I'd better lie down and rest because I'm stressing myself.

7:09 p.m.

I'm still in bed, in a state of shock. When I realised that I'm in shock, the thought of high expectations came to mind, followed by the dream in which I was holding the head of a snake while Louie milked the poison out. Before I started writing this part, the inner voice didn't want me to write about it. *It seems the inner voice is threatened by the truth.* I also noticed that the frozen state I was in when I was shrouded in depression at 4:33 p.m. started to thaw when the depression turned into a state of shock.

Now there seems to be a bit of calmness inside me – I'm not in such a shocking state.

When I said that the frozen state began to thaw, I meant having some ability to write even though there is no strong urge to write, and I could analyse my emotions because now there is some emotion. When I'm shrouded in deep depression there is nothing but depression, which immobilises my mind – just like an immobile vehicle with the engine going. The depression I'm referring to (at 4:33 p.m.) was not triggered by threats. It was like the one I experienced before I got in touch with Ms Jacob.

During this afternoon's session, Ms Jacob asked me, 'Is it really all of you – the whole self/personality – that you want to get rid of, not just part of it?' And I replied, 'There are so many negative aspects to that personality!'

The negative points outweighed the positive points so much that I overlooked my old self. I know that most of the time I was symbolically speaking of a potential Hitler in me, but there were times when I was a real Mother Teresa, especially to Michelle. And what about when I guided Louie about his authoritarian relationship with the kids and that 'two wrongs don't make one right'?

While I was writing the above paragraph, I realised that even if I don't discover anything new in the field of psychoanalysis, my experiences, including conclusions, are going to prove that some theories are right, since I am only a layperson who doesn't know anything about theories.

As for Freud, I found out about him only fifteen months ago. I read a book about his life and another one, *Five Short Accounts of Psychoanalysis*. The first book was written in a way that I could understand. I enjoyed reading the second one too, even though most of the time I didn't know what Freud meant.

Two things that stuck in my mind are the superego and the concept of childhood sexuality. I still don't know much about them. All I remember from what Freud said is that the superego is imperative, and sexual drives originate in childhood.

This reminds me of the common emotions I experienced

recently with Brother Philip and a priest six years ago. On both occasions I refused to be hugged, not because I didn't trust them but because I felt I would be sexually aroused, and then I would end up with an inner conflict (sexual arousal, followed by conflict between guilt and the superego). I couldn't allow that to happen – it's mental and emotional torture, too painful for me.

But the fact remains that there is a sexual desire that needs to be fulfilled.

Friday, 23 October 1987
7:30 a.m.

I have just been over what I wrote yesterday, and I enjoyed reading it – in fact, it made me feel better because when I got up, I was in a state of shock and disappointment because I didn't have any dreams – or so I thought. I just remembered a dream in which there was this couple back home, Vitorja and Ġirġi ta' Garga, whom I knew when I was little. In the dream I was pleased to meet them.

Earlier, when I was preparing Mark's lunch, I realised that the inner voice is not only negative but against my wishes.

Inner voice in relation to wishes

This seems to be leading me to something. Is the inner voice indirectly guiding me to identify my wishes in the unconscious mind? In my case there are two types of desires – sexual desires and future desires regarding my career. Could I have stumbled onto something?
Take threat as an example. I feel there is a double threat in me – a female threat and an academic threat.

As I have pointed out in my diary, I feel strongly threatened by other women in the case of Dr. Garcia. This has to do with my experience as a child, when I felt I had lost my father to another woman.

10:41 a.m.

I just had a feeling that I'm not ready to recover, because it's only through this ordeal that I can study the negative emotions and mental states – that is, the chaotic inner world of someone suffering from mental illness. If I recover completely, there is nothing much to study – there is nothing new. How many qualified people have studied these emotions and mental states while they were experiencing them?

Saturday, 24 October 1987
6:20 a.m.

I don't have the urge to write, but I'll try to give an account of what happened during the night. I woke up before 11:30 p.m. in a mild state of shock, and I tried to figure out the emotional and mental state I had been in just before I went to sleep. I realised that I must have regressed to the stage of my life in which I had already started reasoning. It wasn't the same babyhood I had regressed to in class. I also noticed that it wasn't the stage in my life in which I had experienced loss. It must have been a period in between. At that point my inner voice told me to have a look at the time. I noticed that the time I woke up was the same time I had woken up a couple of nights ago when I was overcome by fear. I realised also that this time (11:30 p.m.) is earlier than the time I have been waking up, namely 2:30 a.m. This indicated to me that I had regressed to that stage of my life when I used to get up at night back home, and I remember my father giving me a piece of bread sprinkled with sugar to eat.

Gradually I was overcome by fear. I didn't cry, but I started breathing heavily and taking short breaths. Louie, who was having trouble sleeping, noticed it. He lifted his head up to see if I was asleep. I told him in an alarming voice, 'I'm frightened'. He stretched out his left arm, and holding me tight, he assured me that nobody is going to hurt me. I was still petrified but I felt safe, so safe that I felt close to him emotionally.

The state I was in yesterday, I felt so far away from him – I must have been identifying with him as my father. I told him that, and he was so understanding. I kept telling him, 'You should be proud of yourself because you are helping me recover.' 'That's all right', he said. I felt so proud of him! After ten minutes or so he said to me in Maltese, '*Qed issaħħanni*' (literally meaning 'You are warming me up', but it also has a sexual connotation). That implied he was sexually aroused, and I got so frightened. I said to him in a gasping voice, 'No! No!' This was definitely no for sex or even for him to masturbate. 'Alright', he said. 'I understand.' Then I was a relieved, and gradually my fear started to subside a bit.

Then all of a sudden, my right hand went completely numb. I got up with a jerk and said in a frightened voice, 'My arm!' I was frightened that I had developed a psychosomatic symptom. And the first thing that came to my mind was that I don't want to lose the feeling in my right hand because I want to write. Louie told me reassuringly, 'It's only pins and needles.' For me it didn't feel like pins and needles. It felt as if that part of my arm, from the hand to the elbow, was not there! Gradually my fear began to subside a bit, and I started to regain feeling in it.

On reflection, as soon as I felt my right hand going completely numb, I realised what was happening. *I strongly believe that realising that numbness was a psychosomatic symptom and having an insight about the little girl using her right hand to masturbate my father helped me end that psychosomatic symptom.*

After a few minutes, I turned around on my left side and told Louie I was going to sleep. I gave him my back. He turned around, too, and put his arm around me. I made sure he didn't touch my breast. When his penis touched my leg, I moved my leg away because I didn't want it to touch me.

From this experience I could see that I was definitely frightened of sex. During that ordeal I kept muttering to myself repeatedly in a low voice 'No, no!' This repetition of 'no' is not the 'no' to the loss of my father.

8:00 a.m.

I am still in bed. I feel so dazed. I must still be in a state of regression. That's probably why I don't have the urge to write and analyse myself. I just noticed that I don't have any sexual drives whatsoever. If I have been regressing to infanthood, that explains why – after all, infants do not have sexual drives.

This reminds me of Freud. From the little bit I know according to Freud, sexual impulses start from childhood. From my experience, Freud is right. This is clearly indicated in my encounter both with the priest six years ago and Brother Philip about ten days ago. I have already written about my sexual feelings on both occasions in my diary.

8:15 a.m.

There is a lot of fear inside me at the moment. In my monologue I can say only a few words, and if I manage to say a sentence, I pause between each word.

8:30 a.m.

Louie, Mark and Craig just went fishing in Werribee River. I went to the window to see them getting ready. I gave Craig, who is eleven years old, one of Mark's jackets, so he wouldn't feel cold. I was concerned about him. Now I feel that gradually I am getting close to children. *I can't wait to relate and connect emotionally to children and babies.* It would be such a good feeling. I suppose that can only happen when all the hurt and fears inside me go away. I'm thinking of Mother Teresa. I wish to be like her in my relation to children. I want to feel close to them.

During psychotherapy I once said to Dr. Garcia how much I care about children in third- world countries. But then I said to him, 'How can I care for other children, if I don't care about mine?' He replied, 'That's possible.' Now I see why it's possible. That part of me that was hurt used Michelle, especially, as a scapegoat. And the other part of me felt sorry for children who need love and attention just like 'Victoria, the little girl'. I never realised how much hurt and anger there was inside me. Why did it take me so long to become aware of it?

11:05 a.m.

I'm still in that state of regression. While I was outside in the backyard, I fell in love with nature again. There is this beautiful small flower in the garden, like the one I gave to Michelle some days ago. I bent down and touched its petals gently. One of the petals happened to bend and I fixed it. There is something special about that flower. It may not be the same kind of flower I fell in love when I was little – the blue pimpernel I picked up and cupped in my hands to protect. The flower that I caressed this morning in the garden means a lot to me. It must be reminding me of that other flower, because it has blue petals too. The state I'm in at the moment is certainly a state of emotional regression.

There is a stillness inside me. Could that be non-aggressive anger? I'm not sure if aggression is the right word. I said 'non-aggressive' because at the moment I don't feel that rage. I have gone calm and quiet. I have no strength to yell and even if I did, I don't feel like yelling. This is definitely *silent anger*. It could be the same anger I experienced during this time of regression. I must have been so little that I couldn't scream in anger. Silent anger – that's what it is. I feel dazed, and I suppose it looks like I'm staring, because I cannot blink. I don't even want to look at my face in the mirror. When I was in Michelle's room a while ago, I did not want to look at my father's photo – in fact I didn't, even though the thought of looking at it went through my mind.

While I'm in this state of regression, I talk to myself while I'm doing the housework. I can hardly breathe, and I'm talking in a low voice, but it needs to come out – I have just realised that I have been thinking aloud, something I couldn't do when I was little. This is the little girl talking, not the thirty-five-year-old Vicky. Perhaps the latter is the instrument that is giving the little girl a voice. How long is this going to last? I don't sound desperate though. Is it because I am not ready for it? I know it sounds crazy, but there has to be a reason for it. What could it be? Maybe this is part of my intensive study (of myself and my chaotic and complex inner world). In fact, I'm sure it is. Before I started writing that last sentence, I hesitated because doubt crept in. Is the inner voice behind my doubt? It was the word 'study' that triggered it. After all, from my previous analysis it was the negative inner voice that felt threatened by my study of myself. Who or what is behind that inner voice?

I'm still in that state of regression. I have been in bed because the little girl wanted to lie down. Vicky assured her that she would take care of her and even Louie. If he were there, he would have done the same. The little girl felt safe. She wanted to have lullaby music and something to cuddle. Yes, Vicky slipped into a sensory stage. I asked Michelle to get me the purple soft toy, which she did without questioning me. She didn't laugh at me when she saw me hugging it against my cheek. I even caressed it, felt its paws, ran my fingers through its crest, touched its hard, shiny black nose and pressed it against mine to see what it felt like. I'm not sure whether to write 'I' or 'she' when referring to the little girl, because I'm still in that state of regression. I suppose I partially regressed; otherwise, I wouldn't be writing. At this time, I have been thinking out loud. I feel that regression is inevitable. I needed to meet that little girl, to nurture her and help her grow emotionally, and this is the only way to do it. I'm experiencing that silent anger again.

2:30 p.m.

The superego and the inner voice are quiet during the time of regression. There are no inner conflicts or inklings towards the future.

While I was hugging the soft toy earlier, I realised that I wanted to keep it against the left cheek, the same cheek I have been getting the numb feeling in for these last two years or so!

6:30 p.m.

I just had tea. I've been trying to analyse an incident that happened as we were having dinner. I was telling Louie about a dirty joke that Mark told me. All I could remember were a few words here and there. I was frustrated because Mark could express himself and I couldn't. Stephanie came to my mind, followed by a fear of not having interest in self-analysis. That was followed by disappointment, which led to depression. This is the analysis:

Feeling frustrated – thought of Stephanie – fear of losing competition – disappointment – depression – frustration – loss – anger. This is what's behind my depression at the moment.

Sunday, 25 October 1987
10:48 a.m.

I feel angry at Michelle. She has just come from church, and she is going straight to Irene's place. For some reason it hurts me when I see her spending more time there than at home. She knows I'm sick. She does help with the housework, but she is not there for me emotionally – to try to console me. She is so different from Mark. There has to be a reason for it. Could it be a result of the negative attitude I used to have towards her? I'm sure she cares, but she doesn't show it – maybe there is too much hurt inside her, which reminds me, if she is so hurt, how can she care for me? When I assure her that one day I'll be all right she says, 'Oh yes, that's what you said last time.' I can see that she doesn't believe me. I must have disappointed her. She must be angry at me – I hope she doesn't think I did it deliberately. It's true that at times I feel so optimistic about the future. That's when I have that inner strength.

I don't blame Michelle and Louie if they feel sceptical about my recovery. There are moments when the inner strength is so strong that I feel optimistic about my recovery. Not only that, I also feel that something significant will come out of it.

Then there are times when I feel that I'm losing not only the battle against mental illness but also the war. It breaks my heart when I think of it. It happened last night, for example. I felt that I had lost my war completely. I was terrified I would end up in a psychiatric hospital for the rest of my life! But then I said to myself, 'I don't deserve it. I've worked so hard all these years to have a happy and united family.' Yes, I worked hard to the best of my ability at the time. I really admire myself. I not only had to deal with my own psychological problems, I also tried and still am trying to undo some of the hurt I have caused Michelle. I even tried (and am still trying) to guide Louie in his relationship with the kids. I give myself a lot of credit.

These last three days I have been also wondering *why people behave the way they do.* Well, from my experience I can see that many people have been emotionally hurt by their parents. How can they love others when they are so hurt themselves? They identify with other people unconsciously, namely the people that hurt them. Therefore, *they direct their anger and fear at other people.*

I've also noticed that people can have different interpretations of the same word. Therefore, they misunderstand each other, which leads to conflict.

My emotions are at a standstill right now. I suppose that's why I have problems expressing myself. The thought just went through mind, 'You're using it as an excuse.' This reminds me of the inner voice. It seems that it operates differently, i.e. directly and indirectly.

3:15 p.m.

I'm feeling down again. I said 'again' because this last hour I noticed a significant lift in my depression. I've been for a driving lesson with Drago. I did extremely well – that's when I noticed the elation. I stayed at his place for about an hour. I expressed myself well, and I was also laughing and smiling with his wife. Then I happened to look at the newspaper, and I thought about the talk we have to prepare for Preparation for Tertiary Studies. Because I'm feeling better, I have no excuse not to do it. After that I went quiet.

On my way out I met Drago playing with the dog. I thought that he loved that dog a lot, and there is a lot of love inside him. Then when I went in, I saw Louie lying down on the couch, watching TV. I had that sinking feeling again. Although I sat next to him for a while, I didn't feel close to him at all. I questioned in my mind my love for him, and *I had the fear of not loving him.*

Could I have been identifying Louie with my father? This is the sequence of the above incident: love – sinking feeling – lack of love – fear of not loving Louie. That sinking feeling seems to be anger.

I want to elaborate on the thoughts that went through my mind when I saw Drago playing with the dog. I thought the dog is affectionate towards Drago. That's because he shows a lot of affection towards it. Then I said to myself, 'Perhaps I was wrong when I thought that Drago takes pleasure in watching the dog playing.' I thought he was a pervert. I thought that he plays with the dog to have a close look at the vagina while the dog is rolling on its back. This incident could have triggered something that led to me feeling down again.

At about 11:45 a.m. I was angry at Michelle. I felt she was abusing my illness. I didn't like the attitude she used with me in front of her cousin Marlene. It not only hurt me, but she also needs to be made aware of her wrongdoing and punished. So, I gave her a half-hour timeout (she was on her way to Marlene's birthday party). While she was in her room, I decided to make her aware of her unacceptable behaviour and why she was being punished, even though I was in a deplorable state. When I started talking to her, I must have been so angry or hurt that I couldn't express myself. I got frustrated – I even banged my fist on the door. Then I yelled out in desperation, 'I have a problem expressing myself at the moment, but that's not going to stop me from saying what I have to say. You'd better hear me out.'

Then I explained to her that I'm quite sick at the moment, and she ought to understand that. I assured her of my love for her, no matter what. I told her I'm still her mother, whether I'm healthy or sick. I told her that I've always appreciated her help around the house. But I'm not satisfied with what she is doing. She did ask me earlier if there was anything to do. I can't go around finding jobs for her. There is plenty of work to be done around the house. I was angry because I felt that she needs to work around the house on her own initiative, as I'm sure she does over at Irene's place. I pointed that out to her.

I felt proud of the way I handled the situation, especially under the circumstances. I felt that I need to help her grow by trying to make her aware of her negative attitude and that there are consequences for it, namely a timeout.

Monday, 26 October 1987
11:00 a.m.

I have just been listening to the radio on 3AW. It's a special day for Derryn Hinch (one of the broadcasters). He has just been released from jail, and the public response to his release was tremendous. He had yellow ribbons everywhere. I had tears in my eyes when I heard the words 'yellow ribbons'. I believe I deserve heaps and heaps of yellow ribbons.

This morning on the way home from my sessions, I felt that being 'victorious over the power of darkness' is and will be my greatest achievement in life. No matter how many qualifications I might have, this achievement beats them all!

Last night before I went to bed, I asked myself what I would do if my father were still alive. I would have faced him, no matter how sick or old he was. I wouldn't have said anything. But I would have stared and stared at him to make him realise that I know about the sexual abuse. If I told him anything at all, it would be that I have some unfinished business with him. I told the psychologist about it, and I even told her that if he admitted it, I would have forgiven him straightaway. I don't want revenge. *All I want is the truth, to be able to make a fresh start.*

When this ordeal is over, I will ask for yellow ribbons. I certainly deserve them. I have been imprisoned within myself for all these years, with so many shackles attached to me – in a dark dungeon – almost inaccessible for so many years.

When I think about the photo my mother is sending me – an original photo of my father with a friend, taken in a studio when he was in Australia before World War II – there are times when I don't want to touch it – I don't want it in my house. It reminds me of my father as a child molester, which I never expected and which nobody else would expect.

9:27 p.m.

I'm puzzled by the state I've been in during the last three and a half hours. I'm breathing normally. There seems to be no depression or fear. My brain feels heavy. Somehow, I feel strange. In class, however, I did well. I even questioned a philosophical question that was brought up in class: 'How do we know what we know?' I seem to be interested in philosophy. To be honest, I don't know what's going on with me – whether this is a healthy sign or not.

It feels as if I am someone else. The events of these last few days seem like a nightmare to me. Even the diary seems to belong to someone else. Earlier, I looked in the mirror and when I saw my hands, it felt like they belonged to someone else (I was wearing red nail polish). Am I in some kind of shock? This afternoon, for the first time, I expressed my anger towards my father in front of Michelle and Mark. On the way to the Institute, I felt angry at Michelle and my sister, who hasn't even rang me to see how I am. Could this be silent anger? I feel emotionally numb.

10:00 p.m.

I feel a bit panicky and frightened. I couldn't go through my diary. My breathing has changed. Am I regressing again? I have just been looking for the essay topics for our assignment. I couldn't find it, and I feel disappointed. I'm frightened.

10:32 p.m.

Since the diary represents my past, could this be a denial of my past? I know I feel disappointed because I have no concrete proof to show Michelle and my sister. They don't seem to believe me about my past sexual abuse.

Chapter 9

Silent Anger

Tuesday, 27 October 1987
7:23 a.m.

When I woke up this morning, I was in a state of shock as usual. As soon as I realised, I was awake, I wondered where I was and what day it is. Since I've been in this state of shock, those are the first thoughts that go through my mind.

I prefer to be in a state of shock where there is fear inside me, rather than the other state of shock – the one I experienced last night.

I would like to go over the events of yesterday afternoon and the emotions I experienced.

After Michelle returned from the hairdresser, I wasn't pleased with her haircut because she spent $12, and she hardly had any hair cut at all. I know that after she washes it a few times, she is going to be annoyed with it. I noticed some brittle black hair from the haircut over the side of her face. Could that have triggered something or reminded me of my father (whose name was Michael)? Then she told me she is going to take the hairdryer to camp, and I felt agitated. It was pretty obvious, and Michelle got annoyed at my reaction. I was also angry at myself for behaving like that. That's when I started openly expressing my anger towards my father.

An argument with Michelle followed. I told her that if she

understood what I'm going through at the moment, she would tolerate me more. She thinks she knows that, but I felt that she doesn't; otherwise, she wouldn't be so angry at my attitude and reactions towards her. Then she made fun of what my father could have done to me, and both Mark and I joined in. At that moment I felt that if I joked about it, I would not only come to terms with it, but it might also help me, and Michelle get closer. When I saw her smiling, I went over to her and tried to cup my hands around her face, and I told her that I still love her. I just realised that I could have been identifying with Michelle as my father.

Joke about something so serious?! – followed by affection.

This explains why on the way to the Institute I felt angry at both Michelle and my sister (whom I could be identifying as my mother) – father and mother both against me.

That *burning pain in my right wrist* is coming back to me. I have it now.

I'm thinking about this burning pain. Is it a psychosomatic symptom? What could my father have done to me? After all, he used to smoke. As a child (and even now), I used to think about the tragic incident of *Ġiġa* and Leli – a Maltese couple who in 1960 inflicted severe torture on their little child, who ended up dying. One of the tortures was burning their child with cigarette butts. I have tears in my eyes as I write. I have just pointed to where the burning pain is and said, 'This is where my father burnt me.' I hardly remember any stories, whether religious or not, that I must have heard when I was growing up. But the above story of *Ġiġa* and Leli stuck with me.

There is another story I've always remembered. It's about the devil dancing on the roof of a house in which people were doing things they shouldn't. When the old lady next door told us that story, as a child I used to think they must have been doing 'rude' (sexual) things. She never told us what the activities were. Why did I come up with this? Why was I impressed with that story? *Why did I have such a strong fear of the devil?*

Speaking of the devil, I remember as a child looking in the mirror and saying to myself that I looked like the devil. In our bedroom, we had a holy picture of the Archangel Michael in a suit of armour, piercing the devil with a sword in one hand and holding a shield in the other. The devil was naked and looked like a man with horns. *As my father's name was Michael, could have I identified with Archangel Michael as my father and the devil as myself?* If that's the case, the devil and I had something in common – we were both victims! This is making a lot of sense to me now as I am analysing and questioning myself. No wonder I used to think that I looked like the devil as a child!

Another possible reason why I identified with the devil is that as a child I must have blamed myself for the incest. As I mentioned in my diary, a part of me enjoyed being involved in sexual activities with my father. It was another way of getting attention. At the same time, I must have had some awareness that it was 'rude' and immoral. At some level I must have been harnessing guilt, shame and fear. *These were perhaps the core elements that constituted the shackles that kept me imprisoned in such a dark dungeon for so many years.*

4:30 p.m.

About fifteen minutes ago, I noticed a small burning mark in the same area where I have been getting the burning pain. It occurred to me that it might have been caused by the oil while I was frying an egg for Louie. As far as I know, no hot oil splashed on me.

Anyway, the day turned out to be a good day. After I got out of bed at about 11:00 a.m., I spent some time in the garden. I enjoyed every moment of it. Sitting on a log near the prickly pear tree, surrounded by the beauty of nature, I started recollecting those happy times in my childhood when I used to go to the fields at *Għajn Xejba* during the summer. The bamboo shoots in the far corner of the garden, the fig trees, the glorious sun shining above me, birds twittering and chirping in the trees – all these elements really set the scene and took me back to the neighbourhood where I grew up and the fields at *Għajn Xejba.* As I was sitting on the log, I thought of the valley that meandered through the fields and recollected the beautiful experiences I had. Those are happy memories I will treasure for the rest of my life. While I was sitting on the log in the garden, I was free from fear – even the fear of snakes. That's the only fear I had when I used to spend time near the valley.

I went near the ferns in the garden and kept touching the lacy leaves. It was such a good feeling!

My sister came to visit me at about 1:30 p.m. When I saw her coming, I wasn't sure how I was going to relate to her. As the conversation went on, I felt better.

I am now thinking of an incident that happened today. While I was washing my white jacket, I noticed a travel ticket in my pocket. I tried to take it out, but I couldn't because it wasn't in the pocket – it was in between the lining. I couldn't figure out how it got in there. But then I did and felt relieved – not for long though! I thought, 'What if the ticket inspector had asked for the ticket, *and I wouldn't have been able to find it? I wouldn't have been able to prove it, no matter how right I was*!' Fear struck. This explains why, when I'm travelling on the train and the inspector happens to come on board, I get this fear even though I have a valid ticket. This is definitely a disguise for another fear. I remember Dr. Garcia once telling me that *where there is a fear, there is a wish.* This really makes a lot of sense. There must be a wish inside me to prove I am right. Why do I want to prove it? Because nobody would believe me.

Wednesday, 28 October 1987
12:55 p.m.

I have just been talking to Stephanie on the phone. She rang me up before 11:00 a.m., and we had a long conversation. Although while I'm writing I feel that sense of loss (due to her being a threat to me both academically and personally), I'm proud of myself because I gave her lot of encouragement. I told her not to be afraid of unfolding and facing the past, no matter how painful and frightening it might be. 'Wounds are very painful, but scars, no matter how bad they look, are not sore at all,' I added. She said she related to what I told her. We must have been destined to have this conversation.

I was about to go to Deer Park this morning. But after I got dressed, the little girl wanted to sleep. Yes, that little girl is very much within me. There are times when she wants to cuddle the soft toy against her left cheek and go to sleep. Other times, she wants to be pampered by eating a chocolate-coated muesli bar or a piece of cake. She doesn't want herbal tea or cod liver oil or any other vitamins – she doesn't think she needs them at all. Physically, no matter how fragile and haggard she looks, she is quite strong. *All she lacks is affection and security.* And that's what she'll be getting from now on.

The little girl seems to feel cold too. Last night I felt close to Michelle. As I was sitting beside her watching TV, I kept touching her to see if she was cold. I wanted to make sure that she was not feeling cold. That little girl must have felt hungry too – a hunger that at times couldn't be satisfied. That's why I was always over-concerned about Michelle and Mark when they didn't eat properly. I would say that hunger is a symptom – the actual hunger is for love!

10:46 p.m.

I got the application form for the Bachelor of Arts for next year. I don't feel optimistic about it right now. Before the lecture, I went to see one of my tutors, Marion, and told her about the painful inner journey of self-discovery I'm going through and the effect it's having on me – including my academic commitments. I told her that I won't be doing the essay as required, and I need special consideration regarding the application form.

I feel that I'm using it as an excuse. In a way, I also feel disappointed because I cannot test myself to see if I'm capable of doing it or not. I feel so confused regarding returning to study. Why do I feel so pessimistic about it now? A couple of months ago, I was looking forward to it so much. What am I frightened of now?

I just realised that I haven't written anything about Michelle today. This evening she rang me up from camp, and she was so keen to talk to me – she even put extra money in the public phone. She seems to be having a great time. She deserves it. *I can't wait for the day when I feel close to her – feeling the actual connection.* What desperation it has been for me! I don't think anyone can fully understand what it's like when you don't feel that emotional connection with your loved ones. Fear and anger – how destructive they can be with regard to this emotional connection! I consider the feeling of connection as being at the core of my inner self –

just like an onion, I need to peel layer after layer to get to the core of it. *And like an onion, it makes me cry.*

I am puzzled about this emotional state, in which my emotions are at a standstill (this is the most accurate word I have come up with). When I'm in this state I don't feel panicky, there are no fears/anxiety, there *seems* to be no anger, the little girl is not there. My intellectual ability is poor. I can't communicate with people, especially if there are three people in the conversation. It happened last night at the Institute's cafeteria when I was talking to Bob and Stephanie. I got embarrassed by the way I expressed myself. When I heard Stephanie talking, I kept saying to myself, 'Why can't I express myself as well as her?' It's not a language problem – it's only a matter of putting words together. What's wrong with me? Is it an emotional handicap caused by my emotional state or some other kind of intellectual disability?

When I was at the cafeteria last night, I tried to think about the diary and the intellectual ability I had displayed in my self-analysis. But I couldn't think about it at all – at that moment the diary didn't mean anything. But why? *Could that state indicate that I was in some kind of depersonalisation?* I felt perplexed. However, the fact that I am denying the diary when I'm in that state might explain why my intellectual ability is so poor. The question then is, what kind of state could it be? Is it a state of denial? Is it anger depression? But it couldn't be, because there is no sadness, and on the other hand there is no peace within me. *Could this be silent anger* – the same anger I wrote about in my diary few days ago?

9:33 a.m.

I have just decided not to attend the Child Development course. I don't want to be influenced whatsoever by any qualified person regarding child development. Even yesterday when I was in the library, I got hold of a book by Sigmund Freud regarding man's soul. I was tempted to read it. But then I felt that I didn't want to be influenced by that book. Why is it that I don't want to be influenced by anybody? Is it because I want to discover these emotions by myself, thus giving me some kind of satisfaction? Is this the mission I felt some time ago – that I'm going to embark on something nobody has ever embarked on before? I have already told Dr Garcia about it, and I even mentioned it in my diary (9 August, and clearly described on 19 August).

9:24 p.m.

Although I don't have the urge to write, I can't let the day go by without giving an account of what happened today. At about 11:00 a.m., I went into the garden and spent about an hour and a half there. I sat down on a heap of bamboo leaning against the back fence, enjoying the beautiful sunshine, observing every minute thing around me. I found great pleasure in touching the bamboo and feeling the fresh green leaves. Louie cut the bamboo only recently. We have some shoots in one of the far corners of the garden. What a beautiful feeling it was! I felt I was discovering a sixth sense, and I was in a heaven of delight! I felt that I am awakening from a prolonged sleep – to such a beautiful environment, which was lying dormant for so long! The thought of going inside the house and getting my diary to record what was happening went through my mind. But I didn't want to, in case it interrupted this wonderful ecstatic experience, and I was also concerned that I would lose it. I kept saying to myself, 'I wish I were a poet, to express my experience through poetry.' I thought about the well-known British poet William Wordsworth – the poet of nature. *I closed my eyes and was in ecstasy for quite some time* as I felt the warmth of the sun gently stroking my cheeks, while listening to the dove cooing on the oak tree close by.

At about 3:00 p.m. I was overcome with fear. I was thinking of that sequestered nook in the garden and the time I intend to spend there, when all of a sudden, I thought of Drago (the man who lives next door) and vaguely remembered a dream in which Drago made love to me. That's when fear struck. I kept thinking of my experience in the garden earlier and trying to relax. The thought of being interrupted by him when he is on afternoon shift kept coming to me. I was disappointed because I wouldn't be free to have such an experience again. I also felt frightened. Then I said to myself, 'I will have to find another place, where he won't be able to see me.' My fear of Drago was so intense that I didn't even dare to stay at the kitchen window that overlooks his house – lest he see me when he comes home from work. I went to my bedroom and stayed there on the bed. *I was so frightened of Drago!*

No doubt I was identifying with Drago as my father. It looks like my father disturbed me in my sleep when I was a baby. That must have not only annoyed me but also frightened me. I never realised how much fear is still inside me! I believe that the sexual abuse by my father started when I was still a baby. Not only that, the psychosomatic pain in my left groin that I identified a while back seems to indicate that my father hurt me during the sexual abuse. Since I had the insight about this, that psychosomatic symptom has gone away.

9:54 p.m.

I just remembered that I have to record the phone calls I made these last couple of days. Panic struck because I have forgotten to do something I am supposed to do. This kind of forgetfulness, that is, when I'm asked to do something and forget, seems to press the panic button. I have noticed it a few times.

Friday, 30 October 1987
12:15 p.m.

I've just come back from Footscray. I was looking forward to shopping, but it didn't turn out as well as I wanted it to. In a way I'm not disappointed, because I was closely observing my emotional swings, like a hawk, and I discovered a few things.

When I was shopping for a pair of white clip-on earrings, I got annoyed because most of them were for pierced ears. I kept saying to myself, 'It's not fair. People who have their ears pierced not only have a lot of variety to choose from, but they can wear both kinds of earrings (clip-ons and pierced). I don't have a choice. I can only wear the clip-on ones.' *That sense of restriction pressed the panic button.*

As I was analysing myself while shopping, I kept thinking also about why people behave the way they do. I seem to be interested in this area, but somehow when that thought comes to my mind, fear strikes – fear of studying, fear of not coping. A few weeks ago, while I was reading *Dibs In Search of Self*, I kept thinking, 'If I were his therapist, would have I used the same techniques that his therapist did?' No doubt there is some sort of ambition inside me.

I've just remembered something else I've noticed lately – time seems to press the panic button too. Before I start writing in the diary, I'm precise with time. If I am not, panic strikes and I feel guilty for not stating the exact time, even if it's only one minute off. Why am I so precise with time? And why do I feel such guilt?

Even forgetfulness presses the panic button. When Louie asks me to do something, no matter how trivial it is, I get panicky and frightened, even though I know he is going to be understanding. Incidents like these are indirectly telling me many things – that there was a time when I was supposed to do something and I forgot, with negative consequences – keep an appointment with my father perhaps? *Time* and *forgetfulness* and the emotions (guilt, fear, making sure of being precise, panic) that accompany them are certainly giving me a lot of clues.

These last twenty-four hours, I've also noticed a couple of instances when for the first time I felt angry at the little baby (that is, the little baby that is part of me). I just realised that at that moment I must have been identifying with my father. Lately, when I pass wind, I have been feeling angry at her. Even when there is a motion of the bowels, an inner voice says to me in Maltese, *Tarraqlek qalbek, issa ġiek il-ħara* (Damn you, you had to have a shit now). Is that what happened to the little girl/baby and what my father told her? It seems my father sexually abused me as a baby, who experienced physical pain and fear to the extent that I had a motion of the bowels, which upset him.

I am questioning the inner voices again. Could some of them be the same voices that we heard and stored in the unconscious mind, like the above example? There are certainly different kinds of inner voices. There seem to be voices or inner messages that emerge from our emotions. If they are negative emotions, the messages are negative. On the other hand, if the emotions are positive then the messages are positive.

6:50 p.m.

The last forty-five minutes or so, I have been in bed – I regressed. As usual, it felt like there was someone frightened inside me (this is different from fear that arises from thoughts). I was frightened – it's pretty obvious I am blocking something in my mind. I kept saying, 'I don't want to hear that voice again' (I was referring to my father's voice). And then I was overcome with fear, followed by saying 'I hate everybody' repeatedly.

Mark just brought me a nice piece of Vienna bread with fresh tomatoes, oil, salt and pepper and olives. I really enjoyed it. *And hatred turned into love*. I told Mark how much I love him, that I love everybody, including God. I even told him that my father must have been sick to do what he did. I begged him not to hate him, but it's reasonable for Mark to be angry at him. While I was talking to Mark, I kept touching his face – what a beautiful feeling it was! That beautiful sensation can only be there when there is no fear, anger or hurt – just when there is love – peace coming from the centre of my being.

Saturday, 31 October 1987
11:00 a.m.

I am sitting in the car by myself at Queenscliffe. Louie, Mark, my nephew Charles and I arrived here before nine o'clock. There were hardly any cars. The boys went fishing, and I stayed by myself in the car. Somehow, I didn't feel at ease. I didn't feel safe. Louie parked the car on the side of the road. I preferred it in a car park. I didn't know what to do. I lay down on the back seat, and gradually I settled down. As more cars arrived, I felt even better.

Fear of not being safe – anxious to be relaxed and enjoy that peace within myself. This certainly reminds me of that part of babyhood when fear started to take over and interfered with inner peace. It's sad indeed when I think of it. No wonder I'm yearning so much for inner peace, which apparently, I only enjoyed for a short period of time. What a pity! While I'm writing all this, I'm not feeling that little baby as part of me. I feel so detached from her.

Am I angry at the little baby? I wouldn't be surprised. I noticed it when I was in the back seat of the car. I just had a recollection from childhood. When I was about ten years old, I used to spend time over at one of the neighbour's, who had a few children. On one occasion, the mother asked me to keep swinging the cradle that was attached in the corner of the bedroom, so her baby girl would go to sleep. I *clearly remember* wanting to swing the cradle hard, hoping the baby would fall out and get hurt! I can't believe this. This must explain why I wanted to hurt that baby at such a young age!

Yesterday, I was puzzled and even embarrassed by my reaction when I spoke to Dr. Garcia about the inner voice in Maltese with regard to the baby having a motion of the bowels, which I wrote about yesterday. I went hysterical with laughter. Was it the little girl or baby laughing because she found a way to protest or even stop the sexual abuse, even for a while, and felt like laughing her heart out because she was victorious over her father in terms of power?

I just reached for something out of the bag. My first intention was to have a muesli bar –something sweet for the little girl. I ended up eating a Vita Wheat biscuit. It's pretty obvious that the little girl and myself are at odds at the moment. I seem to be avoiding the baby; I'm writing 'girl' instead of 'baby', even though I'm referring to the baby. I keep associating the word *ħara* (shit) with the baby!

I just noticed that those Maltese messages are nasty comments or remarks. As I was turning the radio on, the comment that went through my mind was *Trid tisma' il-music issa* (she wants to hear the music now), which in Maltese is a nasty way of saying it. Although I am fluent in

Maltese, I have spoken English 95% of the time since migrating to Australia.

5:30 p.m.

I just went for a walk, and now I am back in the car. All day I have been mostly in that state where my emotions are at a standstill – silent anger. I felt (and still do) so indifferent and so alienated, even though I'm talking to people. I met a lady on the pier. She had a one-year-old boy. Although I touched the baby, I felt so indifferent. I tried to imagine myself at that age, but nothing ticked. At one stage, I was impressed by the baby. I kept looking at him, and after looking at me, he would look at his mum as if he wanted to tell her something. Even when he diverted his attention somewhere else, he would look at me again as if he were saying to himself, 'Let me see if she is still looking at me.' Yes, babies are clever, even at such a young age!

There was a girl whom I also seemed to be interested in – about four-and-a-half years old – looking at me. I tried to imagine myself at her age, but nothing ticked. One of the men that was with the girl's family did remind me of my father – the muscles on his arms.

The little girl doesn't seem to be angry at her father. It's the little baby who is. That's why I'm experiencing so much silent anger. I've noticed that when I'm in this state, even my vision range is limited – I tend to look around me without turning my head, instead of looking in the distance. I hear noises such as music, but there is nothing happening inside me – no sensation whatsoever, no matter how nice the music is. There seem to be pins and needles in my head at times, and my head feels heavy, as if someone were pressing it down.

Sunday, 1 November 1987
6:34 a.m.

I'm in bed listening to the radio program 'Praise to the Lord' on 3LO. I was deeply moved when I heard the song 'How Great Thou Art'. In spite of the agonising pain that I'm going through, I still feel close to God – at least at times. It's true that there are moments when I get into those fits of rage, and I turn against God and Our Lady. I'm sure God knows I'm using him as a scapegoat, and he knows how much hurt there is inside me.

Today is All Saints Day – a special day in Malta. My sister Carmen, who passed away when she was eleven years old, is surely a saint, and she probably knows what I'm going through. I asked Mum to send me her only photo because I want to make a copy of it. We have been unfair to her, because when she died, we buried her completely, as if she had never existed. I want to bring her back into our lives through our thoughts and spirits. Carmen doesn't need prayers – all she wants us to do is to remember her and tell our kids that she existed. After all, she is their auntie.

11:07 a.m.

I have just spent some time in the garden and fell in love with nature again, even though I wasn't by myself – Mark, Louie and Michelle were there. I was a bit apprehensive at first, but when I touched the bamboo and its leaves, it was such a good feeling. Even Michelle and I seem to have come closer together, although she is grounded for her attitude towards me yesterday.

Before she went to sleep, she came into the bathroom for the radio. I told her not to put it on, or if she did, she would have to put it off herself. 'Alright then, I'll put it off', she said, and as she walked away, she mumbled, 'Get out of here.' That really hurt me. She not only doesn't believe what I'm going through, but she also abused me when I was so sick. As a punishment, I grounded her all day today. I'm so proud of myself. I've certainly done the right thing by punishing her. And at the same time, I'm showing her my love. I'm not going back on my word as far as punishment goes, but that doesn't mean I need to hold grudges. Even Louie, I'm so proud of him. He really stood up for me last night, and this morning I'm so impressed with the loving and caring way he is relating to her.

Just before I came in, Michelle asked me how I was. I told her that I feel better in the garden. 'Why don't you stay in the garden then?' she replied. I can see she does care about me. What worries me is the way she shows her concern. Will she ever change her attitude – not for my sake but for hers? All I want for her is to have a happy future and have a life, not just be alive.

9:15 p.m.

I feel furious at my bastard father – if he deserves to be called a father. YOU ROTTEN BASTARD! That's what you are. You can roll over in your grave. It's a pity you're not alive. I would have humiliated you in front of everybody – that would have been my revenge. How am I going to take my revenge on him?

I'm thinking of my mother now. Has she any idea what my father was up to when I was so little? How I wish to face her and find out more about my babyhood. I wonder how much she remembers. I had a dream a couple of nights ago in which I was talking to my mother, and she asked me about my children. She seemed to know what I was getting up to, and she told me gently, '*Why don't you leave the past behind?'*– as if it was too painful to know. That's how the dream ended.

This afternoon as I was washing the clothes, I got angry at my father because he not only ruined my life but also Michelle's. He deprived me of so many things. What hurts me most is the fact that I never enjoyed my pregnancies (becoming a mother) and Michelle's babyhood. I looked at her through the eyes of fear, rather than love. That is so painful for me. I can never make up for it. I feel so broken-hearted. As I was thinking aloud, I kept repeating, 'You rotten bastard.' No doubt there is a lot of anger and fear inside me. If he was still alive, I would have faced him no matter what, even if he was on his deathbed!

Monday, 2 November 1987
2:10 p.m.

I am thinking of my father's photo. I've just been outside to check if there are any letters in the letter-box. I seem to be looking forward to receiving that photo. There are times when I doubt whether my mum will send it to me – I feel she has an idea of what I'm up to. I could be right. After all, I dreamt about it.

During therapy this morning, I told my psychologist that there are so many things I would like to know about my babyhood. One wish came particularly strongly. I would like to know where my mother used to leave me at night, in the zinc bathtub that served as a bassinet – in the room where she and my siblings slept or in the small room where my father used to sleep.

I told my psychologist how strange I feel – I seem to be miles and miles away, even with people around me. I feel so dazed. If I am partially in a state of regression, that would explain why I'm feeling like this. Even in my dreams, the scenery is back home, and the people living in Australia are in the same dream. Last night, for example, I dreamt of Stephanie and Ron Adams at a fete at *Għajn Xejba*, and Saturday morning I dreamt that my sister and I were going to the fields (in *Pergla*), and I was running late. In fact, we got up late to go fishing.

10:08 p.m.

It seems such a long time since I wrote last in my diary. It has only been eight hours. So many things have happened since then. As soon as I stopped writing in my diary, I started writing the journal for Preparation for Tertiary Studies. In the journal, I wanted to tell Jacob, the tutor, that I won't be doing the student presentation and the essay. *I felt obliged to tell him that, and because I felt obliged, I had to tell him*. I wasn't pleased with the way I was expressing myself. I decided to rip the paper off later and copy it again after rewriting it on a rough work paper. As soon as I decided to do that, I felt relieved. I still wasn't happy with the way I was expressing myself, and I got frustrated.

From this incident I've noticed a couple of things. Because I felt obliged, I *had to do it*. That must have triggered something. Could I have been identifying with Jacob as my father? Also, as soon as I was not restricted to that paper, I felt relieved.

Restriction is certainly pressing the panic button. I've been reflecting upon it a lot these last few hours. It annoys me often in everyday life. If I happen to have some perishable ingredients in the fridge, for example (like ricotta and cold meat), I feel restricted and annoyed because I have to use them.

Even when it comes to cooking, I'm torn apart by the conflict inside me – part of me is annoyed because I have to do something, and another part is desperate to fulfil her duties. Oh God, how painful that conflict is! It's psychological torture. I end up losing control of myself and I despair, just like I did this afternoon. *The rage that comes out is expressed in Maltese*. It is so emotionally draining!

Tuesday, 3 November 1987
8:50 p.m.

The day is almost over, and I haven't written anything in the diary yet. I seem to be losing interest in continuing with my studies next year. I got the application form, but I'm not so keen to fill it out. Why did I lose interest in returning to study? When I started the short courses at the Western Institute, I was so excited about it. I felt like I had found an integral part of myself. What happened? Is it just a temporary lack of interest due to the emotional problem I'm going through? I wouldn't be surprised, especially now that I have also lost interest in my diary, which meant so much to me.

Today is the Melbourne Cup – a public holiday. This morning I stayed in bed till 10:00, and at 2:30 I came to lie down again. I hugged the soft toy and Louie came in. I tried to hide it. I was embarrassed when he discovered it, and I wouldn't face him. He told me that it doesn't matter, and there is nothing to be embarrassed about. I slept peacefully. I even had a dream that I was on a ship, and if I'm not mistaken the ship was heading to Gozo. Yes, it has become evident now that I'm desperate to go there in my dreams. About a year or so ago, I had two dreams about going there. In one dream, I never told Mum that I was going and took her by surprise. In the other dream, I told her that I was going, but apparently, she wasn't too keen to see me, because she left the key in a hiding place and went into the fields. When I arrived, she wasn't there to welcome me.

Would I have to go to that extreme and see my mother to find out exactly what happened to me? I'm so frightened. I hope it doesn't come to that. What am I going to tell her? What if she blows the whole thing out of proportion? Or insists that nothing happened? How am I going to handle her? I am so fragile, not only physically but also mentally and emotionally. Will I ever come to terms with my insight that I am a victim of incest?

I feel so desperate for some confirmation of this insight. I am frightened. My right hand feels weak. What if I get paralysis in it? I am so scared.

Wednesday, 4 November 1987
2:01 p.m.

At about 10:00 this morning while I was still in bed, my sister came over to see me. She wanted to take me to the doctor, but I refused. So, she rang up Dr. Murdoch herself, who apparently still remembers me. He also seems to be concerned about me, because he wanted the name of the psychologist to get in touch with him. At first, I felt angry at my sister, but then I realised that she meant well, even though I didn't approve.

Erica, one of the neighbours, came to see me too. She even got me a doyley, cotton and a crochet hook to occupy myself. She was understanding when I briefly explained to her the reasons behind my emotional and psychological problem.

Fear of lying (not telling the truth) is certainly pressing the panic button. I just received a phone call from Louie's lawyer to go to court regarding his compensation claim for hearing loss at work (he is a wood machinist). Louie hasn't told his solicitor that he was in the army during the Vietnam War. In me, there is that fear of not being honest, which would mean he did it deliberately to cheat, which would work against him in court. That's when panic struck. I felt desperate that his lawyer should know the truth. I suppose I was afraid that Louie would be falsely accused and lose the case.

Analysis: Fear of lying – guilt must be behind this fear. Could I have lied when I was a child for the sake of getting attention – in other words, when I lost my father through incest? I wouldn't be surprised. I must have lied. That's why I feel guilty about not being honest, even when recording the time in my diary.

I was concerned about Louie being falsely accused as a result, when he didn't do deliberately. There is so much conflict inside me. I'm thinking of Louie. Perhaps he didn't tell his lawyer deliberately, for fear that it would work against him. But if she did ask him, he would have told her. I don't think his having been in the army would work against him; but rather, the fact that he omitted it. I need to discuss this analysis with my psychologist – I cannot think at the moment.

10:40 p.m.

I seem to feel a bit better this evening. When I came back from the Institute, I walked over to Michelle, who was lying down on the couch, and sat beside her. I felt close to her. I kept touching her, and she seemed to like it.

The lesson this evening was on psychology. At first, I was apprehensive about it. But then I felt at ease during the lecture. Rose, Cynthia and I held a conversation during the break, and I communicated well.

Psychology fascinates me. However, I am a bit apprehensive about it because of the exams we have to sit for.

Mikieli Bajada

Chapter 10

Conflict

Thursday, 5 November 1987
1:30 p.m.

I've just received my mum's letter and the photos. When I recognised the envelope, I felt a bit excited about it – there was definitely no anger. When I opened the envelope and looked at my father's photo, nothing ticked – *he looks like a stranger to me*. Nobody in the family looks like him at that age. I've been looking at his hands – do I see something in them?

This is not the reaction I expected, and I feel disappointed by it.

As I was opening the envelope with the knife, first I thought of my mother licking the envelope, and then the idea of stabbing went through my mind. As I was taking the photo out, I felt like ridiculing my mother, as if I have taken him away from her, and she had no idea what I was up to. I imagined her going through the trouble of walking up the stairs to get the photo from the cabinet, and I'm laughing behind her back. This must be the little girl who enjoyed incest. She must have fallen in love with her father's hands. I can't tell how old my father was when this photo was taken. All I know is that it was taken in a studio when he was in Australia, before he was married. He was 38 years old when he got married.

What happened to the baby? Why isn't she angry? I feel so

indifferent. I'm stunned. Is this a state of denial? After all, there are moments when I want to continue with my work as if nothing has happened.

Friday, 6 November 1987
12:20 p.m.

I've just made an appointment to see Dr. Murdoch this afternoon. Louie was upset with me last night because I'm losing a lot of weight, and he is concerned about me. I don't blame him. The deplorable state I was in last night was frightening. I even thought I was about to lose not only the battle against mental illness but also the war. It is so scary when I reach that point. No words can describe it. It has been a tough war for me – a war in which I've shown so much courage, strength and hard work.

Last night I cried and cried wholeheartedly by myself in bed, especially when I was thinking of my current lack of interest in returning to study at the tertiary level. It took so much courage for me to go to the Western Institute for Women's Access Day, and I was proud of myself.

9:23 p.m.

I'm pleased with the way I conversed with Dr. Murdoch. I told him the reason behind my psychological problems and that I was considering returning to study at the tertiary level next year. He encouraged me to go ahead and fill in the application form.

During the session this afternoon I was much better than yesterday. What a mess I was in yesterday! I can't believe it. I told my psychologist about this man whom I identify with Sigmund Freud. I usually see him at the shopping centre. This man reminds me so much of Freud. He is always in a suit, wears a hat and uses a walking stick, even though he doesn't seem to have any difficulty walking. In fact, he walks smartly and briskly. His gait impresses me a lot. Yesterday, on my way home after the session, this man came past me just before I turned into our street. I usually see him at the shopping centre in St Albans. Could Freud be haunting me? When I told my psychologist about him, we laughed about it together. It felt so good to be laughing again!

These last few hours I've been doing a lot of thinking out loud. *I've noticed I am defensive about psychoanalysis and psychotherapy*. That's why I don't want to go on any medication, and I keep assuring Louie that this is my only way to recovery.

Saturday, 7 November 1987
12:45 p.m.

As I was doing the laundry, I felt sleepy – I must have regressed to babyhood. I was intending to leave everything and come have a nap after I hung up some of the laundry. But Erica saw me over the fence, and we chatted for a while. She said that her father once told her, 'Respect your husband as a man, and treat him like a boy.' That struck me, because that's what I have been doing with Louie these last few years. While I'm writing, my stomach has been rumbling a lot. I don't know why, because I had lunch. I'm at home by myself – Louie and Mark went fishing, and Michelle slept over at my friend's house because she went to a disco with the twins. I think I'd better lie down, even though I have lots of things to do.

4:33 p.m.

While I was lying down, I heard light footsteps in the hallway. I sat up in bed – not exactly petrified, but more anxious to find out whether I was right – if there was someone in the house or not. Yes, I was right. It was Marlene. I told her to call out next time because she frightened me. But deep down, I was more relieved that I was right. It seems I'm still after the truth.

I have a number of sores on the palate of my mouth. I'm not sure if it's thrush. While I was thinking about it before, an inner voice said to me that I had been drinking a lot of hot tea and coffee lately. As far as I know, I've always had my tea and coffee at more or less the same temperature. If it's thrush, could it be another psychosomatic symptom? This morning I started feeling a pain running from the thumb to the wrist, as if I had strained or sprained it. How could that happen when I have only been doing light housework?

When I was lying down this afternoon I couldn't relax, partly because I knew I had a lot of housework to do and partly because of the noises in the background – dogs barking, Samantha yelling, the guys at the back of the house hammering. I ended up having a lot of fear inside me.

I just vaguely remembered a dream I had this afternoon. I dreamt that something sticky came out of the diary, and I had to rip out two pages. I was disappointed, partly because I couldn't replace those pages and partly because even if I could, they wouldn't be the original pages. What could that sticky stuff be? In the dream I was puzzled because there is no glue in the diary. The pages are spiral-bound.

Sunday, 8 November 1987
10:00 a.m.

It is a beautiful day outside – part of me is yearning to go out in the garden and enjoy the beauty of nature; another part of me wants to be by herself. She is avoiding everything, including Louie. I feel *so far away* from the people around

me. When am I going to be fully in touch with reality? It's heartbreaking. When Louie is close and looks at me, I feel so far away from him. I'm sure I'm identifying with him as my father – the look on his face and even his posture reminds me so much of him. There is certainly some unfinished business with my father. Lately, when I picture Louie naked from the waist down, I picture my father.
Last night I had a dream. I was sick, and Fr Jude from St Bernadette's Church came to visit me. In the dream I was in the small room where my father used to sleep. He knew about my problem, and he asked me to have a medical check-up because the doctors could tell if I was a victim of incest and if I had been tampered with when I was little. I did end up going for a check-up, and the test proved that I was a victim of incest. In fact, the nurse told me there was some kind of bag inside me still full of infection and pus or fluid from it. I was stunned. *I must be so desperate to find some concrete evidence that I'm a victim of incest.*

I want to be by myself, free of any expectations as a mother and housewife. That's why I get so frustrated when I realise there are chores to be done. And then, when everybody is at home, *all my negative emotions* (fear, anger, irritability, guilt due to lack of competence as a wife and mother) *surface, and my personalities are at war.* I end up getting frustrated, followed by a fit of rage in which I start swearing in Maltese. I turn against God completely: *Nirraħ Alla jgħallaqni, joqtolni*, etc. (May God hang me, kill me, etc.). Interesting that the anger is also directed at myself!

Then I calm down, especially if Mark or Louie tells me not to worry about housework or cooking. That reassurance makes me feel better, and I end up staying calm in bed. *Usually that whole inner drama is followed by affection.* When either Louie or Mark comes next to me to make me feel better, I assure them of my love. The word 'love' holds the key to the emotional problem I'm going through.

10:52 a.m.

I have been thinking of Dr. Garcia. I felt sleepy. As I was thinking in my room, I remembered the photo of my father. I didn't want to look at it. I still don't feel like looking at it. Looks like the baby is angry at her father, even though the man in the photo is a stranger to me. I just realised that the man may be a stranger to me, but he is not to the baby.

7:20 p.m.

Louie and the kids went over to our neighbour Drago and I'm at home by myself. Actually, I was looking forward to being by myself. I wonder why! Could it be because I want to be in touch with my emotions and don't want to be disturbed? Or is it because when I'm by myself, there is more of a chance to regress to babyhood? When I regress to babyhood, I really enjoy the peace within myself. *I suppose that baby missed out on a lot of inner peace.*

I'm imagining my father looking at me with his hands on his hips, wondering what is going through my mind. I suppose he would be thinking of his relationship with me. I feel embarrassed of my father. I wonder how many times I reminded him of his sexual activities, and I had no idea what was going through his mind. How did I manage to block the past? Will I ever get a breakthrough in my memory? I feel so desperate to remember something.

I am in search of the truth and am proving to myself that I am right. Yesterday's incident with Marlene clearly indicates that. Even this afternoon when I was in the garden, I heard Drago's back door slamming. I thought to myself, 'I bet he is coming.' And as soon as I got a glimpse of him, I was relieved, not because I was looking forward to seeing him but because I proved to myself that I was right.

While I'm sitting up in bed writing, I'm avoiding my father's photo, while on the other hand I'm imagining my father standing in front of me, looking at me. Does he want to tell me something? I seem to be frightened, lest he haunts me. I've just noticed I don't want to look up. Am I scared to see him? What if I do? Part of me wants to see him, especially if he confirms that he sexually abused me. This shows how desperate I am for some confirmation of my conclusions – in other words, of the truth. Why did I call it 'the truth'? If I regard it as the truth, it doesn't need to be confirmed – I suppose only doubt needs to be confirmed.

Monday, 9 November 1987
8:37 a.m.

I got angry at Mark this morning before he left for school. He doesn't seem to be so keen to go to school. It's a wet morning, and when he noticed the dark clouds he said to me, 'If I get caught in the rain, it will be your fault.' He later said he was joking, but it didn't sound like a joke to me. That must have made me angry, and I kept pushing him to go to school because he was running late. After he left, I was worried that he wouldn't concentrate, not only in class but also on the road. Then I became angry at my father. He is the one responsible for all of this.

Mark was an intelligent boy, but now he is losing interest in school. I'm sure his intellectual development has deteriorated for a number of reasons. His relationship with his father was poor when he was little. That's because Louie and I had many problems in our relationship, mostly due to my psychological problem. It has only been in these last few months that Mark has become close to his father. It makes me so happy when I see them together. Mark also has another problem with Michelle, who was using him as a scapegoat. Instead of directing her anger at me, she was/is directing it at Mark. This was a vicious cycle that affected all of us.

If I didn't have emotional problems, Mark wouldn't have any problems in school whatsoever. He would have been more secure and therefore happier. Now that I know the reason behind my emotional and psychological problems, I blame my father. I got angry at my father this morning, but I realised that he must have had psychological problems himself; otherwise, he wouldn't have hurt me sexually, physically and emotionally. Then my anger subsided.

I can see that the real me is interfering with the anger that needs to come out. But is this really interference, or does that anger need to be vented through rage or by reasoning? At one stage, the little girl could not reason. And yet she needed and still needs to express that anger and rage.

I just had a long pause. I have been going through my diary. On 9 August, in spite of the hurt inside me I wrote, 'Now that I understand the reasons behind your actions, I don't have any grudges against you.' And then I felt close to my father. It is clearly depicted in the paragraph preceding that quotation.

This makes me wonder if, for the inner child who is so enraged, reasoning is good enough. From my experience, this rage needs to come out. *Apparently, reasoning is not enough, or rather, is not applicable as the child cannot reason.*

9:18 p.m.

After I returned from the Institute today, I felt disappointed by my performance in class. During class a thought went through my mind: what if I'm not accepted for the Bachelor of Arts next year? Fear struck. That would be a great disappointment for me, and it would be difficult to come to terms with. After that, I felt pessimistic about being able to cope with my studies next year. Why do I have this fear? Could it be because, at the moment of thinking about it, I am partially in a state of regression?

In class I found it hard to communicate with my friend Rose, even though we were talking about psychological problems in general. It seems that the only person I can communicate with right now is my psychologist. During the session today, however, at one stage I couldn't communicate with her. That was when I thought she had lost interest in what I was saying. I felt down. Could that be anger depression?

I haven't had that premonition I used to have for quite some time. Not only that, I have been feeling pessimistic about it. While I was flipping through the book about Sigmund Freud, *Man and His Soul,* I felt discouraged by the vocabulary and asked myself, 'How am I going to express myself if I write a book about psychoanalysis?'

Intellectually, I feel so helpless at the moment.

Tuesday, 10 November 1987
4:35 p.m.

Louie is over half an hour late from work. My emotions are at a standstill. I don't feel panicky at all. Am I experiencing silent anger through regression? Could be. I went to Deer Park Shopping Centre this morning, and at one stage I felt panicky – I was longing to see Louie. If I had seen him, I would have run to him like a little girl.

4:56 p.m.

Louie is not back yet. I have no emotions. Something must

have happened to him. He left work. Michelle rang up to find out. Before, I rang up Ġuza's (his sister's) place. I am emotionally frozen. My left arm is very weak.

Louie just rang me up from Monsanto. He worked overtime. I burst out crying when I heard his voice, but not for long.

5:39 p.m.

Michelle put her arms around me earlier, when she saw me upset. That meant a lot to me. She is also enjoying doing housework, and she seems happier. Now she is playing with the dog outside. I feel happy when I see her happy. This is a good sign because my anger towards her is subsiding, or at least I'm not directing my anger at her.

6:47 p.m.

Still in bed thinking out loud. I have been holding the soft toy all this time (since 4:35). I have become attached to it. I have been caressing it, playing with its crest, touching its eyes and nose and I even kissed him (it). Michelle brought in Butch (our Boston terrier) before, and as soon as he came in, he jumped on the bed. I was so pleased to see him – I even felt affectionate towards him. It was a good feeling because it broke up that frozen emotional state.

I am in search of my real self. I have just been thinking of Dr. Garcia – the little girl still needs him; the baby hardly ever gets angry at him, and the real self can be very understanding about my relationship with him.

I have just remembered an emotional moment. This morning when I was about to get off the bus, I felt close to my 'real' mother – the baby felt like crying for her mother. I was in a public place, and that's why I didn't cry. But it was certainly a special moment for me. As I was writing this last sentence, the fear of not being able to express myself came back to me.

I was thinking of the book I heard about on the radio this morning – it's a fictitious story about Marina, who couldn't communicate with people except through her journal because she had an emotional problem. Apparently, it's going to be a famous book. This morning as I was listening to the radio, I was thinking of myself – I am another Marina (our nickname back home was *tal-merina*)! The difference is that Marina's story, although based on true emotional problems, is fictitious, whereas my story is real.

This incident clearly depicts that the fear about expressing myself verbally or in writing is certainly associated with my childhood.

On the way to St Albans this morning, I was haunted by the fear of snakes when I saw a black hose in a front garden. I had that creeping feeling about snakes, and even a stand made up of curved black pipes at the petrol station reminded me of snakes (in Malta, the male snakes are black, and the females are brown). A real snake – that's what it reminded me of. As a child, could I have been frightened of a real snake, perhaps as a threat or a punishment, or is it a disguise for a penis?

10:20 p.m.

I have been watching 'Never My Child', a documentary on TV about incest and sexually abused children. Louie and I watched it together – the kids started to watch it with us but fell asleep. Louie was moved by a comment (or rather advice) to *believe children*. At that point Louie came next to me and held me tight. I recollected that scenario I made last night when I thought he didn't believe me. The part that struck me most was when one of the incest victims said that she carried it unconsciously for thirty-five years until it came out in therapy. She certainly is another me. That lady had a lot of psychological problems without being aware of the reason behind them. While I was watching the documentary, I noticed that my emotions were at a standstill, and I was intellectually frozen – a lot of pressure on my forehead. I suppose that was silent anger. I also had a craving for a chocolate-coated muesli bar – a sign of regression in my case.

Wednesday, 11 November 1987
8:29 a.m.

I took out my secondary school certificates from Oxford University this morning. For all these years, I have left them rolled up in a drawer as if they didn't exist. I was thinking about what Stella, one of my grammar school teachers, had advised me to do with these certificates before I came to Australia. She told me to put them in a frame. That teacher was proud of me and happy about my academic success, even though she only taught me in Form 1. While I was writing this last sentence, I burst into tears – when I was at secondary school, people cared a lot about me. I suppose that interest and care camouflaged my emotional deprivation. Many times, I've wondered how I managed to be so content during those years. But now I understand.

Yes, teachers and school principals alike were all willing to help me. They must have detected some intelligence in me to have encouraged me to go to secondary school, which in those days was not compulsory. There was Ms Farrugia, who was more than a teacher to me. She was the one who encouraged me to sit for the entrance examination. Ms Carmen Rapa, who happened to be my sponsor/godmother for Confirmation, was willing to have me in her Italian class after school. Then, when I passed my exams, Ms Natalina Sultana invited me to attend the private lessons she was offering without charging me anything, because my parents could not afford it. Apparently, she wanted to help me.

At the time of writing, I don't feel close to the above people – I suppose that's because of silent anger. I want to feel close/intimate with these people, who all cared about me – I'm mentally frozen again. My left arm is weak at the moment. I feel like fiddling with the corner of the sheet.

3:20 p.m.

Just rang Mr McFerguson at the Western Institute to let him know that I'm filling in a Special Consideration Entry Form regarding the Bachelor of Arts, and I also told him the reason behind my emotional and psychological problem. The impression I got from him was that now it's up to me whether I let it interfere with my studies or not. He said, 'You've got to keep in mind that the past can't hurt you anymore.' *I felt panicky because it's up to me whether I let the problem interfere with my studies or not.*

The message I got from my inner voice was that I'm using this illness as an excuse, as if I don't really want to continue my studies. How can I believe that, when I know how excited I was when I started these short courses at the Western Institute? And what about when I was in bed a few nights ago, when I imagined myself in front of the interviewing panel and couldn't stop crying as I kept saying, 'I'll be back. I'll be back'? Although I feel apprehensive about going back to my studies, handling my certificates today was a special moment for me.

Thursday, 12 November 1987
7:00 a.m.

Last night I rang up my brother Laurry to let him know that we won't be going to Sydney at Christmas because of my illness. He wasn't home, so I spoke to Mary. She was disappointed and sad about the news, but she was also understanding. That meant a lot to me, and I told her that she is more than a sister-in-law to me. She wondered about the underlying causes for my psychological problems, and she seems to suspect something – she told me so herself. I have a feeling she suspects that I'm a victim of incest. I told her that one day I will find out the truth and even promised her to tell her.

Louie definitely doesn't want me to tell anybody about my findings. At one stage I was quite angry at him. I said to him, 'I don't know why you are so protective of ~~your,~~ my father.' The little girl or the baby was the one who was angry. Whom was I identifying Louie with? *Could I have identified with him as my brother?* After all, in the above quotation there was a slip of the tongue, 'your' instead of 'my'. Yesterday I thought I identified with Louie as my father, who didn't want me to tell the truth.

Last evening after I hang up and told Louie about the conversation, I felt panicky. I kept thinking, 'How am I going to continue with my life without telling Mary the truth?' And then the superego took over, and I felt a strong compulsion to tell her. I felt panicky: on one hand there was Louie, who strictly doesn't want me to tell her, and on the other hand there was the superego compelling me to do the opposite. *Could I be identifying with Louie both as my father and my brother regarding telling the truth?*

5:30 p.m.

I just had a fit of rage after I clashed with Michelle over her maths problems. While I was washing the runners in the backyard, she came over and asked me if I could help her with her maths – how to find the interest. I can't remember exactly what she said, but I realised that she was referring to compound interest. For a moment I felt excited because I was extremely good at them in school. But then fear struck. What if I don't remember them? On the way inside the house Michelle said, 'Or else I can ring up Catherine to explain it to me.' Then I replied, 'Why should she know how to do them, and you don't?' If her friend knew how to do them, I expected Michelle to know how to do them too. Michelle said to me abruptly, 'Well, we are not all the same.' When I realised my mistake, I also realised how damaging that comment was for her self-esteem.

I had a look at the sum, and I got mentally frustrated because I couldn't figure out the formulae. When I did, before I explained it to Michelle, she started showing me how to do it her own way. She worked the formulae right, but then there was an improper fraction in the denominator, and she didn't do the reciprocal of the fraction. I could *clearly* see her mistake. Michelle, on the other hand, was so sure of her answer. I didn't want to upset her. So, I tried to explain to her that she was right, in a way. But to explain the complicated fraction to her was too much for me, even though I knew how to do them. I gave up and asked her to ring up her friend. I ended up in a fit of rage in the laundry.

Friday, 13 November 1987
7:30 a.m.

These last couple of nights I haven't been sleeping well at all. When I got up this morning, I was stiff all over, including my back, and I was also mentally exhausted. When I told Louie, he said he was having the same problem. That reminded me of something. Some time ago I noticed that if Louie has trouble sleeping, I sense it, become uneasy and end up having trouble sleeping myself, even though he is not tossing around and looks as if he is asleep.

Could I identify with Louie even in his sleep as my father? I wouldn't be surprised. That's why I end up being uncomfortable in bed, even though he doesn't approach me sexually. Could it be the baby who feels uneasy with her father? I never thought of it before, but it makes a lot of sense. I never sleep close to Louie; on the contrary, I sleep at the edge of the bed. And there was a time when I used to have sleeping problems because of the tension in my back, and I would go and sleep with Mark. *That tension in my back is definitely associated with my father.*

11:15 p.m.

I don't feel sleepy because I had a good nap before, from 5:30 till 8:30. I must have slept so deeply that I didn't even hear Michelle cleaning up the kitchen.

Just before I started writing, I was going over some parts of my diary. I really enjoyed reading it, even though there are times when I wish I could express myself better in writing. But when I take my deplorable state into consideration, I feel good about it. During today's session I told my temporary psychologist that at times I wish Dr. Garcia were here to share my diary with, especially when I discover something through my self-analysis. I feel so excited about it that I want to share it with him. I suppose I feel that now he is an important person in my life. The first time I had that feeling about him was the Saturday morning when I discovered the little distressed girl. That was a special moment in my life – so special that I wanted to share it with Dr. Garcia, and I ended up ringing him up at home for the first time.

This afternoon I also told Ms Jacob that to me this therapy is now more than just therapy; I feel the need to work with someone regarding my findings with the inner voices and the whole area of study that I'm interested in. I also talked about my obsession with Freud and the man I identify as Freud. Why am I so interested in Freud? I don't know much about his theories, but apparently, I know enough to be interested in him.

P.S. This morning I handed in my application for the Bachelor of Arts for next year. I wanted to mention it in the diary, even though I'm not so sure about my studies. I suppose the fact that I wanted to record it in my diary means that deep down I feel that today, Friday, 13 November 1987, could be another special day in my diary [12:06 a.m.].

Saturday, 14 November 1987
1:50 p.m.

At home by myself – Louie is at work, and Michelle and Mark went to West End Market. This last hour or so, I have been trying to figure out what state I'm in. There is no sign of depression or anger. On the other hand, I'm not in a state of elation, and I haven't got the capacity to connect emotionally. While I was in the garden, I didn't feel that close to nature either. However, I still spent about ten minutes touching the water lilies and trying to attract the goldfish in the waterfall. For a few moments, I fell in love with this particular water lily, which hasn't fully blossomed.

Susan, one of the neighbours, just dropped in for a visit.

Sunday, 15 November 1987
1:30 p.m.

In the car by myself in Williamstown, close to the pier. Mark and Louie are fishing a few metres away. I have just been interrupted by Louie. He came for a cuppa. He is now sitting next to me enjoying a nice cup of coffee and some sandwiches. Louie just went back near Mark.

Speaking of Louie, he does anything for me. Before we came to Williamstown, we were in Werribee. We arrived there at about 9:30 a.m. I stayed in the car. I couldn't be bothered with writing. So, I stayed lying down on the back seat, trying to relax. Although I lay down for about two hours, I couldn't relax. When I got up, I was so weak that I couldn't even butter the sandwiches.

At one stage I felt like writing, but I didn't have the strength. While I was sitting down, I saw a little boy and a little girl playing on the beach. They seemed happy and looked like normal kids. I wondered, however, if they have any emotional problems. I also wondered if they are victims of incest. If they were, would that problem affect them now or later on in life? That prompted me to reflect upon my childhood.

As a five-year-old girl, I suppose there were times when I was happy too. I did play with other children in the neighbourhood, and I really enjoyed those happy moments. However, I clearly remember tearing up a rag doll in anger when I was about three years old. This took place as I stood in front of the barn, which was not attached to the house.

When I was doing the Childhood across Culture course, I tapped into that part of myself that enjoyed my childhood. I started writing an essay about recollections of my childhood. I really enjoyed writing that essay. At that time, I had no idea that I was a victim of incest, and the essay didn't trigger anything. It was when I started writing similar essays in Maltese that something pressed the panic button.

It seems the Maltese language does take me back to my childhood. When I get fits of rage, I swear in Maltese. Since I've been in Australia, I have avoided the Maltese language. I hardly ever speak to the kids in Maltese. Lately I've noticed that both Michelle and Mark have been using a few words of Maltese, and I feel uncomfortable when they do.

I can't seem to run away, not only from my childhood but also from the environment in which I was brought up. On the way to Werribee this morning, I couldn't help thinking about the fields – the green veggies, crops, wooden boxes, old sheds, the red colour of the soil, cart wheels, agriculture, irrigation – all these certainly took me back home. And when I saw the coloured boats at the bay, I felt excited like a little girl.

Could those boats have reminded me of the times I went to the main island by boat? After all, I used to get excited about it, even though I would get seasick. Going to the main island of Malta was a treat. This morning I certainly felt like that little girl.

Even the tugboats, ships and cranes around me definitely remind me of Gozo. I feel so far away from everybody. People have been walking up and down the pier, and I still feel so alienated. When Louie came to the car before, I had such a fright when I saw him at the car window, and while I was having a cup of tea, I felt so far away from him!

This lack of intimacy is so painful for me. I can't write about it now because that emotional pain is not there. My head feels so heavy. I don't know how I managed to write.

7:00 p.m.

I am in my bedroom. Just a few minutes ago, while I was lying down on the couch, I was thinking about my Christian name, Victoria. I felt that I preferred that name rather than Vicky. But somehow, I still liked Vicky too. This uncertainty about the preference for my name prompted me to reflect on it. For me, the name Victoria implies power, courage and leadership. Whereas Vicky implies informality, immaturity, being casual. Where does the one with doubts, fears, anger and frustration fit in?

I'm thinking of Victoria again. She is the one who has

authentic peace within herself – thus possessing all the other virtues that inner peace entails, namely love, caring, compassion and understanding. She is also the one whose key to success is patience, perseverance and tolerance. By success I mean not only in achievements, but most importantly in her relationships with herself and other people, especially her husband and her beloved children.

Before I started writing, I was thinking of that day when I christened the little girl and called her Victoria. That was Friday morning, 7 August 1987. Victoria is my Christian name, and when I find my real self, or rather when I will be in control of my real self, I will, metaphorically speaking, convert to that name. It would certainly be an appropriate name. *I am a victim of incest (and much more) in search of her real self.*

Monday, 16 November 1987
1:39 p.m.

I've just come from a driving lesson. I'm a bit disappointed with my performance. I feel that I'm always learning from my mistakes – yes, mistakes do teach me a lot.

During this morning's session I talked a little about the fact that through regression, the real me seems to be observing many things. Yesterday, for example, while I was near the pier in the car, I regressed to babyhood. I noticed it when my eyes fell on a small toy that Louie has dangling over the dashboard. I kept looking at it without blinking, as if it meant something to me, and we were communicating with each other. I felt that the soft toy was telling me something – perhaps that the two of us needed each other because we were both lonely. I wish I could have written my feelings about it while I was experiencing it. But somehow, I couldn't be bothered. It was such a good feeling that by the time I started writing, I would have lost that regression. After all, babies don't write. So, the best I can do is recollect it.

As I was lying down on the back of the seat, I kept looking at the patterns of the upholstery. I was fascinated by it even though it was a tiny pattern, a diagonal cross made up of small holes. At one stage, I observed my right hand. During these times of regression into babyhood, I want to concentrate more on what goes through my mind. This may be tricky, because intellectually I don't know how much I regress. *I wonder if emotional regression is equivalent to intellectual regression.* I did tell my psychologist this morning that the real me is interested in observing this regression through an adult's eyes. I'm not sure if I expressed myself properly during the latter part of this last sentence – but I know what I mean.

So far, during regression I have discovered the serenity inside me (I'm thinking of when I had this regression in class for the first time). That time when I was in the garden, I discovered a 'sixth sense'. I kept touching the bamboo and the leaves – it was such a good feeling – or should I say sensation, which has nothing to do with sexual sensation as perhaps we adults think. However, during that regression I certainly noticed a sexual sensation – it was such a beautiful feeling! I call it a sexual sensation because I felt it in the genital area, not because it was an impulse or desire. It seems that childhood sexuality is preceded by that sensation, which later develops into impulses and desires. I'm thinking of Freud and Dr. Garcia. I wonder what the latter will think when I tell him about it. I also wonder what other people's reactions might be when I bring it out in the open. Then again, this discovery might be new to me but not to other people.

9:00 p.m.

Just came from the Institute. I feel depressed. Even in class, I hardly said anything. And most of the time I felt pessimistic about the Bachelor of Arts. Students discussed the essay that has to be handed in soon, and I felt the odd one out because I'm not doing it. At one point I even felt sad about it. I feel so helpless. Michelle came to ask me some questions regarding the book list and stationery for the next academic year – I could hardly follow them.

It's not only sad, but the fact that it is interfering with my relationship with the kids is frustrating. Mark just made a comment about Michelle, saying, 'She is walking all over you, and you don't even know it.' That certainly triggered anger.

When will I be able to continue with my life? Will I ever be able to? I feel so helpless. Before I started writing, I rang up Brother Philip, but he wasn't there. As I was looking through the phone book, I came across Dr Garcia's number. I thought of him and wondered if he thinks of me while he is away. I suppose I was experiencing loss depression.

Tuesday, 17 November 1987
9:57 a.m.

I was looking forward to today because I have nowhere to go, and I hoped I might regress into babyhood and enjoy a couple hours of sleep. I stayed in bed this morning, but I couldn't sleep. I held the soft toy, but I didn't have any attachment to it. There must have been no regression then.

Since I got up this morning, I have been having abdominal pain. There is no panic whatsoever – I'm just breathing. I feel uncomfortable because of my sharp abdominal pain, and there is also some sensation in the vagina/urethra because I feel as if I want to pass water. Even the tension in my ear is bothering me.

I've decided to write about the dreams I had these last couple of nights. Sunday night, I dreamt that my father attempted to commit suicide. In the dream it was Sunday morning, when my father and my sister Mary went to the 11:00 mass. My mother and I were at home waiting for them. They were very late – so I went outside to see if they were coming. When I saw them coming, I noticed that my father had bloodstains on his shirt and a horrible bruise on the right side of his neck. When he arrived in front of our next-door neighbour's house, I also noticed a knife in his head – the same knife I'd wanted to butter the sandwiches with the day before. My father headed towards this paddock. I knew what he was going to do. I felt the knife was not sharp enough to commit suicide with, and I wanted to stop him because it would have been a painful way to die. Eventually, in the dream my father ended up committing suicide by hanging himself. I was upset because that was a disgrace to the family, and now nobody would want to marry me. As a result of that disgrace, I was concerned about my studies; but at one point I was determined to study mental health.

2:08 p.m.

Just before 2:00, my brother Laurry rang me up from Sydney. He talked to me in a loud and strong voice. *Inti taf x'għandek? Ħara ma' sormok għandek. Int xejn m'għandek. Dak il-mard int trid tiġġielidlu. Int għandek raġel joqgħod għal kollox Mur itma dawk it-tfal . . . ixtri zewgt it-tfal oħra ħalli jkollok x'tagħmel* (Do you know what you have? You're spoilt. You haven't got anything. You need to fight that sickness you have. You have a subservient man. Go and feed those kids . . . get another two kids so you have things to do). I told him that I have a lot of fear inside me, and something must have happened to me when I was little. *X'seta'ġralek?* (What could have happened to you?), he replied abruptly.

During the conversation I also told him that one day I will sit down and talk with him. I even told him that I'm interested in studying mental illness. When I was telling him that, I didn't feel strongly about it, but I said it, and then I had that fear of expectations. I'm emotionally and mentally frozen.

Wednesday, 18 November 1987
8:30 a.m.

I've just been looking for the pen I usually write with. I couldn't find it. So, I ended up using another pen. When I couldn't find it, there was disappointment inside me, perhaps even a sense of loss. Why did that pen mean so much to me? And why was I so disappointed?

Loss: Does losing my father mean so much to me that I can easily get attached to anything, no matter how trivial it is? This particular pen was special to me because I have been writing the diary with it. I also got attached to the other pen I started writing my diary with. This attachment to pens reminds me also of another special pen – the fountain pen I used for my exams. I still have that pen, and it and the pencil case are invaluable to me.

Writing about my attachments to certain pens was definitely unpremeditated. What I was intending to write about was my impressions as I was looking through Michelle's photo album. But I just couldn't help mentioning the loss associated with that pen in my diary.

This morning I felt like looking at Michelle's photo album. I wanted to recollect how she looked, as if looking at Michelle as a baby would be like looking at myself as a baby. When I was looking at Michelle's christening certificate, something struck me – Michelle's second name is Victoria, and my second name is Michaelina. Michelle Victoria (daughter) and Victoria Michaelina (mother). Mother and daughter – we not only look alike, but our names are the other way around. What a coincidence! I want to point out that it was my mother-in-law who gave Michelle her second name, Victoria.

The first photo that impressed me was the one in which my sister and I are holding our babies on the day they were christened. In the photo my sister's son, Charles, is crying his heart out, and Michelle is bending her head over slightly, looking at him. I was impressed by her alertness at only forty-five days old!

Was I as alert as she was? I looked at the photo of the bassinet where she is sleeping peacefully. I thought of the other baby. The photo in which I'm bathing Michelle. I noticed that sense of loss when I was thinking about it. I was also thinking of the other photo in which Louie is holding Michelle. The photo in which Michelle is in the bouncy – she looks like a doll. In some photos she looks much like my father. In others she looks like my mother. When she was born, she looked like my mother.

Thursday, 19 November 1987
7:00 p.m.

It took me quite some time to get up and start writing. I have been lying down since 5:00 because I had sharp abdominal pain. This last half hour it seems to have eased a bit. While I was passing water just before, I felt lot of pressure on the abdomen. Could this abdominal pain be another psychosomatic symptom? I wouldn't be surprised. When I had a tubal ligation, I experienced that pain for quite some time.

9:40 p.m.

I couldn't continue with my writing because I was so hungry, I couldn't concentrate. And after tea the pain was so sharp, I had to lie down.

Last night I had a dream. I have been thinking of it all day. In this dream Louie and I had just finished building a second house. This house was in Gozo, next to the nuns' convent at Nazzarenu. For this house, I bought a baroque lounge suite like the one I have at home. In the dream the nuns had another building on the other side of our house. Michelle was in this dream too, but I can't remember what she was doing. In that separate building, there was a nun who was more understanding, because she said that she herself has sexual problems.

I kept thinking about this dream all day, and it seems to be unfolding another chapter. Lately I've been thinking about the Spanish Inquisition. The thoughts that came to my mind in relation to it are being questioned about something having to do with religion. If I'm not mistaken, a couple of years ago Dr. Garcia must have asked me a personal question, and I replied that it sounded like the Spanish Inquisition. These last few days when I have been thinking about the interview at the Western Institute, I felt that the little girl is being questioned. Could she have been questioned by the nuns?

As I was about to doze off this afternoon, I felt someone pulling my left ear, followed by a sudden fright. At the moment, I'm thinking of Mr Kelly from St Albans South Primary School. He keeps reminding me of the Madre (Mother Superior) who used to teach at the preschool I attended that was run by the nuns. I made the association this morning when I was waiting for Irene to get ready to go shopping together. This afternoon I also vaguely remembered my father working in the garden of this same preschool.

I remember the classroom where the youngest nun used to teach. I also remember that nun doing some sewing in the yard. I remember where the toilets were, the 'apron' we wore as a uniform, hiding the pacifier under the apron, the room on the left, which was used as an office and an interviewing room and the first classroom, which belonged to the Madre. I also remember being in that room, using the small blackboard and holding the counter, which was in different colours.

Friday, 20 November 1987
10:45 a.m.

As I was doing the laundry this morning, I felt close to a breakthrough regarding inner voices and conflicts. I was reflecting upon the origin of the fear I had with regard to Michelle and facial hair. I was thinking of when that fear started – a few days after she was born, when I bathed her for the first time, while I was still in hospital. It reminded me of the way my mother used to hold me when she washed my hair and how traumatic it was for me as she held me with my face under the water. The more I cried, the more she held me under the water.

Till this morning, I thought the fear that has haunted me day and night since then was a disguise for the fear I must have experienced while my mother washed my hair. This morning, however, I came to the conclusion that embedded in this fear are four fears: (i) the fear I experienced while my mother washed my hair, (ii) the fear of my mother, who also had fine, fair facial hair and (iii) fear of my father, because I feared Michelle's facial hair developing into a beard; (iv) fear of Michelle turning into a monster.

This morning I realised that I not only have been unconsciously identifying with people when I see them, but inwardly there was/is another way of identifying. I want to elaborate on the latter.

In my experience there are different kinds of voices; in other words, there are different personalities behind these voices. These personalities unconsciously become part of us. I said unconsciously because I wasn't aware of it, and I wasn't obsessed by it like people who suffer from schizophrenia. I also said they are part of us because they (personalities) talk inside us through inner voices, messages and conflicts.

In my case, the different personalities are:

i) The angry and frightened baby who has been trying to tell me what happened to her. There are moments when she encourages me to keep hanging in, and there are moments of despair.
ii) The little girl who is still sexually after her father and still experiencing loss.
iii) Then there is the old self, the one that is a by-product of negative emotions and experiences – the one that is so emotionally hurt, constantly psychologically tormented by conflicts, doubt, guilt, shame, jealousy, fear and anger, including silent anger and rage.
iv) Part of the real self – the one that showed moments of affection, the one who has a tiny ray of hope and at times is so optimistic about a highly successful prospective future; the one that has been trying to emerge, especially these last few months.
v) My father, who is attempting to defend himself by imposing his guilt on someone else through the superego; the one who made nasty remarks to the baby.

My mother – where does she fit in regarding the inner voices? Whenever I see a child crying, the inner voice saying *Ibki kemm tiflaħ* (cry as much as you can), with no compassion or understanding, always comes to the forefront. My mother is also affecting me through a psychosomatic symptom, namely bad breath, which she used to have and which I have become obsessed with these last ten years or so. Through this symptom I'm suffering from embarrassment, which results in withdrawal and an inferiority complex. I'm sure there is more to this embarrassment.

Now that I have become aware of who is behind these inner voices, I'll watch out for my mother's. I've just remembered someone else behind another voice – *the devil*. Do I have a fear of him? Am I psychologically possessed by him too? I wouldn't be surprised! It's important to point out that in Maltese the devil is masculine, considered an enemy who embodies evil.

After all, as a child I used to look in the mirror and say to myself that I looked like the devil. And when I came to Australia, I put the sticker saying 'Verbum Dei Caro Factum Est' with a cross on it on the inside of the front door. We used to be told that the devil is frightened of those words and goes away when he sees or hears them. Oh yes, I was/am frightened of the devil.

And what about God? I feel his presence in me when I have authentic peace inside. Somehow, I don't believe in God as a person, as I used to. I took the notion of God very literally until recently.

I would like to comment on the word 'personalities', which I used before. Although there are moments when I am 'possessed' by these personalities, they are not fully in control because I am still in touch with the real world. I deliberately used the word 'possessed' because as I have already pointed out, we are 'possessed' up to a certain point. Otherwise, we don't have those voices inside us. And they are powerful – at some times more than others.

Sometimes those personalities are in conflict with each other. It's obvious when they are. I am completely torn apart. And it is so horrendous. Through these conflicts and contradictions, there is doubt. *It's the real emerging self that is in doubt* – the real self that is so torn apart through these conflicts and so overcome by them that it has no strength to fight back and ends up being doubtful.

4:20 p.m.

Before I got dressed to go for my session, I was not sure whether to wear casual – something with runners – or the white shirt and Michelle's black and white baggies/pants. I decided to wear the latter. When I buttoned up the shirt, I felt it was too constrictive, so I unbuttoned another button, and the result was the opposite. The little girl took over and felt it was seductive. Together with the gold choker chain, I put on the long chain and pulled it backwards to get just below the choker chain. That meant that I had most of the long chain in the back. Part of me felt that another part of me would do anything to be seductive. That same part wanted to make sure it didn't show from the back. As I looked at my back through the mirror, that length of the chain at the back reminded me of priests. Back home during processions, priests used to wear this long cord around their neck that hung from the back.

As I was writing the above paragraph, Dun Baskal came to my mind. I also remembered when Michelle used to put the scarf around her neck. This reminded me of confession, and I would feel uneasy when I used to see it around her neck like that. Could my mother have taken me to that priest to confess incest, and he ended up interrogating me? Could this be 'the inquisition' that seems to be unfolding?

Chapter 11

Stillness

Saturday, 21 November 1987
8:30 p.m.

I don't know how to describe the events of today. I'm not sure I want to remember them. At about 1:00 p.m., Louie got drunk. It's the events that preceded this that frightened me.

After Michelle and I got back from shopping I must have regressed, because I wanted to lie down, and I felt irritable because Michelle wanted me to help her sew the bootie for the Christmas decoration. We clashed. As I went to my room upset, I could see this head being chopped off by a pair of scissors. I wonder whose head it was! Before, I thought it was a nun's, because I've noticed that when it comes to helping Michelle with some handicraft, I get into these fits of rage. But when I was mentioning the scissors just above, I thought of my father and clippers – it must be the same clippers he used to shear the sheep.

In the meantime, Louie was back from work. He was still angry at me from yesterday because the kids were watching a movie, and he wanted to recite the Rosary. I stood up for the kids, and somehow, he got it in his head that it's always my way, as if he has no authority in this house.

He took his anger out on Michelle, who came to my room and threatened to go to the police. She said, 'Why doesn't he rape me?' as if she really wanted him to harm her, so she'd have every reason to call the police. Her words infuriated me. I threw the lampshade on the floor and yelled 'NO!'

What did I mean by that 'NO'? Was it the rape or the 'no' for losing my father to someone else?

When Michelle saw my reaction, she quickly changed her mind, and crying, said 'No, mummy', as if she didn't mean it. That's when Louie lost control of himself and wanted to leave home. He even took the shotgun out of the cupboard. Michelle tried to stop him from leaving. He begged her to apologise, which she did. I can still see her kneeling down in front of him to apologise.

After that, Louie drank about one-third of a bottle of whisky and some brandy. Michelle came down the corridor, her face looking pale and cold as ice. 'I don't care', she said. 'I don't care.' I went to see what had happened and there was Louie, standing with his face against the wall in a deplorable state. Although there was that emotional stillness in me, mentally I felt sorry for him. I put my arms over his shoulders and tried to make feel him better. Even Mark was there, holding him and comforting him.

A few things struck me during this ordeal in the lounge while Louie was drunk:

- My emotional stillness. I felt sorry for him, I cared for him, but I couldn't feel any affection for him. I kept caressing him and telling him how much love there is for each other. He kept telling me how much he loves us and that he will never leave me. He kept saying how sorry he was for threatening to leave. He kept looking at our wedding photo and saying how beautiful I was. He even told Mark, 'Isn't she beautiful!' Every time he said that I burst out crying, even though I couldn't feel it emotionally.

- Louie's love for us really struck me. He kept saying how much he loves me and Mark, because we were beside him. How much he loves Michelle and Mark – that he loves them both the same. He kept asking for Michelle. He was concerned that she will never forgive him. I could see how sorry he was. As soon as Mark went to sit on the couch, he kept asking for him in a feeble voice, and Mark would come straight to him. I shall never forget the expression on Mark's face every time Louie asked for him. He was certainly glad that his father was calling him. They both cried on each other's shoulders. Mark stayed with Louie all the time. I was so proud of him!
- And what about Michelle? While Mark was so affectionate, she was so cold! She ended up going over to Irene's place. I kept assuring Louie that she will forgive him and told him to give her time.

Who was I during that time, when I wouldn't move away from Louie because I wanted to be with him? Was I the little girl who was trying to comfort her father or the real self with her husband, even though I was so far away from him emotionally? I did tell him there is no doubt how much love there is for each other. However, mentally I knew it was one-sided love at that point in time. Louie loves me sincerely, but what about me? I've questioned this before and even now at the moment of writing, because there is no affection for him whatsoever. But then, during this emotional stillness there is no affection for the kids either. This stillness has certainly immobilised my emotions, especially affection. How am I going to overcome this fixation?

What does God want from me? During the drama that Louie created, the reassuring thought went through my mind that nothing serious was going to happen, as if we were safeguarded, and that I am going to be helpful to other people, and the first person I'm going to help is Michelle. I want to help people but not at the expense of my family.

During that state of elation, when I experienced a great sense of inner freedom, there was so much love between the four of us. Even my sister-in-law Mary could see it. She told me so herself.

Sunday, 22 November 1987
3:00 p.m.

I seem to have a problem expressing myself in writing. I don't know where to start – because there is conflict inside me. I'm thinking of Mark and Louie. They have just been to West End Market to buy a treasure chest for the aquarium. It wouldn't work. On my way to the bedroom to start writing, I joined them. They were trying to figure out why the chest wouldn't open. I figured it out! I was surprised at myself.

Monday, 23 November 1987
9:00 a.m.

During the night I had a fright. I was sleeping on the side facing Louie, when all of a sudden, I felt someone touching me from the back, just behind my left armpit. I got a terrible fright, and I yelled something. I think I said 'NO!' Louie woke up, and realising I must have had a fright, he stretched out his arm to hug me and told me not to be frightened. As soon as I yelled out, that voice was clear to me, and it reminded me of Michelle. That's when the real me took over and tried to remember the dream and the point at which I had the fright. I couldn't remember. So, I started observing, and the first thing I noticed was that my left leg was out from under the blanket, and the way it was bent reminded me of babies in their sleep. Then I remembered that before I went to sleep in my long-sleeved pyjamas, I thought that I might get hot and would be uncomfortable. So, I started wondering if it was the baby who had screamed in her sleep. Then, looking at the clock, I realised it must have been 2:00 a.m. when I had the fright. At the same time, this lady from Chile came to my mind. She did the Speaking Up course with me. That lady then reminded me of Ġuseppa ta' Lażru – a lady from the neighbourhood when I was growing up who owned the bakery. What does she mean to me? Is it because 2:00 a.m. was the time she would start working in the bakery? Or is it indirectly associated with another fear?

I figured out this second fear last Saturday afternoon, while Louie was sleeping in bed after he drank the whisky. I was in bed getting ready to start writing. I was waiting for Michelle to go to church, because I didn't want to start writing while she was still around. I must have regressed, because I felt sleepy. *And while I was dozing off, I felt this abnormal heat coming up as far as my knees*. As the heat reached my knees, I expressed this fear inside me, and then I felt this feeling in both arms. With that 'tight' feeling (as if someone was holding me tight), I saw part of a hand, the Y shape of the first two fingers of the left hand. *I recognised the fingernail – it was my mother's!* And my mind went straight to the bakery that belonged to Ġuseppa ta' Lażru. Did my mother hold me tight, close to the roaring fire that was heating the oven, to frighten me of the fire of hell?

I haven't written about this abnormal heat in my legs before. But I have noticed it a few times. Even that day when I was lying down in the car at Queenscliffe, as soon as I felt the heat of the sun on my legs, I got up in a fright and yelled out, 'It's the sun!' In hindsight I must have said that to assure myself that it was not something else!

Looks like this abnormal heat in my legs is/was a psychosomatic symptom. *What a wonderful way for my inner child to communicate with me and let me know what happened!* What a way to be victorious over the power of darkness!

Speaking of fears, one night in my sleep some years ago, I felt someone trying to choke me. It felt so real that I got up and looked around to see if anybody was in the room. There was no one, and Louie was sound asleep. Who was trying to choke me then? I did mention this incident once during therapy, and I thought then that it was related to the devil. Now I feel that it was someone else. Could it have been my father or mother? Or perhaps some other man?

Last night I also dreamt of my father. My brother Laurry, my father and I were in the same room upstairs. My father must have made a nasty remark about my genital area. I turned around to my brother and said to him, 'You see how rude he is', as if he knew that my genitals were ugly. The fact that he knew seems to confirm incest. I'm not sure whether it was during that dream that I felt the touch that frightened me.

Yesterday, while I was in the toilet at my mother-in-law's place, the noise of the buckle of my belt reminded me of my father's belt. I was wearing the white shirt and the black dotted pants. I looked so smart in them. But somehow that outfit makes me feel uncomfortable. Maybe because I wear the belt. I know that the pleats and the colour of the pants remind me of Mr Thompson, the principal of St Albans South Primary School. I have been associating that priest Dun Baskal with him. I realised it while I was doing the ironing. I was thinking of Mr Thompson and wondering with whom I could have been identifying him, when all of a sudden, I thought of Dun Baskal. They have the same complexion, and from the back, the neck and shoulders are the same. Since then, whenever I think of Mr Thompson, I think of Dun Baskal.

Yesterday I realised also that Saturday afternoons seem to trigger something. How many times I used to lie down in bed on a Saturday afternoon. Could it have reminded me of confessions or perhaps even one particular confession? After all, my mother used to take us every Saturday afternoon to San Wistin chapel to Dun Baskal for confession. And then, when Dun Baskal was too old to hear confessions in church, she used to take us to his house for confession. I still remember standing up in front of him in the small room where I used to go for confession.

Tuesday, 24 November 1987
10:00 a.m.

Michelle is at home. She didn't go to school because she has a sore throat. That annoyed me because I cannot concentrate when she is around the house. I feel uncomfortable because of the fear of being interrupted. When that happens, the baby identifies with her as my father.

When I was writing the last sentence, I wasn't sure whether to use 'I' or 'the baby'. This is an area in my study that I'm interested in: the pronoun 'I'.

What prompted me to study the concept of 'I' is the fact that when I'm writing the diary, especially when I'm giving an account of an incident, I have to stop and think whether I should use 'I' or 'the baby' or 'the little girl' or 'the real me' or 'the old self'. In other words, the 'I' who experienced the incident is sometimes different from the 'I' at the moment of writing.

In my diary I have already talked about my different personalities [20 Nov]. Besides the extreme cases when I turned completely into the little girl or the baby, those personalities are still active inside me, even though I remain in touch with the real world.

Wednesday, 25 November 1987
10:00 p.m.

I'm just breathing – no tension in my head either. I don't know what's happening. All I know is that I don't feel close to the family at all. I can't say it's sad at the moment because there is no sadness. Could this be silent anger? There is no sign of regression. It has been a long time since I held the soft toy.

What part of the 'I' am I at the moment? I really can't tell. During today's session I wasn't much into it either. I kept changing from one subject to another.

This morning I went for a pelvic ultrasound test. After drinking two litres of water, I got this unusual feeling down the throat and stomach. It wasn't painful, but it bothered me. Could that be another psychosomatic symptom? When I mentioned it in therapy, I thought of oral sex and semen.

I'm finding it hard to write because of the emotional stillness I'm experiencing. I'm thinking of Mark. I feel so far away from him too! There is so much stillness inside me! I am so quiet. I'm not even thinking out loud.

Thursday, 26 November 1987
12:34 p.m.

Today I slept in till midday. I really enjoyed that sleep, in which I dreamt that I masturbated twice and reached an orgasm each time. *A sexual desire fulfilled in a dream.* What a great way for nature to take care of itself.

This morning I tried to figure out the emotional state I was in yesterday, and even this morning before I went back to sleep. I noticed that during that state there was only one 'I' – the only fraction was the real me/observer who was puzzled by this state. I kept saying every now and then, 'What on earth is going on?' During that state I couldn't write because there were hardly any thoughts. I was more focused on looking (not necessarily staring) at objects. There was definitely no intuition. Could I have been in a state of regression to another stage of babyhood – a stage between the babyhood that I regressed to in class, in which the vision was blurry, and hearing wasn't very clear either, and the sensory stage? I believe it certainly was a state of regression.

When I was writing the expression 'sensory stage' above, I thought of the sexual sensation I experienced during that stage while I was in the garden. *It seems that during the sensory stage, we start experiencing sexual sensation.*

I'm now thinking of myself as a victim of incest. Yesterday and this morning I had that feeling in my throat, which started after I drank the two litres of water. Part of me is wondering whether it is another psychosomatic symptom. If it is, then that's when incest started, during that stage I regressed back to yesterday. While I was writing these last two sentences, part of me wanted to write it, and another part of me didn't even want to think of it (oral sex/semen could be represented by the water). It's really sickening. Could my father have gone to that extreme? Am I imagining things?

Was my sister Carmen a victim of incest too? And was the paralysis in her hand a result of that? If I'm not mistaken, she developed paralysis when she was eleven months old. If we were victims of incest at such an early age, when did it happen, and where was my mother when it happened? It could have happened while she was downstairs washing the clothes. I don't know if she used to go to the fields when we were little. When she was at church in the morning, where was my father?

I remember having a dream just before Dr. Garcia went on leave. In that dream Michelle, who was about three years old, was with my father in the room where he used to sleep, when my mother turned up. She was wearing a black veil. She must have just come back from church.

Friday, 27 November 1987
7:00 p.m.

While I was sewing Michelle's jumpsuit about an hour ago, I realised that I'm still in the state of regression I discovered yesterday. There is some sort of stillness/peace inside me. However, it's not the same stillness (silent anger) I've already written about. And on the other hand, it's not authentic inner peace either. I called it 'peace' because there are no fears (emotionally), and there are also no conflicts, doubts, inner voices and superego. *There is a regression to that part of babyhood when I knew no fears, but at the same time my inner peace was already lost.*

This morning when I was shopping, I felt at ease because there were no conflicts inside me. I thought the real me mostly took over, because I wasn't disturbed mentally and emotionally. That's what I told my psychologist this afternoon. This morning the real me felt disappointed because she didn't feel any inner peace (elation). During therapy I was puzzled about which part of the self I was. I also said that I feel strange.

Now, however, I realise what's going on. I'm still in that *state of regression, which I'm going to call Stage 1 of incest.*

This state of regression explains why these last two days I haven't been thinking about my childhood – namely Dun

Baskal, the nuns, my mother, my father and the environment back home. The little girl has not been there either. There have been no fits of rage and hardly any thinking out loud.

The difference between Stage 1 of incest and Stage 2 (when the baby, through instinct, started to realise she was being abused) is that during the former there was no fear or silent anger, because she didn't realise what was going on.

This morning, because I had peace of mind, I expected inner peace. I was wrong when I thought the real me was mostly in control. This explains why in therapy I couldn't understand my emotions in relation to the state of mind (peace of mind).

Saturday, 28 November 1987
9:00 a.m.

Could the state of regression I talked about yesterday have been a regression to when I was still in the womb? This is what I've been wondering this morning since I got up. What triggered it was an image that went through my mind during the night.

At about 2:00 a.m. I felt a fright inside me. As soon as I felt the fright, I saw myself from behind, frying fish in the kitchen. That reminded me straightaway of my mother, who was cooking fish when she started going into labour with me. I lifted my head up and looked at the clock. It was just after 2:00 a.m. After that, I experienced sharp pain in the lower back. I couldn't sleep because of the pain, and I kept turning around from one side to another. I almost went to the kitchen to have a cup of coffee.

While I was having breakfast this morning, I was thinking of the possible regression to when I was still in the womb. Yesterday during therapy, I told Ms Jacob that I am puzzled and feeling strange. I didn't know where I was (not literally of course), whether back home or Australia. I told her that I must be somewhere on the ocean. As I was reflecting upon what I said this morning when I thought of the ocean, I thought of Michelle's conception! She was conceived on the ship on the way to Australia.

Last night Mark offered me a piece of his Mars bar. At first, I said no, but then on second thought I said yes. And I had a small piece, *għax-xewqa*. (In Maltese culture, when a woman is pregnant, it's important to offer her whatever you are eating, in case the unborn baby desires it. If it is denied, the baby might end up with a birthmark.) Was it the baby still in the womb who wanted that little bite of chocolate? Even when I'm putting away the ham, salami, etc., I get the craving to have a small piece.

Could the two litres of water I had to drink on Wednesday have reminded me unconsciously, or maybe not so unconsciously, of the fluid in the womb during pregnancy? I do know that the words 'ultrasound test' reminded me of pregnancy and of my sister-in-law Rita, who had an ultrasound test when she was pregnant. Was it the unborn baby, then, who kept smelling the *ġobon tal-bżar* (Maltese preserved pepper cheese) every time I opened the fridge to get the bottle of cordial? I just realised that the bottle of cordial must have reminded me of the womb, because I used the cordial bottle to measure the two litres of water! By the way, when I smelt *il- ġobon tal- bżar* I was puzzled because although I do have some in a jar in the pantry, nobody has handled it, and there is no smell coming from it. It was the unborn baby who was smelling it!

I must have been 'carrying' that unborn baby, and I wasn't aware of it. What is she trying to tell me?

Sunday, 29 November 1987
10:48 a.m.

Overall, I had a good night. I did wake up with a mild fright at about 1:30 a.m. Apparently, I didn't stay awake for long. Both my back and left arm are better this morning.

While I was putting the rollers in my hair, I noticed some tiny pimples on my right cheek. They reminded me of newborn babies and the placenta, which also reminded me of my mother-in-law and the superstition she told me about the placenta. I am now thinking of the *landa tal-kunserva* (tomato paste tin), where it was placed before disposing of it in the sea.

It now seems that I have entered a new dimension – *inside the womb. That's because the unborn baby has some unresolved matter.* It seems she experienced fears and had some cravings that were not satisfied. *(Note: Years later, I found out through my inner journey of self-discovery that I had a twin who apparently was murdered at birth. This was a family secret!)*

Chapter 12

The Lost Girl

Monday, 30 November 1987
10:22 p.m.

As I was writing today's date, I felt I should write it in bold letters, as if there is something special about it. Maybe one day when I look back on this day, I'll realise why. Today I went for the interview at the Western Institute. Could this be an academic turning point in my life? During my interview with one of the tutors, I emphasized that my emotional problem might slow the pace, but it's not going to stop me from continuing with my studies.

Speaking of studies, today was the last lesson for the Preparation for Tertiary Studies course. Towards the end, I felt that my last lesson meant as much to me as the first one. We did this psychoanalytical drawing on the board. I had no idea what it was all about. One student was asked to draw a path, another was asked to draw the sun and so on. I was asked to draw a path. Jacob, the tutor, was impressed by the way I drew it. *It was a bold, wide path leading to the house and was in perspective with it. Its width was from one corner of the house to the other.* Jacob explained to us what the elements of the picture symbolised. The house symbolised the self, and the path symbolised ambition!

No wonder Jacob was so impressed by it. I still remember the expression on his face when I drew it. Out of all the students, why did he ask me to draw a path? Many times, in class I have sensed that he thinks highly of me. I suppose today's experience confirmed what he has been thinking of me since the first essay I wrote for the course.

Although the feeling is not there at the moment, today is a special day for another reason. About two and a half months ago, I sent an essay to the community radio station 3EA. At about 4:30 p.m., halfway through the program, I decided to listen to the Maltese program – and my essay was read today. What a coincidence! Unfortunately, although I seemed excited, I couldn't *feel* the excitement. It hardly meant anything to me. What a pity! When I wrote that essay, it meant so much to me. I was so proud of it! I did end up taping it.

Today I also received a letter from my mother. She advised me to be careful regarding letting Michelle sleep over at other people's places. While she was listening to Rediffusion (radio) about two weeks ago, she heard about a sixteen-year-old girl who got pregnant by her grandfather, and she told me that these things also happen between brothers and sisters. I'm afraid I had no reaction to that part of the letter – except a thought went through my mind that both my mother and I, so far away from each other, are thinking of incest.

Before I go to sleep, I want to give a brief account of a dream I had last night. In this dream, my paternal grandmother, who died in 1963, appeared as a spirit, first to my mother and her mother (my maternal grandmother). Then she appeared to me and after that to Louie. She appeared in a corner of the skylight in her room back home. What struck me most was the fact that my grandmother appeared just exactly above where I remember myself standing next to her when I was little, while she was cleaning the cobwebs around the skylight with the broom. In this apparition there were pictures of soldiers going to or coming from war. Did my grandmother have some unfinished business too? That is, did she know of my father's involvement with incest and never say anything?

Somehow, I am too scared to go to the toilet and the kitchen.

Tuesday, 1 December 1987
8:00 a.m.

I had a reasonably good sleep – I didn't experience any fears. I had a dream in which I emotionally *felt close* to this bedridden little girl. Part of me thinks she was an image of myself, or rather, a miniature of myself. In the dream she was bedridden – she was a bit too old to be a baby. I just noticed that feeling in the air pipe/vent again. I believe that was myself as a baby.

Since I got up this morning, I've been feeling stiff all over, and there is lot of tension in my back – it's like the old days again! Even mentally, I have been 'carried away' by yesterday's drawing while I was lying down in bed, and I felt excited about it. There are no conflicts inside me, either mentally or emotionally. I feel far away from my children. When I went into Mark's room to wake him up, I felt close to him.

Which part of the 'I' am I at the moment? I just rushed to the TV to watch my horoscope – I was just in time. When I put it on, Libra was on the screen, and it said, 'Personal Relationships: Overcome Barrier'. The barrier I'm thinking of at the moment is between Mark and myself. Although I haven't recorded it in my diary, lately we have been at loggerheads with each other.

Whom could I be identifying him with today? Just before I got up this morning, I had a dream in which I opened a wardrobe where there were some baby boy's clothes. I handled one of them, which was on a hanger that was too big for it. I tried to fasten the top button but couldn't make the ends meet. However, as I was attempting to do so, this coat hanger folded by itself, thus making the ends closer together! It was an unusual coat hanger*: a self-adjustable one*. Whom or what is that hanger representing? And what about the garment on it? It was definitely for a baby boy. Which part of me was responsible for that dream?

As I was thinking of the above question, the real me realised that I have just imitated one of my father's gestures – touching one of the nostrils with my right thumb, while the left hand supported my right elbow. My father used to do that a lot while sitting down on the limestone in front of the house. That posture and the expression on his face are still vivid to me. I wonder what was going through his mind. Another part of me can imagine what he was thinking of, especially when he saw me. His eyes say it all, and that same part of me feels angry. I've just muttered to myself, 'You rotten bastard.' I imagined us looking each other in the eye.

9:00 p.m.

I'm emotionally and mentally frozen. There is lot of pressure on my forehead. Cannot write. I'll give an account of what happened this afternoon as soon as I feel better. I'm going to lie down now.

Wednesday, 2 December 1987
11:41 a.m.

Still feeling stiff. The back tension I had yesterday, and this morning has now eased. I still have the *qtiegħ ta' laħam* (aching muscles) on my thighs, which I had yesterday too. Speaking of yesterday, while I was lying in bed at about 6:00 p.m., I had a regression. I would say it was to the stage before the sensory stage, because I didn't have the urge to fiddle with the corner of the sheet. However, I noticed that I wanted my left cheek to cuddle against the sheet. During that regression I turned to my left side with my knees bent. I didn't move for about half an hour, while I experienced this *intense fear inside me as if someone else were in there, fully alive.* I kept mumbling, 'This is all repressed fear; it needs to come out.' At one point I was even stammering. Besides fear, the baby felt cold during that regression. I felt there were two bodies in one. One was warm because I was fully clothed, and I even had the electric blanket on. I touched my hands and put my feet together to see if they were cold, but they were warm. The other body, however, was cold all over. It was pretty obvious that it was a regression.

During that regression, I felt not only tension in the back but also stiffness all over the body. The stiffness in the upper parts of both arms struck me – even the pain (*qtiegħ ta' laħam*) on the upper part of the legs was sharp.

I'm trying to remember the thought that went through my mind. I'm not exactly sure, but yesterday I was thinking of my driving instructor, who kept spitting on his hands and then rubbing them together. It really put me off. It also reminded me of my father, who used to do that while he was digging in the fields.

Saliva does trigger something. After my father's death, when I received letters from my mother, I used to get this yucky feeling while opening them. I remember clearly when I received the first letter after his death, thinking my mother had probably kissed his body and now had licked the envelope. I had a dream in which I clearly felt this kiss on my lips. Could that baby boy have been my father? I don't even want to think of it. I'm imagining him with his hands on his hips, looking at me while I'm writing. How am I going to come to terms with it? Last night I was hoping that my paternal grandmother would talk to me in my dreams.

I just remembered that during yesterday's regression, my right hand didn't feel stretched and wrinkly. This is another psychosomatic symptom I've experienced over these last two years or so. It has been only recently that I realised it is a psychosomatic symptom that has to do with incest. I wasn't sure whether or not to put 'probably' there. I didn't feel the conflict, but apparently, unconsciously there was one, and therefore I ended up with doubt.

Doubts arise from conflicts, whether we are conscious of them or not. This conflict is between different personalities.

Tuesday, 3 December 1987
10:52 a.m.

Just before I opened the diary to start writing, I reflected upon the picture on the front cover. Yesterday Ms Jacob asked if she could have a look at it herself. I told her there is a reason why I chose an exercise book with that particular picture – pink ballet shoes and a white pearl necklace. The little girl fell in love with it, and I bought it in memory of her. While I was looking at it before, the real me felt that this particular picture has some significant meaning for her too – a ballerina means coordination between mind, body and soul, which results from authentic inner peace – peace at heart.

I'm feeling down again. Before, I had to come and write because there was something I really wanted to write. While I was doing the washing, I was thinking of what my mother told me in the letter. I asked myself, 'Is my mother trying to make up for some guilt by making it her responsibility to advise me about incest?' This is the translated version of what she told me in the letter:

> Vitor, you told me that Michelle went to sleep over at Stella's place. Don't trust her anywhere, because about a fortnight ago I was listening to the radio. They were talking about problems. This sixteen-year-old girl got pregnant by her grandfather. These things also happen between siblings. Don't be offended by what I'm telling you, because I love you and whenever I need to, I speak up.

When I went into the kitchen, I read this part of the letter again, and this time it meant more to me than it had initially. For a moment I even felt close to my mother. I was thinking of elaborating on incest in my next letter to my mother. Could this letter be the first step towards resolving the traumas/conflicts between my mother and I and the first step towards confirmation of the truth?

In the kitchen I was also thinking of in-nanna Karmena (my paternal grandmother) and my father – they both have unfinished business before they will be able to enter the kingdom of heaven. This morning as I was walking from the washhouse towards the bathroom, *I smelt burning candles*, which reminded me of the burning candles in the chapel of the village cemetery back home. There were *no* lit candles at all, but I just realised that some months ago, when the electricity was out, I used a candle in the bathroom. When I lit the match to light the gas stove, I experienced the same smell. Smells seem to have a lot to do with the unconscious mind. Even our emotions play an important part in the sensitivity of smells. This morning, for example, when I picked some mint from the garden, I not only enjoyed its smell, but somehow the smell was more poignant. What made the difference for it to smell so strongly? It must have been my emotional state.

Friday, 4 December 1987
10:00 p.m.

Today's session seemed to be the longest one I've had so far with Ms Jacob. There were many moments when I went quiet – it was like the old me again during therapy with Dr. Garcia. I was experiencing silent anger. After I came home, I went to my room thinking about the emotional state I was in. I had complete stillness inside me – no conflicts, no fear, no rage. I also realised that during that state of regression, I had no frustrations regarding expressing myself. And I had no urge to fiddle with anything. This must have been a regression to a time before the sensory stage.

I have just been reading through Stage 1 of incest, because I wasn't sure if today's experience was the same as Stage 2. The difference between these stages is that during Stage 1, there was no silent anger; whereas during today's stage, it was pretty obvious that I was experiencing silent anger, and I also had that light tingling feeling and slight tension in my head – a sign of mental blocking. This silent anger came out strongly during therapy when I made it clear that I don't want to be 'possessed' by my father through his inner voices. I was referring to yesterday when I told Michelle's friend, Elizabeth, to bring her seven-month-old sister over to my place. *The inner voice said that I only wanted her for sexual abuse*!

I am going to call today's regression Stage 2 of incest.

P.S. During Stage 2, my right hand didn't feel stretched and wrinkly. There was no tension in the back either. After I figured out this stage, I felt drowsy and had to lie down in bed – definitely a sign of regression.

My emotional state when I was writing is clearly depicted in my handwriting – there was lot of anger inside me because Michelle didn't take no for an answer. She wanted to continue with her sewing – she *interrupted* me just after I had started writing. That of course infuriated me – that is, it infuriated the little girl whose father wouldn't take no for an answer – the baby who was interrupted in her sleep.

Saturday, 5 December 1987
1:15 p.m.

I have just checked my father's date of birth – it's 4 December 1909. I thought it was 5 December. Somehow, I felt doubtful about it – that's why I checked it. Why did I feel doubtful, and who was responsible for triggering that doubt? Yesterday morning I did think it was his birthday, but that's because I thought yesterday was the 5th. So, part of me was right. I don't know why I'm making such a fuss over this, but there is some truth in it. I did look at my father's birth certificate some weeks ago. I just realised why I came to the conclusion that his birthday is on the 5th. While I was thinking aloud in the kitchen, instead of saying 5 December, a couple of times I said 5 October, which is Louie's birthday!

1:57 p.m.

I have just written a letter to my mother on a rough piece of paper. I feel I have worded it properly – so properly that my father feels threatened. After reading it, I started feeling the burning pain on my right wrist. I haven't felt that pain for such a long time. My father feels threatened. I will be sending that letter, and with that letter will be my father's photo. My mother is clever enough to realise what I'm getting at and read between the lines.

2:14 p.m.

Going over the letter again. In the letter, it's the little girl who is talking[2], and this is what she has to say (translated):

> Dear Mother
>
> . . . In the letter you told me not to trust Michelle anywhere. I was not offended because you pointed that out to me – not at all. On the contrary, I really like it when you advise me because as you said, it means that you love us. Mum, you have every reason to advise me not to trust Michelle anywhere because there is lot of evil, and there is sexual abuse by parents, especially to girls, even though they are so little and sometimes even babies. These things have happened for a long time, but no one took any notice. Now, even priests and psychiatrists advise mothers to be mindful of the evil acts of their husbands and believe their children if they tell them something. Because what the children say is true, and when these things happen, they shouldn't blame the children, because they are innocent – the responsibility is that of the fathers. In Australia they have found that one in every four girls is a victim of this evil.

Saturday, 6 December 1987
6:00 p.m.

Nirra l-Madonna tirkbek Alla (May Our Lady fuck you, God), I am saying repeatedly. The colour white is coming to mind – white horse – in relation to the bishop of Gozo.

The little girl is so angry that she cannot write! It's not the little girl who enjoyed incest. Far from it. It's the little innocent girl who is so furious. She has just identified

[2]At that point I went to the toilet. I 'forgot' about my period, and when the little girl saw the blood on the pad she was frightened! (I have a staring and vaguely blurring look at the moment . . . a sign of regression.) That was the third day of menstruating!

Michelle with so many people – Madonna, *Alla* (God), male, female, clergy, bishop. No wonder she has just been so rebellious – she also bit her right hand. This anger will only go away when I discover the reasons behind all this. While I'm writing, I'm mumbling sometimes, even stuttering what I'm writing. I'm taking shallow breaths. Earlier, Michelle said, 'You're not in labour, Mum.' That is, 'Stop breathing like that.'

Fits of anger, not rage. The little girl is so little that she stammers, she doesn't yell, she doesn't bang anything – she is also missing her pacifier – she's got something missing from her mouth, not a craving. This is a regression. I'm thinking of Rabat (the capital city of Gozo) again. I remember when my mother took us to the dressmaker to make me this beautiful red dress with a bolero. I was so little.

That's the earliest experience in Rabat that I remember. The little girl believes (conflict) that she was taken to the bishop, maybe not for 'inquisition' but for a special blessing or absolution. My mother might have been so concerned about my spirituality that she took me to the bishop. She probably asked Dun Baskal for advice. That's probably why the little girl is so angry at him.

Yes, Dun Baskal came back to me today. After I came from the 11:00 a.m. mass, I identified both Peter and Drago with Baskal – they both have his stature. The little girl was angry. I was wearing this Italian pink lipstick, and while I was eating, some of it came off on my finger. That colour reminded me of cardinals, that is, the hierarchy within the church. After helping clean the kitchen a bit, I went to lie down – the little girl was so exhausted from anger!

As I was lying down, my thoughts led me to the bishop of Gozo – in those days it was Ġuseppe Pace. Then I remembered Bishop Cauchi, who succeeded him, and the white horse he was riding as he entered the citadel for the ceremony when he was officially appointed as bishop. Then I realised I have been identifying with Joseph Cauchi, who comes from Għarb too, like the bishop. It seems the little girl was frightened of the bishop. As I was lying down, however, there was no fear. Could the little girl have been frightened of the bishop before she met him? I don't know where I'm getting all these ideas from. I've just noticed that my right hand is not so stretchy. But it seems that someone pulled the little girl by her right wrist. I've just remembered an incident when I was in Grade 1 in Miss Vena's class. While the whole class was lined up for confession at the school, I accidentally urinated in front of the priest, who was sitting down on a chair while hearing confessions.

I just remembered many dreams in which I ended up shopping at Rabat, especially around the bishop's palace . . . pause . . . During the pause, I remembered that dream in which I (my mother) have just come from church (I had a veil on), and I was embarrassed. Michelle was with Dr. Garcia, and she was wearing that hat in the photo at the studio with Mark. In that photo Michelle was about three years old. Was that when my mother discovered incest and took me to Dun Baskal and the bishop? What about the nuns? At that age I was not going to preschool. On second thought, I suppose I was. I remember my mother saying that I started preschool at about three years of age.

Monday, 7 December 1987
3:00 p.m.

Just finished writing the Christmas cards. I really rushed writing them. I wasn't in the mood at all. Felt panicky, especially when it came to write the ones back home. My head was buzzing – I had to draft my letter to Pawla on rough work paper. I hesitated to tell her that I was returning to study. There was fear inside me – fear I will never make it. There was also fear of high expectations. When I came to write Maria's letter, I felt panicky because I had to tell her a white lie for why we are not going to Sydney this year. I told her that Louie can't take the holidays this Christmas. Fear of getting caught lying – I wished I could have told her the truth. At the moment of writing, the real me is not present. I feel uneasy because the kids will soon be back from school. But I decided to write something in the diary. Tonight, we're having a break-up party at the Western Institute. I baked pizzas this morning.

Speaking of this morning, I had a session at 8:40 a.m. Walking at that hour of the morning certainly brought back memories, especially the paddocks near the hospital.

5:46 p.m.

Just numbered the pages of the diary. Number forty triggered something – the number of the house back home.

I didn't know what to write. My last day at the Western Institute for this year. Will I ever go back again as a student? When I came home, I was quite upset and even cried. I was in a frozen emotional state at one point. I had (and still do) a certain numbness at the back of my head. As I was lying down, my left leg felt numb too. Michelle was sitting on the bedside, and twice I felt panicky when I couldn't move my left leg. Actually, I feel panicky about it now too. Could I have experienced numbness when I was a baby as a result of incest? Even my left arm is bothering me. Earlier I felt itchy in between the toes of my left foot. The left leg is bothering me a lot. In spite of this numbness, I feel optimistic. I'm looking forward to sleep. I might have a dream that could shed some light.

10:18 p.m.

Just had a fit of rage in relation to my numbness (left leg and arm and top of my head). I kept biting my right hand in anger, saying *Nirrah Alla iwebbsek* (May God stiffen you). I've been saying this word '*iwebbsek'* (stiffen you) often since yesterday. *I seem to have been angry at myself!*

Tuesday, 8 December 1987
7:19 a.m.

I'm cold and shivery! These last fifteen minutes or so, I've been thinking of something that I wasn't going to record in my diary. *Was my father responsible for selling me for prostitution?* I'm thinking of Fortun ta' Baxu, an old man who lived in the neighbourhood. I do vaguely remember being over at his place. I remember an incident that happened in Adelaide about two years ago – a dwarf man was being thrown around for entertainment. That incident struck me so much that every now and then it comes back to me. There was an expression I used to say to myself: *Jiena qaħba ta' l-Ibirba* (I am a slut from Iibirba – North Africa).

Is this another chapter of my childhood? There is a part of me that seems to be happy about it! Another part of me has just muttered, 'Oh no. *Dan mhux veru'* (this is not true). Where am I getting these ideas from?

These last couple of days, I've been hearing *in-nanna Merina* (my paternal grandmother) saying '*U Mikel'* while my father was passionately involved in incest with me. *Tgħid missieri wasal biex għamel hekk?* Is it possible that my father sold me for prostitution? Did such things happen in those days?

I don't know how I'm going to tell Louie about this. I'm scared of his reaction – that he won't love me anymore. Is this going to put my self-esteem down?

I'm stunned at the moment – my emotions are at a standstill, and the upper part of my head is numb.

10:00 p.m.

I just had a fit of rage at my father. I suppose it was the little girl who was angry – the little girl who witnessed her father fucking that old man, Fortun ta' Baxu. I kept biting my lips and my finger while saying, 'Have fun. Fuck each other in hell. Have fun, you rotten bastards' and looking at my father's photo. I didn't feel like calling him my father at all. How could he be my father if he went to that extreme? This morning she was angry at him because he sold her for prostitution. The reason I said 'sold' is because money was involved.

There is a little innocent girl inside me – she is frightened and definitely has lot of anger inside her. She is angry at her father, who had sex with another man in front of her, probably getting her involved too. This morning she was angry at him because he sold her for sexual activities.

Mark didn't end up going to school this morning. He came back home because he was concerned about me. He stayed outside by the bedroom window. I didn't notice him straightaway. But after hearing some light tapping on the window, I turned around and saw him. I went to the window, and as I drew the terylene curtain he told me, 'Mum there is something I want to tell you.' When he came in, he told me that while he was peeping through the holes of the embroidery of the curtain, he saw a man between the dressing table and my bed. I was on that side of the bed. He said he saw the side of his face. He had bushy eyebrows and whiskers. His nose struck him most – he said it was sort of twisted. Mark seemed quite sure of what he saw.

I told my psychologist about it, and she asked me if that description reminded me of someone. I told her that if it was my father, Mark would have recognised him. I told her the whiskers reminded me of Freud. But then in the evening I remembered il-Barbuto (the bearded man) from the Italian book at school. Could I have been identifying the Barbuto with Fortun? The Barbuto used to come to my mind often.

I just remembered that before Mark went to school, I had a fit of rage in my bedroom and yelled, 'I will not leave a stone unturned. I want to find out who hurt me.' I was thinking of Fortun and his house. When I looked in the mirror, I could see that I was pale. That is probably why Mark was concerned about me.

There is another girl inside me – she enjoyed prostitution, and she is in conflict with the real me, who is angry. This morning after Michelle dropped the sugar, I sensed an underlying smile as a sign that she was pleased to upset me. That underlying smile infuriated me. It must have reminded the real me of the little girl who is smiling 'undercover'.

This little girl is the one in the photo with my maternal grandmother Vitorja and my brother Tony. In that photo she is about seven years old. This may explain why when I imagine that girl, she is always without underpants, and sometimes she is putting her dress up (exposing herself) and is happy doing it. I do not have any other photos from when I was younger.

This also explains why when I discovered the little girl for the first time, I always imagined her younger than the one in the photo. In the memory I have of walking down the street behind my father, coming from Fortun's house, I was much younger.

Wednesday, 9 December 1987
9:42 a.m.

I just handled the original photo of my father and the letter I wrote to my mum. This seems to be an important moment in my life, so important that I had to drop everything and write about it. I felt sad when I handled the photo. What a contradiction to what I have been telling my father these last two days: 'Go back where you belong.' I even spat at him this morning. And now that I'm sending the photo back, there is sadness. I suppose the real me does feel sad about what happened. The little girl, however, wants to see him in hell. She must have been hurt a lot. And for the little girl that's not so innocent, she *is* innocent too – it's not her fault that she ended up the way she did. This prostitution was brought on her – she was led into it. She is innocent too. She didn't know whom to turn to.

I'm now thinking of Mark. This emotional fixation is affecting my relationship with him. Part of me is scared to let him go emotionally; another part of me does not trust Vince, the boy next door. These last few days they have become close. Part of me trusts Mark so much and knows he is sensible, and if Vince gets into trouble, he knows what to do. And later on, if Vince is not his type, then Mark would look for someone else. Please help me, God, to help these two boys grow – the real me likes Vince and wants to help him if she can. Showing them trust is important. Yesterday I felt momentarily close to Samantha too. I want to record these moments because they are *special moments* for me.

Thursday, 10 December 1987
2:46 p.m.

I'm afraid I haven't got much time to write because I'm cooking, and Michelle will soon be back from school. I had the urge to come and write. There is fear inside me. After lunch I had to lie down – I couldn't even be bothered to have a cup of tea. The baby wanted to have a nap. It must have been the baby, because babies want to sleep. I'm not sure which part of babyhood I regressed to. I didn't have the urge to fiddle. My mouth was moist with saliva, and I enjoyed the sweet taste. Actually, I still have that taste and don't want to lose it. Even yesterday I had it! I just thought of Ms Jacob. With a smile on my face, I said to myself, 'I'll tell her tomorrow.' Yes, I am excited about it – I should be, I suppose. However, there is a lot of fear inside me. The baby must have already experienced fear.

I've noticed that in spite of my negative emotions, I haven't been having any mental conflicts – the voices are not there. *There are moments when I do have emotional conflicts but not mental conflicts. This is an area I want to explore.* By emotional conflicts I mean fear, anger and loss. What happened to the voices? It seems that since I have discovered who is behind them, I haven't been hearing them.

Emotionally, however, there has been a lot going on these last couple of days. Part of me is angry, sometimes at the baby and sometimes at the 'lost girl'. Yesterday the real self felt sorry for the latter – she wouldn't call her a prostitute; instead, she called her the lost girl. She decided to look after her, and she will be taking her for a holiday to Queensland, together with the other parts of myself, for the New Year.

7:00 p.m.

The little girl has just been feeling angry again at her father for involving her in prostitution and making his own daughter a laughingstock. There are times when I feel like telling my sister about my father's activities. The little girl is so sure about them that she is not scared of her father. She believes that if it wasn't true, he would protest by appearing to her. I would like to ask my mother how close he was to Fortun ta' Baxu. No wonder my father was always scratching his bloody bum. The little girl just muttered *Daħħlu f'sormok* (go and have anal sex – a very common colloquial expression).

There is another little girl, however, who got excited by this homosexuality. That explains why when I was in the car at Queenscliffe some weeks ago I got excited, even sexually aroused, when I saw these two slim divers kissing. I thought they were both male, and I felt disappointed when I saw that one of them was female.

This morning the little girl turned her anger at Louie in her imagination. In her anger she involved him in homosexuality.

I wish I could ask my mother how close my father was with this man. I'm imagining my niece at Fortun's place when she was about four years old, laughing at what she is seeing. Was Fortun the only man involved? Part of me believes he was not the only one. There is another man that comes to my mind – Dun Angelo – he is also a priest. God, please forgive me if I'm jumping to the wrong conclusions.

In that nightmare in which my hands were tied up, I was running away from the Pergla fields, where both my father and Dun Ang had fields. The latter also had a barn. In that nightmare [2 Aug] I was running away from more than one slave . . . pause . . .

I just went through the nightmare again. I'm wondering what the lethal weapon actually was. Could it have been a penis?

Chapter 13

Waiting for Breakthrough

Saturday, 12 December 1987
4:23 p.m.

Yesterday I didn't write anything in the diary, but I still want to record what happened.

For yesterday's session, I didn't take the diary with me for two reasons: first of all, I had to go to Footscray, and second, I wanted to observe my reaction. I did feel strange without it during therapy. At one stage I went quiet – there was stillness inside me. Then I thought of the photo – Michelle's photo up to the age of four. I carried it deliberately in the bag. That struck me. Part of me was desperate to find something constructive. I don't blame myself for doing that, because mentally nothing was happening due to the stillness inside me.

I have just been interrupted by Louie, who threatened to burn my diary as a joke, and I told him that if he did, it would destroy me.

This diary means a lot to me because it's proof of what happened to me – not only these last few months but also as a child. Once I get better, these experiences will be like a nightmare to me.

5:17 p.m.

I just had to prepare tea. Charles and Alex were here too. As I was cooking, there was a Maltese Christmas carol on 3EA.

I was moved when I heard it – all I want this Christmas is to feel emotionally close to my immediate family. That's what I told Louie this afternoon. Yesterday I told Erica that too. This is the saddest part of this ordeal – not being able to feel that emotional connection with my own kids and my husband. I wish I could express myself better.

At the moment there is that stillness inside and a bit of pressure in my head too. I've still got that beautiful taste in my mouth – it feels so good that I don't even have to eat anything to kill the bad taste I usually have. The real me just realised what I wrote in the last sentence. I had to do so many things in my life – even eating. *It seems that the bad taste had control over me.*

Was my father indirectly controlling my life? I said 'my father' deliberately, because this fits in with what I was thinking this morning regarding the part of me that is frightened of psychology. Some time ago in my diary, I said that I am 'possessed' by my father because of his being behind some of the inner voices. If I am possessed by my father, then it's my father who is frightened of psychology (I'm not sure if he hates it too). If he hates it, it's because it was through psychology that these scandals (incest and other sexual abuse) were revealed.

This is an area I need to look at – I'm thinking of schizophrenia. At the moment, I cannot concentrate because I have to get tea ready, and Michelle and Louie are washing the car.

Yesterday I told my psychologist that part of me is frightened of psychology, and part of me[3] is happy getting a degree without majoring in psychology.

[3] At that point I said loudly and firmly, 'I don't want to get a degree unless I major in psychology.'

I noticed that during yesterday's session my self-esteem lifted up a bit. I spoke of my real self as being an analyst – sometimes even too much of an analyst. And I told her about my observations in church last Sunday when my eyes fell on Pauline's brother, who is very religious. I was mostly impressed by his fidgeting after Consecration and before Communion, when the priest handled the Host and the people stood up. I also told her that Michelle will be my first patient and how the real me guides Louie in his relationship with the kids. The real me is capable of so many things!

Last Wednesday I bought a special card for my mother – it's a musical card with candles that flicker with the music. I didn't care about spending $7.00 on that card. I felt she deserves it. And I sincerely hope it will make her happy. I can see that I am trying to reach out to her emotionally. Those moments I feel close to my mother are precious to me, even though they don't last long.

Sunday, 13 December 1987
11:10 a.m.

Sunday morning – what a glorious day! Every time I go near the waterfall, my eyes fall on this white water lily, standing up majestically like a champagne glass. It looks so perfect, not marred by even the smallest dot. I wish I could explain myself better. As I was looking at it, I wished I was a poet or a painter to capture that beautiful scene – it is certainly quite a scene! The water lily, so beautifully erect with the leaves around it. Even the combination of the shade and the sunlight on the leaves impressed me so much! How I wish to capture that impression, at least in my writing – but I'm afraid I can't – maybe one day I will. I'm thinking of the writing I did during that state of elation – how it came out *so fluently*. I certainly found pleasure in writing, especially creative writing. I really enjoyed it because I felt free to write about anything I wanted. That made a big difference to me. When I came to write the essay on 'Images of Women', I felt panicky because I felt restricted. The real me, however, wanted to do it. She handled it pretty well. Restriction must certainly have been a frightening experience for me. It's even affecting me in everyday life.

I'm now thinking of an incident that I analysed and haven't recorded in the diary. Michelle told me that in the afternoon she is going to take the kitchen curtain off to wash it. I felt panicky. I thought of the dust and dirt that will be revealed after taking the curtain off – I couldn't bear the thought of it! Dust and dirt – I wanted to leave them concealed because I know they are there. This triggered the panic button. Apparently, there are lots of things (experiences, I suppose) in my life that I want to leave concealed. Which part of me is behind this blockage? Doesn't this coincide with what I wrote yesterday about fear of psychology? The real self is after the truth, and she won't be satisfied until it all comes out. She wants nothing but the truth.

I told Louie that I'm not afraid of my father haunting me – *he* is afraid of me. At the moment, I do feel frightened of the other man involved. I want to turn each and every tombstone and look for the people who might have hurt me. I feel that blocking in my head. The little girl was so sure that she was hurt by at least one other man (Fortun ta' Baxu). There are no feelings at the moment, and I feel that blocking in my head. I'm still experiencing that beautiful taste.

12:09 p.m.

Mark has just cut his finger a bit. I was apprehensive about it – the little girl seems to be frightened of blood. I said 'the little girl' deliberately because just before Mark came in, the little girl felt panicky because there is a lot of housework to be done, and she finds it hard to cope – a sign of regression. When I was handling one of Michelle's statuettes, one of them reminded me of the pasture back home – it's a lady with a scarf.

5:35 p.m.

As I was dishing out dinner at 12:30, panic struck. I felt I was not going to please Louie with what I cooked (meatloaf and veggies) – in other words, the little girl was afraid she won't please her father.

Monday, 14 December 1987
9:53 a.m.

I have just been looking for some information about the sensory stage in the *Encyclopaedia Britannica*. In Vol. 9, I was reading about childhood development when panic struck. I reflected on it to see what triggered it – first of all, the different stages were too much for me because I needed to know the differences between one stage and another; and second, I couldn't compare and contrast Freud, Erikson and Piaget.

After I became aware of my problem, I continued to read on about the preoperational stage, the period from ages two to seven. I was greatly impressed by the phrase 'but can deal with one problem at a time'. That struck me because it not only explained but also confirmed my above problem. That's why during this emotional state I cannot compare and contrast – a confirmation of an emotional and intellectual regression/fixation.

No wonder there is panic inside me, because the little girl cannot handle it. I just said to myself, 'Psychology is such a beautiful thing.' However, there is fear inside me. There is also heavy pressure on the top of my head. I'm afraid the bad taste is back. Psychology is an interesting subject indeed – it's fascinating – I'm so desperate to get hold of psychology without any fear. After writing 'get hold', the real me realised why I said it – it's because I'm yearning to get hold of it so much that I don't want to let it go – I want to hang on to it.

The little girl is talking metaphorically – *no,* she is talking literally because she is little, and she means it that way. She can only speak in concrete terms. It becomes metaphorical to the adults. The little girl inside me is doing a great job. Keep it up, sweetie (I have tears in my eyes). The real self will be proud of her – apparently, she is not there at the moment. But the fact that I noticed her is there.

The five-year-old (maybe even younger) girl is interested in psychology! The little girl has just experienced a mild conflict. My head is buzzing so much, and I keep repeating my thinking in a low, gasping voice – gasping because of the fear inside me. Fear – yes, there is lot of fear inside me.[4] This morning the little girl wanted to know about childhood amnesia – she wanted to know about the sensory motor stage – she even looked up the word 'narcissism' (self-love). As she was looking that up, she was thinking about her study regarding sexuality in childhood. She also wanted to know what 'phallic' means.

[4]As I was writing all this, the real me realised that the little girl managed to overcome previous conflict regarding her interest in psychology. I suppose if she wasn't interested, she wouldn't have looked up those words. As she was handling the dictionary, she was on the lookout for the pictures of snakes – she was and still is very frightened of them. A few minutes ago, when I went into the garden to pick some parsley, there was that fear of snakes, especially the snake our neighbour killed recently. 'What if that snake went on the parsley?' I thought in a yucky way.

11:22 a.m.

While I was preparing the *bragjoli* (stuffed rolled meat), they reminded me of a penis. I also started experiencing abdominal pain, which to the little girl felt as if there were something inside her. This reminded me of the same pain I experienced Sunday at about 2:00 a.m. I've still got that pain, which is sharp at the moment – it feels like period pain in the centre of the abdomen, just above the pubic hair.

12:14 p.m.

As I was getting ready to go for my session, I felt that today is another special day in my life. It seems I am now identifying with Anna Freud (Sigmund Freud's daughter), even though I don't know much about her.

4:00 p.m.

This pressure in my head – does it mean I'm getting close to a breakthrough in my childhood amnesia? As soon as I came up with this question, I felt it was an important one, so I wanted to record it in the diary. This morning I told Ms Jacob that the feeling in my head is a sign of blocking something – it feels heavy, like local anaesthetic – like the upper lip and sometimes even the nose feels heavy when dental anaesthetic is wearing off. The heavy feeling is a sign that the numbness is going away. This is what prompted me to ask the above question.

Short pause.

As I looked at Victoria in the photo, I mentally saw a lot of black snakes moving. I'm now thinking of what the brain looks like. I'm also thinking of black snakes in relation to the brain. I need to get that frozen part of the brain activated again. In these last few minutes, I have that feeling in my throat (air vent) again. The pressure is still in my head. And emotionally I am just breathing. *Is the unborn baby trying to tell me something*? Since I noticed that feeling in the throat, my stomach has stopped rumbling – pause – I've just got that bad taste, and my right hand doesn't feel stretchy at all.

I'm now thinking of that soft part on the skull that babies have – pause – Is this pressure a psychosomatic symptom? Is the baby that still has that soft part of the skull trying to tell me something? These last few minutes my stomach has been rumbling again.

7:39 p.m.

I've been thinking out loud in my room for the last thirty-five minutes. I came up with another question: *Has the little girl witnessed a crime*? She seems to be frightened of blood. Some nights ago, I had a dream in which there were pillars in front of the shop *tad-dejdu*, stained with blood. There were fire engines too. In relation to fire engines, I think of Fortun tal-Merguli who started a fire when he was a boy.

I'm getting period pain again, and in relation to that I thought of blood. As I was writing this sentence I thought of my father, and a thought went through my mind:[5] If Fortun ta' Baxu was strangled, would anybody inquire about it? Maybe my father (I was going to write he) didn't choke him completely. When I started writing, I noticed the feeling in my air vent came back. Was my father responsible for Fortun's death? *Has the little girl witnessed a crime*? Could the man Mark saw in my room want me to reveal this crime? Does he also have some unfinished business with my father? I am stunned – pause – I am now thinking of the dream in

[5]I also argued with myself that if blood was involved, other people would have noticed it. That's when I thought of strangling. How many times have I thought of choking Michelle? Or wished to see her hanged in the shed? This is crazy!

which there were disturbed spirits in the room above Fortun's house.

Tuesday, 15 December 1987
5:15 p.m.

There is so much repressed fear inside me, God! I have said this so many times today. What a day it has been! My pubic hair this morning (after intercourse) reminded me of this old man (*missier Sika* – Sika's father) and his bushy black eyebrows. Then my thoughts were centred around the neighbourhood that is St Anthony's Street in front of *tal-Bajda*. I thought of those two middle-aged men being involved in child prostitution. Then I had an insight/conclusion that I had witnessed a crime. As I was near the kitchen sink, thinking about what I'm going to tell Louie regarding the possibility of my having witnessed someone being bashed, I had a flashing picture of a man holding the handle of the *imgħażqa* (a tool used for digging the fields). It disappeared before I recognised him. I think fear struck. Since that moment I've felt I am another Jessica Blake (an investigator on TV). Even when Louie and I were shopping in Footscray, I kept thinking about the possibility of my having witnessed a crime. Could this be another chapter of my life? There is no doubt about how much repressed fear there is inside me. I keep thinking of this inscription in limestone on the outskirts of the village, in memory of a man who died in the fields.

At about 2:00 p.m. there was so much fear inside me that I couldn't continue folding the clothes. I went to lie down on the couch. After a while Louie came over to have me thread the needle for him (he was rolling cotton thread around the fishing rod), and after he got up a certain smell came out of the vinyl – an anal smell, which certainly triggered something (Louie didn't fart at all). Lying down I kept saying, 'No. No' in a gasping voice, as if I was forced to do something against my will. As I was in that state, my thoughts were centred in that neighbourhood near *tal-Bajda*. Louie came near me because he realised there was fear inside me, but I ended up going to my room. As I was walking in my room, I started feeling cold and shivery (it was about 30 degrees Celsius!), and my teeth were chattering with fear. I lay down in bed. At 2:30 there was lot of fear inside me, both emotionally and in the head – all that pressure disappeared – it was like complete calm after a storm. However, it only lasted for few minutes. Then I dozed off.

This morning I wasn't an analyst at all. I was a criminal detective.

I have abdominal pain. Which part of me has this psychosomatic symptom? There is no fear at the moment, and there is a light pressure on the head. Could this be the little girl who experienced penetration? I'm seeing myself as a little girl trailing behind my father, who has his hands crossed behind his back in our street near *ix-xagħri ta' Pupull*. I remember that well – following my father down the street after visiting Fortun's house.

I told Louie this afternoon that the fear the little girl experienced is during the day.

Wednesday, 16 December 1987
8:58 a.m.

I now feel I'm getting close to a breakthrough in my amnesia. Yesterday evening I spent some hours in the lounge waiting for a breakthrough. I told myself that this is the waiting period. I'm even preparing myself for it so I can face it. However, there are still some moments when I don't want to know what happened to me. I'm now seeing the little girl trailing behind her father, who took her for her 'rounds', just as Ġanni tal-Ġus used to make his rounds with the *muntun* (ram). I remember this man, who used to go around with the ram to mate the sheep at various houses, where sheep were kept in the barns.

As I was lying down about forty-five minutes ago, I got a glimpse of my brown sunglasses, and the tinted glass triggered something. It didn't dawn on me straightaway, but when I looked at it a second time, it reminded me of the globe of the kerosene lamp when it was dirty. It also reminded me of the lanterns at the cemetery.

At one point as I was lying down, I could smell shit, and that smell instigated fear. Nobody had used the toilet.

It seems that even smells are repressed in the unconscious mind. The smells I have been experiencing seem so real to me!

7:27 p.m.

I've been thinking on my bed for the last hour or so, and while I was repeating to myself what I told Ms Jacob this afternoon, 'There is a lot of work to be done' (that's what she told me when I had my first session with her), my eyes fell on Michelle's photo when she was about a year old, and I stared at that photo while I was thinking of work. It seems the one-year-old girl had a lot of work to do regarding incest. *No wonder she is so afraid of high expectations!*

During this afternoon's session, I also told Ms Jacob that I am now going through a stage of smelling. This afternoon I put my little finger in my belly button and held it close to my nose to smell it! I even ran my finger behind my ears and smelt it.

During the stage I'm now in, I'm moving away from my

bedroom – yesterday I was on the couch, and even this morning I spent a lot of time lying on my back on the couch. As I was lying down, I looked at the vent on the ceiling and thought, 'What if a snake comes out of the vent and falls on my face?' Yes, it seems the little girl experienced a 'snake' over her face.

7:42 p.m.

Since I woke up from my nap, I've been experiencing abdominal pain – abdominal pain in the afternoon! I'm thinking of prostitution. This morning I figured out why my father had an irrational fear of making ends meets – it's a fear involving money. It explains why I myself experience that fear, especially at the St Albans Market – European men, fruits and veggies! It also explains why at times the bad taste in my mouth tastes of money (copper). As kids we used to put money in our mouths. *Like Judas, my father betrayed the little girl for money.*

Thursday, 17 December 1987
7:00 p.m.

At 6:40 a.m., I discovered the pillar in the dream I had recently – *it's the same pillar my father is sitting next to in the photo*. If that pillar stained with blood represents my father, who actually ended up getting hurt? The fire engine represents or is associated with Fortun.

During the night, the little girl had a frightening experience. I didn't feel like going to bed because I didn't feel sleepy. I stayed up watching TV. I thought of my mother receiving the letter. I even looked at the telephone, expecting her to ring. I didn't have any fears – I was emotionally calm. At about 12:45 a.m. I became drowsy, so I came to bed. As I was walking in, I could smell the leather binding of the encyclopaedia (I hadn't smelt it since we first got it, one and a half years ago), and as I was walking further in towards the bedrooms and the toilet, I could smell shit everywhere (except in Michelle's room). I even went in Mark's room, and the strong smell was there too.

As I was in the bathroom, I became self-conscious about my facial hair, which looked very fair (except one hair under the chin). Fear struck, and as I was lying down in bed I was completely overcome with fear – there was a great deal of fear inside me. Mentally I was obsessed by the fear of my facial hair. Then I got angry. I started swearing, involving first Our Lady and then God. The fear of facial hair kept coming to me. It was pretty obvious that this fear involved my mother. I kept seeing myself battering my own head! *I felt suicidal.* The fear of facial hair was so strong that I couldn't bear the thought of being obsessed with it again – I experienced that fear for over eight years, twenty-four hours a day.

During the night as I was experiencing that strong fear, I said to myself that if I became obsessed with that fear, I would commit suicide. *The little girl's head must have been battered during the anal stage.*

Louie woke up because he realised that I was in fear. As he stretched out his arm, the deodorant smelt of shit to me, and even his breath as well.

I told Louie not to be frightened, because I'm reliving my childhood. I told him the little girl's head was battered. I said it twice, and he told me not to repeat what I say. That repetition must have frightened him. Then the little girl burst out crying. She sobbed as if she had been crying for a long time. This was at 1:35 a.m. Then I fell asleep, and when I woke up this morning, I was still in a mild state of fear. I noticed the fear flared up again when I was writing.

3:10 p.m.

I don't feel like writing, but part of me wants to record what happened. When I was at Jewels supermarket, I kept thinking of the pillar and my father. I did feel a bit panicky, but overall, I was calm, maybe too calm – I suppose I was in a state of a shock. Was the little girl who was battered the same one who wrote the letter to my mother? I wouldn't be surprised – after all, a few minutes before, I had been thinking of that letter and my mother.

After I came back from shopping, I wanted to be on my own in my room. As soon as I lay down, Mark and Charles had an argument. I said to myself, 'I'll let them sort it out. I have my own problems. I'm too fragile to interfere.' I turned into the little girl, who apparently had been sobbing wholeheartedly and *asking for help*. Could the little girl have tried to stop the argument or fight her father was involved in? It felt like two bodies in one. That was at two o'clock.

There have been no inner voices for quite some time. Does this mean I am in a state of regression, both emotionally and mentally?

Friday, 18 December 1987
12:15 p.m.

I'm sitting by myself in the lounge, looking at the Christmas tree.

I am now entering, or rather unfolding, another chapter of my life. *It seems the little girl went through a re-enactment of the Passion of Jesus Christ for masochistic purposes*. Like him, she was ridiculed, mocked, spat on, tied up, blindfolded . . . She was made to suffer for her 'sins'.

Apparently, her father got the little girl involved in more than he had bargained for. He must have felt sorry for his daughter – a scuffle followed, and blood was shed. Yesterday afternoon, I mentally saw my father's arms covered with blood.

I'm looking at the Christmas tree. The purple colour of the silver foil strip reminds me of Lent. Like Jesus, the little girl was stripped of her clothes. The purple thistle reminded me of the crown of thorns. Did the little girl's molesters use anything else as a substitute for thorns? Lately it feels as if there is something heavy on my head. A few days ago, it felt as if something tight had been put into the back of my head (I imagined a potty!).

I have just been looking at the star on top of the tree. I went through every colour and associated something with each: red – bloodshed; purple – penance; green – anger; gold – money; silver – hope (every cloud has a silver lining); blue – sky – immensity, stars, a blue sky means no clouds! No dreariness – there must be sunshine during the day and plenty of moonlight during the night. In other words, there is light, day and night. This fits in well with a dream I used to have years ago. In this dream, which takes place in North Sunshine near the church premises, there is *sunshine during the night*.

This is the colour chart of the star. I didn't do a good job in the drawing. But the star and the colours and their associations mean so much to me that I wanted to draw them. That star, which is holding a prominent position on the Christmas tree, encompasses so many things – past, present and future! The past and present, no matter how painful and shrouded (past) they have been, will always have a prominent position in my life. As for the future, this star *as a whole* means something to me, but the feeling is not there at the moment.

As I am unfolding this chapter of my life, I am going through another critical period – a painful and frightening one. Yesterday I kept saying to myself, 'I overcame the critical period regarding the insight about incest. Will I be able to pull through this one?' Pause – The prominent colour in the Christmas tree is purple. Even the pink of my nail polish seems purple to me. Emotionally there is stillness inside me, and the top of my head has that heavy feeling. There is mild abdominal and back pain. My right hand feels stretchy too.

6:00 p.m.

At 2:15 I came to lie down in my room. I dozed off till 5:00. I didn't have any fits of fear. As I have been lying awake in bed, I have even been questioning myself. Why did it take me so long to realise that the pillar in the dream was the same pillar in the photo? I was recollecting what I told Ms Jacob this morning regarding my initial associations with the pillar – Roman Empire, slavery, chains, Julius Caesar – when at 5:40 I realised why. Indirectly, I associated the Roman Empire with the Passion of Jesus Christ! – the procession on Good Friday in my village – Roman soldiers, high priests, Pilate[6] and many other characters from the Bible, pompously and accurately dressed up.

Yesterday afternoon, when the sobbing girl took a deep ~~breath through the nose, some~~thing triggered. It felt like

[6]As I was writing down the word Pilate, I thought of the man who used to dress up as Pilate -it was *ir-raġel ta' Roża ta' Plejlu* (Roża's husband). Then I realised why the scene in the dream took place *għand tad-Dejdu*. It was indirectly associated with *ta' Plejlu. Just as Pontius Pilate was indirectly responsible for Jesus' suffering, so also was my father.*

water through the nose! Apparently, the little girl's head was *imgħaddsa ġo l-ilma* (immersed in the water). As soon as I said that, I mentally saw a hand doing it, and I related the pressure on my head with it.

Since I woke up from my nap, I have been having abdominal pain, and the pressure in my head is still there. My nipples are sore too. Yesterday I experienced muscular pain in the chest. There is also slight pain in the chest.

Who was the ringmaster responsible for my afflictions?

Earlier in my diary I said the little girl was 'crucified'. That is because there were times, during fits of anger at Michelle, that I felt like telling her *bħal Kristu insallbek* (I will crucify you like Christ). This expression must have been familiar to the little girl.

Pause – These last couple of days, the little girl has been asking for God's help. It seems they have a lot of things in common. That's why the little girl inside turned so much against God – *indirectly, to the little girl, he was responsible for her afflictions.*

I have just been looking at an analysis on pages 124–125 [13 Dec]. No wonder part of me wants to conceal something – it must be too painful for her! Isn't that what my mum told me in the dream a while ago? Apparently, the breakthrough in my amnesia that I have been waiting for is not going to happen the way I expected.

Saturday, 19 December 1987
8:00 a.m.

I've just realised why in the dream I had recently, in which disturbed spirits shook the room above Fortun's house, I moved back when two people were carrying the crucifix –

because I didn't want it to touch me.

I had a good night's sleep, and when I woke up, I was relaxed. I did have a fear inside me as soon as I opened my eyes. I also noticed that after intercourse (I just made myself available for Louie), I started getting abdominal pain. I experienced tension in my back because of problems and pain with penetration.

Pause – I've just been through the diary to look for the above dream. I only talked about it *very briefly* on page 129 [14 Dec]! It seems these two dreams I've had recently (disturbed spirits and the pillar stained with blood) have a lot of *significant meaning*, but initially I didn't think they were important at all (the crucifix, for example).

9:37 a.m.

I have just been having cereal with linseeds in the lounge. I was thinking of poo in relation to snakes (something I was never aware of until yesterday, when Ms Jacob pointed it out to me during therapy), when all of a sudden, I crushed a piece of shell I had found with the linseeds. I had to rush to the rubbish bin because I felt like vomiting. I spat it out, but I still had the vomiting urge for a few seconds.

This incident confirms the conclusion I came up with about fifteen minutes earlier, while I was doing the laundry. It seems there are two fears associated with poo. One is the battering on my head during the anal stage, and the other one is *that real poo was stuffed in my mouth during the mockery experience*. The latter explains why as a child I remember being with a friend under the carob tree. We filled a soft drink bottle with wee and some poo to play a trick on Roża tad-Denfil (an old lady who lived nearby). I'm now thinking of a pathetic case about this girl Gene, and the faeces that was stuck to her for so long. I also thought of her case this morning while I was in bed. This also explains why there are times when the bad taste in my mouth reminds me of *ħara* (faeces).

Sunday, 20 December 1987
6:05 p.m.

At home by myself – I didn't feel like going to church because I needed some time on my own. Being by myself makes me feel so good because I feel free regarding my emotions – if I want to cry, I cry; if I want to get angry, I get angry; if I want to lie down, I lie down. My room, for example, is a mess at the moment – the bed is still undone (Michelle washed the sheets), and there is so much dust on the furniture. But that didn't worry me a bit. I just made myself comfortable on the bed and started to write.

Yesterday afternoon we went for a barbeque over Marthese and Charlie's place. They really made us welcome, and I appreciated their hospitality. However, at the moment I prefer to be on my own. I didn't feel my real self at all yesterday. Every now and then I thought about it – I felt so alienated from the one that spends her time by herself and the one that goes for therapy; in other words, the analyst wasn't there either.

I suppose one of the most important features of the real me is being an analyst. This is my new identity. Last Friday I told Ms Jacob that on Thursday the analyst (the real me) wasn't there at all – a sign of complete regression. Wednesday night, however, while I was lying in bed in a fit of fear, she was certainly there. I thought of the study I'm doing. I was even concerned about it when I imagined her beside me, and bending over, she caressed me and gently told me, 'Don't worry. Leave that for me.' I imagined Victoria, the one in the identity card. *That moment when the future Victoria reached out to me was, is and will be a very special moment of my life*. I did tell Ms Jacob about this incident.

The real self is going to be not only an analyst but also a loving and understanding person.

This afternoon I was thinking about the year 1987, what it means to me. This is an important year for me. I would say it is the second-best year:

1st	1952	The year I was born
2nd	1987	The year I found my real self
3rd	1972	The year I was married

That was a special year for me too. Louie and I were meant for each other. I told him that this morning. I also added, 'Don't you ever feel guilty about being responsible for my giving up my studies, because I don't regret it at all.' I couldn't have found my real self without him. This morning I also told him about my recent findings regarding the terror that the little girl went through. He certainly believed me. That meant a lot to me, not because I want sympathy but because he will be more understanding, especially when he sees me in a fit of rage, like he did this morning. I banged my hand so much on the bench in the kitchen – he thought I was beating the meat. He put his arms around me and took me to the couch, while assuring me that he will help me pull through. When I told him what happened to me, he said, 'I could never believe there were so many cruel people.' While I started writing this part, I began crying.

I have now decided not to ring up Mum, because if I do, I will not only be putting on an act, but I'm also afraid I may have a fit of anger on the phone – I don't want to upset her. I am determined, however, to ask her in my next letter if I had any frightening experiences when I was little and see what she says. I'm sure she will try to help me.

The 4th important year is 1973 Michelle was born

The 5th important year is 1975 Mark was born

Monday, 21 December 1987
9:30 a.m.

I have just experienced a mild fit of rage. Mark asked me to make him a toasted sandwich (he has a sore knee). That triggered something. Apparently, to the little girl, Mark abused my generosity. I was willing to make him a *bela te* (cup of tea), as he put it himself. I felt pleased to hear him say that. But when he asked me to make him a toasted sandwich, the feeling in my head went berserk. The sandwich maker was dirty – *it was too much* for the little girl to do – she also was irritable.

In the fit of rage, the little girl said (before I said little I said 'real' girl), '*Il-Madonna Alla rikiba*' (God fucked Our Lady). I initially thought of my father in relation to the word '*tirkeb*' (fuck). And then a thought went through my mind in relation to the mocking experience. Is this what the little girl heard? Did the *men* that mocked her make fun of religion? That explains why in my fits of rage I identify with Our Lady. How many times have I said *Nirra l-Madonna Alla jirkiba* (May Our Lady be fucked by God) as a curse?

Tuesday, 22 December 1987
8:46 a.m.

Today is another special day for me – I'm going for my driving licence test at 11:00 a.m. Although the feeling is not there at the moment of writing, for me it's already an achievement, considering the emotional state I've been in these last few months. It's certainly been a critical time in my life. As I already mentioned in my diary, there is a lot of fear inside me. These last few days, I've been obsessed with the fear of my facial hair. Even last night I had that fear and told Louie about it.

At about 1:00 a.m. the little girl had another fit of fear – she was sobbing wholeheartedly. The little girl's fits of fear are always followed by sobbing.

As I was up last night, I remembered a dream that took place back home, *ħdejn il-għajn f'salib it-toroq* (near the fountain at the crossroads) of Church Street and Bullara Street. I was approaching the fountain when I recognised this woman I knew from St Albans South Primary School. I can't remember her name. Her husband was Michael. When I met this woman, I was impressed with her beautiful hair, even in the dream. But as I got closer to her, I realised that she shaves the side of her face. In the dream I also noticed that I was wearing my runners, which somehow were too small for my feet, and I could see my toes making a hole in them. I suppose I was stretching them because they were tight, and at the same time I felt embarrassed because I had holes in my runners. We were waiting for the bus.

As I was reflecting upon this dream, I remembered this old man nicknamed *il-bomblu* who lived close to the place in the dream. He had a hooked nose *bħal ta'Roża tad-Denfil* (like Roża tad-Denfil) – her nickname – the same old woman that my friend and I wanted to play the trick on with the bottle of wee and poo. I realised this man is behind my terror. Then I remembered another part of the dream; this time it took place at St Bernadette's Church, in which there were Maltese and Polish people were singing songs about the Passion of Jesus Christ. I preferred to stay near the Polish people because they sang better songs.

There is mild fear inside me, as is clearly depicted in my writing.

After I went to sleep, I had more dreams that took place in that neighbourhood, namely around the intersection of Shaft Street and Bullara Street. In one of the dreams there was this boy (*ta' Ċikku* who made a pass at Louie, who almost ended up having sex with him – he even undid his zip and took the penis out. In another dream, this male horse went crazy when he saw the female horse. They ended up having sex, and after that the male horse went extremely tame.

When I think about this dream, I ask myself why I don't remember anything. At which point in my life did I start suffering amnesia? Did it happen gradually? If not, was the little girl aware of it, and was she frightened by it?

I need to ask my mother about the frightening experiences of my childhood. I remember my mother taking me *għand Frenċ ta' l-Għarb minnħabba l-ponot u il- ħżież* (to Frenċ – a person who had great spiritual powers). I used to get sores and patches of dry skin, and I remember him giving me this herbal mixture for frights. According to him I had lots of frights.

P.S. During the night, while the little girl was sobbing, she experienced that feeling again of water going through the nose (I was sobbing and not crying!).

9:35 a.m.

As I'm getting dressed, I'm emotionally moved. I have tears in my eyes – this is a special moment for me – it has taken me a lot of courage to get this far.

12:11 p.m.

I've just come from the driving test. I failed the test because of a single mistake. I am disappointed, but as I said to the officer, 'Better safe than sorry.' He replied, 'I'm glad you see it that way.' I do feel angry at my instructor because he never took me to that intersection where I failed. Otherwise, I still feel calm about it.

I feel disappointed to disappoint Louie. Right now, he would be expecting a phone call from me. What a stupid mistake it was!

Thursday, 24 December 1987
9:30 a.m.

Yesterday I had my last session with Ms Jacob. I was hoping to be in a better mood than I was. I wanted to be more optimistic (I know I didn't explain myself properly. I feel edgy and even angry at the moment). I was impressed by what she told me before the end of the session. She said it has been a great pleasure to work with me. I told her the feeling was mutual, and I also told her to feel free to ask Dr. Garcia about my progress. She was pleased with that – the expression on her face said it all.

We will be leaving for Queensland at about 1:00 p.m. It's going to be a sad moment for me. In fact, at the moment I'm crying. It's going to be sad because I have become attached to my house, which is more than a house, especially my bedroom. Will I feel the same way when I come back? Will I still be attached to it? I can't afford to lose that attachment. I suppose this is the little girl who suffered loss when she was little. But I still have Louie and the kids with me – I won't lose them. All I need is their understanding to allow me to go along with my emotions. I told Ms Jacob that too yesterday.

Allowing me to express my negative emotions means freedom. Freedom to me is very important. This is where my freedom starts. That's why I love Louie so much, because he is so understanding. A while ago I talked about my desire regarding my emotions on Christmas Eve. Will it happen? It's still a long time before midnight.

I will be carrying my diary with me on the bus – I don't want to put it in the luggage. I'll keep it next to me.

Chapter 14

Christmas Vacation

Saturday, 26 December 1987
(No time recorded)

This is the first time I've handled the diary since I packed it away last Thursday. When we were travelling, I did make sure that it was safe – this diary means so much to me! I couldn't wait to have some time to myself to do some writing.

Drago and his wife also came to Queensland, and we are all staying with their friends, Margaret and John. My sister Mary and the family will also be joining us.

Yesterday, Christmas Day, I didn't write anything. I must admit I was disappointed about the lack of Christmas Spirit on the bus. Most of the time I was crying – I preferred it that way though, rather than the usual stillness inside me. Every time Louie noticed I was crying, he would reach out to me – it meant so much to me! I felt close to him. There was this little baby girl on the bus – five-and-a-half months old. I felt close to her too. I wished I could hold ~~me~~ her. I just realised what I wrote. I must admit there is some truth in it. That baby related a lot to another baby – the one who by that age was already a victim of incest, the one who was frustrated because she couldn't express herself.

As I was walking along the beach by myself this morning, I was in touch with my emotions – I was emotionally moved thinking of the inner peace I've never enjoyed in my life except during the state of elation. Until then, I had never realised what I was missing out on, because I'd never experienced authentic inner peace. This morning I had an intimate conversation with Margaret (the lady we're staying with). She was very understanding, and to be honest I looked forward to it.

Sunday, 27 December 1987
10:30 p.m.

I spent most of today in bed. It started this morning when I had a panic attack as I was getting ready to go to church. I ended up not going at all – the little girl felt that she doesn't *have to* do anything. She wanted to be free. It all started when I was in the bathroom and noticed Michelle's facial hair.

During that state of regression, I was feeling cold even though it was a nice sunny day. I also had an upset stomach, which reminded me of getting seasick when my mother took me to the main island on the ferry a couple of times, at the ages of seven and eight. I also had a migraine.

I couldn't do any writing for two reasons. First of all, I was too weak to write, and second, I felt so down I couldn't be bothered about the diary. I was sick of analysis, sick of everything. When I was thinking of my childhood amnesia, I felt panicky because of that mental restriction. Could the little girl have experienced amnesia around that age? If that's the case, I could be quite close to a breakthrough. Will I ever have a breakthrough, though?

As I was walking by myself along the beach yesterday evening, I was frightened, especially when I was walking back, and the ocean was on my right side. The sea seemed treacherous to me. The sound of the ocean frightened me too.

P.S. On his way home from fishing, Louie got me a nice bunch of flowers. That meant a lot to me.

Victoria, the analyst, hasn't been there at all, especially when I was in bed. Somehow, I'm not feeling comfortable in this place. What a difference from last year!

We had a barbeque tonight, and at least I enjoyed it.

Monday, 28 December 1987
2:00 p.m.

I've spent the day by myself. The boys went to the Seagulls. Michelle, Margaret and Suzie went shopping.

At about 8:30 a.m., I decided to go for a walk along the beach by myself. Emotionally nothing much happened, except when I saw this fourteen-month-old girl playing on the beach. She did trigger something. However, a thought went through my mind that I was much younger than her when I became a victim of incest. As I was lying down, I noticed that my nipples are sore – another psychosomatic symptom of incest during babyhood.

This morning I noticed that I have been thinking a lot of Dr. Garcia and Stephanie – it must have been the lost child. I also experienced that sense of loss for a while. I can't wait for my first session, to see what my reaction is going to be.

Last night I had a good sleep. I had a dream about male prostitution. The scene was back home at *ħdejn ta' Ħamet* (near *ta' Ħamet*), on the way to Rabat. I still can't figure out why the scene took place there.

I need to write a letter to my mother. I can't wait to see what she will tell me regarding frightening experiences.

P.S. Before I started writing, I didn't have the urge to write. I don't want to even go through my diary. Before we came to Queensland, I intended to go through my diary and arrange an index.

6:45 p.m.

I just finished writing Mum's letter. This is part of what I told her (translated version):

Mum, about three weeks ago I had to see a psychiatrist because lately I have been feeling lots of fear inside me. The psychiatrist told me I have lots of frights/traumas inside me from when I was little, and he asked me many questions to see if I could remember anything. He said it is important that I know what happened to me when I was little, because otherwise the frights will remain inside me. Mum, I would like you to tell me the reason behind these frights. I remember you taking me to Frenċ ta' l-Għarb, and he gave me this special herbal medicine for frights.

Tuesday, 29 December 1987
8:45 a.m.

I have just been reading what I wrote in my diary regarding part of my studies [24 Nov]. Fear struck. I wondered how I managed to write that. It seems I am comparing my own potential. Which part of the 'I' (self) is so frightened? I know I am in a state of regression, not only emotionally but also intellectually. Here's another thought that frightened me when I was reading: 'Later on, when I go over what I wrote regarding my studies, how am I going to put it together?' At the moment this is too much for me, and I can only handle one thing at a time.

At the moment of writing there is fear inside me, and I'm also self-conscious of the hair above my lips – I can feel a few hairs moving with my breathing.

3:45 p.m.

Intuition seems to be coming back to me. I've noticed it this morning and this afternoon. It didn't last for long, though.

This afternoon, before we went shopping, I was angry at Michelle. While I was at the supermarket, I was mentally obsessed by the facial hair above my lips, and I was self-conscious about it. *Then that mental fear turned into an emotional fear. I noticed that when I had fear inside me, the mental fear was not there* – it was the real me who noticed it, and this is an area she wants to look at. While I was experiencing that fear inside me, I kept telling myself that it's going to be all right. I definitely prefer the emotional fear, rather than the mental fear and the psychological torment that goes with it.

I suppose this afternoon's experience underscores the fact that my obsession with facial hair is a disguise for another fear.

I'm glad I'm going to turn this experience in a constructive way. I now need to monitor my emotions in relation to my mind, just like I did before.

Wednesday, 30 December 1987
11:15 p.m.

We just came back from the Seagulls. Overall, I enjoyed the night, especially on the way back home. John had a cassette playing in the car – it was nice, relaxing music. Emotionally I felt close to Louie, who held me close to him. I really enjoyed his touch.

While we were at the Seagulls, Drago wanted me to dance with him. The little girl did not want to please him. She also didn't want to dance with him because she didn't want him to touch her. She didn't want to be forced to dance – she wanted to be free.

I'm afraid today was one of those days when I didn't feel like writing. The analyst wasn't there, nor was the intuition. This morning I enjoyed walking up to 5th Avenue. On the way I fell in love with this three-petal purple-blue flower. I picked one up and cupped my hands around it, just like I did when I was a child. I really enjoyed holding that flower in my hands.

Today I wasn't so obsessed with the fear of facial hair. As I was writing this sentence, I thought of John's photo in the bedroom. That photo does trigger something. It reminds me of antique photos that used to be placed on the tombstones on November 1st.

Yesterday I posted Mum's letter. I can't wait to see what she has to tell me.

Today I've been thinking a lot of Dr Garcia and my next session with him. I wonder what my reaction is going to be!

Saturday, 31 December 1987
10:30 a.m.

New Year's Eve, 1987. What a memorable year! To me 1987 is as important a year as 1952. No wonder there are times that when I was writing 1987 in the diary, I almost wrote 1952!

This is the year when I discovered my real self and embarked on a study that seems to be so important to the real me – the year in which Victoria mastered something regarding self-analysis.

This is the year that witnessed the biggest achievement of my life: being victorious over the power of darkness. I'm afraid I have problems expressing myself at the moment. I have the obsession with facial hair again. It's centred on Michelle. When we were downstairs, I felt panicky when I was sitting on the bench between Michelle and Mark. I felt that restriction; that's when I felt panicky. I had to get up and sit on the end. As I'm writing, I'm experiencing the buzzing in my head. My sister Mary and her family will be arriving soon. That's why I wanted to write, because this could be the last time I'll be writing this year.

I'm disappointed in the way I expressed myself – my emotions were not there. *I said it before, and I'll say it again: the year 1987 is a very important year for me.* I really mean it – in fact, I have tears in my eyes – that says it all.

1:00 p.m.

As I was having lunch with Louie, the few hairs in his nostrils triggered something – it really made me feel sick, and there was fear inside me too. It's becoming clear now that old men make me sick – *qed nibda nitqażżes* (I'm starting to get a repulsive feeling). Even when I come to use Margaret's cutlery – I think of it as second-hand, and it makes me sick.

Friday, 1 January 1988
7:15 a.m.

I've been up since the boys got up to go fishing with Freddie, and I decided to get up, just like I used to do last year. I started preparing an index for the diary, and the first item I jotted down on the rough work paper is 'Studying'. As I started reading on page 71 [17 Nov], fear struck – there was fear of disappointment (I was thinking of Dr. Garcia) and fear of high expectations (I was thinking of my own expectations regarding my original study – our emotions in relation to the brain). There is fear inside me, and there is also a slight obsession about the facial hair on my upper lip, which I have just bleached – pause – that fear is now the fear of loss. I just compared myself with Stephanie.

8:37 a.m.

After experiencing that fear, I went to lie down in bed and felt sleepy.

8:45 p.m.

I had a good day at the Seagulls. Louie won the capsicum competition. He and I felt disappointed, however, about not winning the poultry call, because one of the prizes was a radio clock. We were hoping to win it for Michelle.

Speaking of Michelle, I've noticed I am not close to the kids at all; I have been feeling close to Louie though. Last night, for example, I really enjoyed dancing with him. And today at the Seagulls I enjoyed his company so much that I wished we could do it more often – going out just the two of us.

On the way home, I started feeling obsessed with the fear of facial hair. Drago was driving the car, and I sat next to him and his wife.

What lies behind the fear of my (and Michelle's) facial hair? It not only encompasses so many things (embarrassment, lack of control over it, having to camouflage it), but it also has different interpretations at different times. For example, there are times when I believe it is a disguise for the fear of my mother battering my head and washing my hair, and at other times it's a fear of men.

I must admit that this obsession with facial hair is frightening.

Saturday, 2 January 1988
5:00 a.m.

What a frightening ordeal I went through last night! After I finished writing, the obsession with facial hair got worse. As I was lying in bed I kept saying, 'I *hate* facial hair.' Although I kept saying 'I hate', I was just saying it, because by that time I was emotionally frozen. Everybody was asleep by then – Louie had no idea what was going on. I thought I was going to regress completely and lose touch with reality. I kept asking for God's help – actually, I felt very close to God. After a while, I went on the balcony and sat there by myself, crying while looking at the bright moon, imploring God for help, thinking of other people (not children) that are mentally sick, how frightening this 'sickness' is. I kept telling myself that I'm one in a million, because in spite of that critical ordeal, I felt optimistic. I thought of these people and how much help they need, and I thought of myself doing something to help them.

At one point I felt close to my father and told myself that he must have been a sick man himself to do what he did to me. I even asked God to forgive such people, 'because they don't know what they are doing'. I felt close to Dr. Garcia – I imagined him sitting next to me, trying to reach out to me because he felt sorry for me – *he didn't care how I looked – he just wanted me to allow him to reach out.*

From last night's experience, I can see how desperate I am to regress into my childhood. Complete regression, however, would be a frightening experience for Louie and the kids. Is complete regression inevitable? Is it the only way to find out what happened to me?

I must go now and get ready because we are going to Dreamworld Park.

Sunday, 3 January 1988
3:30 p.m.

Last night after we returned from Dreamworld, I was too tired to write – we came back just before 10:00 p.m. I would like to give a brief account of what happened. When I saw the double-decker bus coming the little girl felt excited, but I had to control my emotions – later on I felt it was not fair for the little girl. On the bus I was extremely quiet – I was sitting next to my sister. While we were at Dreamworld, I didn't feel excited at all. I did think of the little girl, whom I wanted to have a good time. My emotions, however, were at a standstill. I kept looking out for three-year-old girls to see if I could relate to them. When I did spot them, I wondered if they were victims of incest.

I felt close to Louie. While we were watching the film 'The Grand Canyons' on the three-dimensional screen, he kept making sure I was all right, and when there was a picture of smoke (Louie had already seen the film), he covered my eyes to make sure I didn't get scared – it was so nice of him! Even when we were waiting in the queue for the log ride and the raft ride, he kept holding me close to him.

The incident that struck me most was when sitting next to this plant, *iċ-ċaqċieqa*, (I don't know its name in English), it kept reminding me of Kelina ta' la Pawl – I vaguely remember being over at her place when I was little. I suppose that's why I was relating to the three-year-old girls.

This morning when I was at church, I related to this eight-month-old baby boy. His father was holding him, and the baby leaned over his father's shoulder. He was quiet, hardly moving his head, but his eyes kept moving around. He was an observant baby – he really related to me. I also noticed a much smaller baby, about two months old, who was asleep, and a thought went through my mind: 'That baby might be little, but she knows what's going on around her.' I said to myself a few times, 'I'm afraid we underestimate babies', while thinking of Dr. Garcia.

When we went on the beach, I found a sequestered nook on the rocks and spent some time there by myself. The waves dashing against the rocks sounded angry to me. When I reflected upon it, it struck me because that was certainly in line with my emotions – there was stillness inside me. In other words, silent anger. I wished I had the diary with me to write about it. I also wished I was a poet to better express my emotions. I really enjoyed that experience.

I've noticed that when I'm walking along the beach, I keep an eye out for little footprints – this must be the little girl inside me. Speaking of the little girl, Michelle found a small red toy car on the beach. I fell in love with it and want to keep it. When she gave it to me, I kept rolling it over the palm of my hand, and I enjoyed the feeling of it. Even this morning I played with it.

This morning Louie made a comment that made me feel good: 'I don't know why you're worried about your facial hair. I reckon your sister has more facial hair than you.' That really made me feel good, because to me my sister's facial hair is not abnormal.

Monday, 4 January 1988
8:00 p.m.

Dr. Garcia is back at work. I was thinking about him all morning while I was at the Seagulls. I wondered if Ms Jacob gave him an account of what happened to me or whether she left him a report in case she is away. I also wondered if he would be impressed by what she might tell him. The 'little girl' at the Seagulls, however, was an embarrassed girl. She wouldn't know how to communicate with him verbally; the analyst wasn't there at all. She was embarrassed about telling Dr. Garcia about the bad breath. She kept comparing herself with Stephanie. Her self-esteem wasn't there.

Before I started writing, I spent about three-quarters of an hour thinking about my own study. It seems there is still much to be done. I imagined myself in my bedroom, where I spent hours and hours studying my emotions in relation to my mind. How much intuition I had! In spite of the psychological pain, I really enjoyed doing that study. There are times, however, when it doesn't mean anything to me.

Michelle, Mark and Charles went to Surfers Paradise by themselves – they were really looking forward to it. Poor Alex! He wasn't allowed to go. He got dressed and everything – but at the last-minute Freddie wouldn't let him go. Alex cried his heart out, and I felt like crying with him – in fact I did. I felt like hugging him or doing anything to make him feel better. But I knew that at that moment nothing would cheer him up. I don't blame him. All he wanted was to go with the others.

Last night I had two dreams. One of them involved Drago, who was about to have sex with Louie, who had no idea what was going on because he was asleep. I was impressed by Drago's reaction when I caught him by surprise. In the other dream, I went past this mentally ill woman who was sleeping in the middle of the road on the way to the cemetery back home. At first, I ignored her, but then I changed my mind and turned back to see if she needed any help. I wonder how close to the truth dreams are!

There is no doubt I'm identifying with Drago. Yesterday, as soon as I saw him coming upstairs, I had a fright. I felt he had no right whatsoever to come upstairs. This morning I accompanied John to the champagne breakfast at the Seagulls, and we all joked about it because I was 'Mrs. Josimovic'. While I was writing 'champagne breakfast', I thought of Dr. Garcia. I started questioning myself, why I thought of him. I must have identified with him as my mother, because there was a change of emotions.

Pause – As I was lying down, I felt proud of the little girl who wrote the diary. I asked God to help me fulfil this mission. I was thinking of mentally disturbed people. They need help. If only I have a breakthrough in the recovery process of this illness, which seems to have become an epidemic. There are moments when I feel so strongly about this mission. Why do I call it a mission? Every time I think of mission I think of help – to me, mission means help to humanity.

Wednesday, 6 January 1988
4:00 p.m.

I'm disappointed by the weather – these last couple of days have been rainy and windy. I feel irritable too – the baby wanted to have a nap, but I couldn't doze off.

Yesterday I spent some time on the rocks near the beach – I wished I had the diary with me. Today I was thinking of going there again and taking it with me. But I couldn't because of the weather.

This morning Louie, Michelle, Mary and I went up the mountain (Tumgun lookout) – I really enjoyed it. Every now and then I lagged behind. Actually, I have been doing a lot of that lately. I really enjoy it, especially when I pick a flower that I happen to fall in love with. It reminds me so much of when I was little and picked up that blue pimpernel – I feel like a little girl again – the same girl who fell in love with nature so many years ago.

When I'm walking by myself, I feel like I'm living in a world of my own. During those moments I feel at peace within myself. I wish I could express myself better, but I suppose the expression 'living in a world of my own' says it all.

I'm wearing the blue and white striped jumpsuit – it reminds me so much of one of Michelle's jumpsuits when she was a toddler! I'm thinking about what I've just written above regarding expressing myself.

This morning while we were walking on the nature strip, Louie was walking in front of us when all of a sudden, he stopped and held both arms out to alert us. I sensed danger, but because I felt secure, I wasn't frightened. I was curious, and on the ground there was this big frilly-necked lizard with its head erect. I wasn't frightened at all; on the contrary, I enjoyed looking at it. The thought went through my mind, however, that the lizard could be treacherous (it was standing motionless) and was not to be trusted. That's when I started experiencing fear – my legs felt like jelly. From this experience I can clearly see that with security there are no fears. I told Louie that, and he assured me that whenever he is around, he will always protect me. He is so understanding with my emotional fears!

Friday, 8 January 1988
7:00 a.m.

My last day at Queensland – it looks like it's going to be a nice day. I want to make the most of it. Tomorrow we will be going back home to Melbourne. As soon I thought of that this morning, I automatically thought of my home in Gozo/Malta.

Speaking of Gozo, on our way to Queensland the electricity

poles in the wilderness reminded me of the fields *tal-Pergla.* And what about the flowers here? The red hibiscus reminded me of *nanna Vitorja* (grandmother Vitorja), the pink and white flowers reminded me of the same flowers and trees *ta' ġol-lumija* (in the inside courtyard back home), and there were so many other reminders of back home!

The dreams, too, that I've been having took place in Gozo. Last night I dreamt that after coming back from a holiday, among the mail I found a present from my mother – it was a set of doilies. She also sent a set to Marija ta' Grezzja. Marija ta' Garga was in the dream too. I thought of looking for a block of land to build a new house there. Yesterday in my dream, a railway track was built near *Dun Mikalanċ tal-Pejza* and extended to Ġnien Imrik St towards *ta' Garga.* I could see the silver train running on the tracks.

We spent yesterday at Surfers Paradise. I did enjoy it – it was a sunny day, and the clothes I wore looked good on me – the white shorts and the green frilly top.

4:30 p.m.

This is an account of an incident I never expected to record in my diary. I feel reluctant to record it. Anyway, this is what happened. At about 9:30 a.m., I decided to go to the beach where Michelle, Mary and the kids were swimming. For the first time this year, I decided to swim in the surf. Although the waves were rough at times, I enjoyed swimming. At about 10:10 I decided to join Michelle, who seemed pleased to see me swimming. All of a sudden, I saw her battling with the waves. I swam towards her and held out my left hand to help her. While we were holding hands, the tide took us right out. I sensed danger and started screaming for help. My nephew Charles was close to us, and he grabbed Michelle. I was screaming 'Help! Help!', and I kept looking around to find Michelle – I couldn't see her. A man came to my rescue, but I didn't feel safe with him. Two other men joined in and asked me not to panic, because they were lifesavers. That's when I felt safe. As soon as Mary saw us going out with the tide, she went for help – she didn't waste any time. I was told later that I had been caught in a rip.

Since this morning I've been asking myself a lot of questions. Part of me believes I didn't experience *any emotional fears* during this ordeal. Was I then in an emotional regression? Victoria seems to be interested in this incident as part of her study – because of the emotional regression (my emotions were either at a standstill or frozen). I couldn't experience the feeling of fear. Who was actually calling for help? At times I feel I overreacted in my repetitive calls for help, and with that feeling comes embarrassment.

When I was crying for help, I felt angry at other people who knew I was in danger but didn't come to my rescue. As I was writing this last sentence, I felt burning pain in my right wrist and thought of my father. At the moment I have that tingling, blocking feeling in my head.

Louie is lying on the bed, and he is very upset about what happened. He never wanted Michelle to go swimming in the surf in the first place.

Part of me is feeling embarrassed by the way I am expressing myself, but when I think of Victoria that embarrassment fades away – she is proud of me. It's not easy writing, under the circumstances (during regression).

These last few days I have been doing a lot of thinking regarding the Bachelor of Arts. I have a feeling that I'm going to postpone it for next year. First of all, I'm not ready for it because of my emotional problem, and second, Victoria's mission is not accomplished yet – she has a lot of studying to do. She needs time on her own – she cannot feel pressured by any other study. *She doesn't need books for this kind of study – all she needs is her inner self and intuition.*

Saturday, 9 January 1988
8:30 a.m.

As I was in the kitchen this morning, Mary came upstairs to show me something in the newspaper. As soon as I realised it had to do with the dangerous surf yesterday, I felt relieved, and the first thought that went through my mind was, 'So I didn't make a fuss over nothing after all.'

This reaction really struck me. For me, proving I was right overcame the fear of the danger I was in. I was right yesterday when I realised that I was in a state of regression during this ordeal.

According to the article, I wasn't the only one who was rescued yesterday. The little girl wants to show the article to Drago as proof of the danger I was in.

I am still in a state of emotional regression.

I also thought of Dr. Garcia and of expressing myself better to him after reading the article. I was not familiar with the concept of a rip. That word says a lot – including why I couldn't swim towards the shore.

10:00 a.m.

We are just about to leave for Melbourne – part of me feels sad about it.

Sunday, 10 January 1988
5:15 p.m.

Back in my bedroom! We arrived this afternoon. I couldn't

wait to get back. It was a long trip. At one point I was sick in the bus, especially when we were going up the mountains. This time the electricity poles reminded me of the cross Jesus was crucified on. Fear struck as the mountain reminded me of *il-muntanja tal-Kalvarju* (Mount Calvary). To make matters worse, we were seated in the last row near the toilet, and the 'smell' of poo (or rather, the thought of it) made me really sick. I was obsessed with the smell of poo, and I kept hoping that no men would go to the toilet.

Amongst the mail, I had a letter from Dr. Garcia to let me know about the appointment for tomorrow morning. The little girl was excited by that letter. I can't wait for my next session, even though I don't know how to make the introduction – that's the hardest part of the session. I don't know if I should take the diary with me either – I don't think I'll be using it because I haven't prepared an index, and also at the moment I'm not so keen to share what I wrote – I suppose I'm identifying with him. Emotionally there is stillness inside me – silent anger – and I also have a migraine. I'm looking forward to a good night's sleep.

Chapter 15
Victoria

Monday, 11 January 1988
2:00 p.m.

Today I had my first session with Dr. Garcia. I was in an emotional state of regression – there was silent anger. I told him briefly what I mean by that fear of expressing myself due to embarrassment. I said I don't care how I express myself, so long as I get my message through. There were times when I found it difficult to answer his questions – I was, of course, in a state of regression. At times I felt helpless. Since that session, I've been going over what I said and what Dr. Garcia said.

I told him that as I'm talking, I'm analysing every word I say. This really strikes me. I was talking, and as I was talking Victoria was mentally analysing. During those moments (I said moments because I noticed it many times), which part of the brain does Victoria occupy? This puzzles me – it is an area I'm interested in studying. Talking and thinking – what is the relationship between the two? During the above moments, there doesn't seem to be any connection between them.

I'm now thinking of what I told Dr. Garcia when he asked me who is going to read my diary. I answered, 'There are many times when I believe it's going to be read worldwide. It's not an obsession, either, because it's not there all the time.' I also told him that I don't think I'll be studying for the BA this year, mostly because of the other study I'm interested in. ‘I don’t need any books. All I need is my diary, my inner world and my intuition.’ I told him that later on I will be comparing my findings with Freud’s. I said, ‘I don’t know much about Freud – just enough to be interested in him.’

I also told him there are times when I feel frightened about this study, but there are other times when I feel I have the potential to do it.

Dr. Garcia told me that he will see me twice a week – Mondays and Wednesdays.

12:50 a.m.

Still awake in the kitchen. There is something I want to record in the diary. At the end of the last session, Dr. Garcia didn’t open the door for me as he used to – I opened it myself (before I did, I looked at him – I wasn’t sure if he was going to open it himself or not). Every time I imagine myself opening the door, I see this little girl, so little that she cannot reach the doorknob, and there is Victoria opening the door for her. She is also clutching the diary in her hands – the little girl is so tiny that the diary (A3) seems too big for her to carry.

This mental image means a lot to me – it also amuses me. The little girl is so cute, carrying the diary as if it is so precious, and she is proud of it. I wanted to record it here.

Tuesday, 12 January 1988
11:40 a.m.

Still walking around in my nightie. I’ve been awake since 7:00 and have been thinking out loud since then.

As I was working in the kitchen, I was engrossed in my thoughts when all of a sudden, I heard Mark’s voice on the cassette tape I was playing – the one John taped for us in Queensland. As soon as I heard his voice, I 'woke up to myself' and said, 'It's all right Mark. I'm here.' Mark sounded far away from me, as if I were in one place and he in another, and he needed help. I feel so alienated from my family. I know I will be there when they need me – just like when I risked my life to save Michelle's when we got caught in the rip.

It's clearer to me why I've been referring to this study as a mission. It involves a great deal of self-sacrifice – a suffering that is also affecting my immediate family – Louie, Michelle and Mark. I feel so alienated from them – it's heartbreaking at times.

6:40 p.m.

Sitting on my bed – I can't concentrate on my writing because I don't feel secure. Louie is doing the dishes, and the kids went swimming. I want to be completely by myself, uninterrupted by Louie. I must be identifying with him – pause – I cannot settle down emotionally or mentally. On the one hand, I feel insecure because Louie is around, and on the other hand, I'm hesitating to write because I'm thinking of Dr. Garcia. I feel apprehensive about the way I'm going to express myself in writing. Part of me is cautious about expressing myself because she wants to sound impressive; another part of me is frightened of being interrogated and not being able to speak up for herself (I'm thinking of the little girl who tried to express herself properly). By the time I finished that last sentence, I seem to have sorted out the conflict inside me – it was quite a conflict between the little girl (infant) and the other girl, who wants to get attention by writing impressively.

This afternoon, when I was in the car with Louie on the way

to see the accountant to fill out the tax return, *I was frightened of losing my mind and losing touch with reality* and regressing completely into my childhood. That complete regression does frighten me – not because I won't get out of it but because it would be frightening for Louie and the kids. Part of me is frightened about ending up in a mental institution and being at the mercy of other people, no matter how well-meaning – I would be completely helpless. This must be the baby that is frightened. Part of me is frightened that the diary will be destroyed – but *Victoria believes that even if the diary is destroyed, she won't give up – she is quite a fighter*. She is even ready to go through this experience all over again. This is what was going through my mind when I was in the car. That's when the future Victoria and little Victoria met. It was a very special moment for me – I wished I could have recorded it in my diary as it was happening.

I'm identifying with my four-year-old niece as little Victoria. She is the one who wants to tell Dr. Garcia about her findings this morning regarding that part of the problem I have expressing myself.

Wednesday, 13 January 1988
6:30 a.m.

I'm hesitant to write, not because I haven't got the urge to write but because I don't know how to word it. I'm thinking of Dr. Garcia. There is something important I want to write about.

When I got up this morning, I reflected upon what happened late last night before I went to sleep. I was by myself in the lounge listening to music when fear struck – it was a fear regarding my own study. *One of the inner voices seems to be threatened by this study – it's the devil that is behind this inner voice*. I was petrified and I went to sleep.

As I was thinking in bed this morning, I felt different – I wasn't the one who is interested in the study. In fact, I was in a state of denial and told myself that I'm not interested in my study. I imagined having a session with Dr. Garcia, and during the session I kept quiet. It wasn't silent anger either. I was experiencing fear – not the same kind of fear the petrified and terrorised girl experienced – it was a sort of underlying fear. That really struck me. It was the result of a mental fear. I'm now thinking of the saying (or belief) 'We think the way we feel.' This is the other way around. This fear is a result of what happened or is happening in the mind (I'm thinking of schizophrenics). I want to elaborate because I want to use my case as an example.

The little girl I discovered this morning is that 'seductive' seven-year-old girl – *she is certainly frightened of the devil.* I'm afraid I've lost that intuition and cannot elaborate on it. I've been getting distorted thoughts regarding Dr. Garcia. I'm afraid he will ask me questions because I am not expressing myself properly. There is no doubt that I'm identifying with him. I've noticed that since I had my session with him, and it's interfering with my concentration while I write.

10:12 p.m.

Today I took my diary with me when I went for my session. There is conflict inside me – part of me wants to give an account of what happened during therapy, and part of me wants to analyse myself. The latter is more powerful because I have to go with my emotions. Otherwise, I end up having distorted thoughts due to the conflict inside me. I did tell Dr. Garcia about what happened this morning – that I am identifying with him, and it's affecting my writing. I told him that I came across a sentence in the encyclopaedia that really struck me: 'Sigmund Freud conducted an intensive self-analysis, something which psychoanalysts today consider an impossible feat.' I told Dr. Garcia that self-analysis *is* a feat, but it's not impossible. I also told him that I've mastered something. 'I don't know what it is', I said, 'but I do believe I'm on the right track. Trust me' – I was referring to the truth regarding my past. 'You don't need the conscious mind to find the truth. It's in the diary.' I told him that in time it will become clearer to him. I was referring to self-analysis or whatever it is that I've mastered.

Victoria handled Dr. Garcia pretty well today. I felt good about myself – I even experienced a state of elation. However, it didn't last long. She still has some unfinished business with him, and she intends to bring it up again during the next session. I read out an analysis for him regarding the travelling ticket [27 Oct], and the argument he brought up was unnecessary because he concentrated more on what went through his mind than on what went through my mind, and above all he never mentioned the emotion (fear) that resulted from that thought. He could have done that on purpose.

Victoria believes that in psychoanalysis, it's what goes through the patient's mind and its emotional impact that counts, not what goes through the psychoanalyst's mind.[7] As I mentioned above, he could have done this on purpose to see how I would challenge him. He said that if the inspector caught me, he would make me buy another one. I replied, 'It's not for the money, it's the principle of it.' I also said, 'I

[7]As I was underlining this in red, a thought went through my mind: Could this be Victoria's new approach to psychoanalysis? There are times when I believe I will be teaching many things regarding psychoanalysis, the inner voices and other aspects of psychology (the way we identify differently with the same people at different times, the different parts of the 'I' and many others) to Dr. Garcia. That's also why I told him to trust me. If he does, it means he has confidence in me and will be able to learn many things from me.

cannot challenge him, because I'm in a state of regression, and it's his word against mine.'

Thursday, 14 January 1988
12:27 p.m.

Just after midday I experienced a special moment – it certainly was special, even though it was frightening at first.

I was thinking about my self-analysis – which to me means turning myself inside out, metaphorically speaking of course – but to me it's not so metaphorical. I need to be born again. This thought triggered the panic button. I experienced a great deal of fear inside me – it was the baby that was either about to be born or had just been born – apparently, the detachment of the baby from the mother was an emotional trauma for the baby. As soon as Victoria realised what was happening, she started to console the baby; that was her priority. Part of me wanted to record that experience as it was happening. Holding both hands on my stomach, she kept saying, 'It's OK honey, it's all right', and with that reassurance the baby felt better, and gradually the fear started to subside.

This was a special moment for me because through this experience, Victoria met the newborn baby.

I would like to give an account of another analysis I did this morning in the lounge, but I'm having trouble expressing myself.

I'm now thinking of the word 'honey' that I called the baby. In relation to honey I think of sticky and yucky, but at the same time it's *bnin* (good) and *ħelu* (sweet). A few weeks ago, I called the little girl 'sweetie'.

I just had a fifteen-minute pause. During the break I started experiencing an upset stomach, just like when I was pregnant with Michelle – this must be a psychosomatic symptom of the unborn child. I heard a similar expression before – in the Christmas carol that has the words 'a child is born'. I now feel weak. I'm looking at myself in the mirror, and my posture reminds me of women in labour (I'm not covered, my knees are bent and I'm wearing just a t-shirt). Michelle has just been in my room, and her khaki shorts and legs are reminding me of my mother. The unborn baby must be behind these thoughts. As I was saying this to myself, I got the same kind of 'burp' my mother used to get as she talked. This is not exactly a burp, but it's a noise that interferes with your speaking. The air cooler is on, and it's reminding me of water.

Self-analysis is a feat that is not impossible; however, it can be difficult if you want to continue with your life. Maybe I'm saying this because I have *so many unresolved traumas*. For self-analysis, *trid tidħol f'qoxortok* (you need to get into your own shell), because each and every thought that goes through the mind is there for a reason.

12:30 a.m.

In the kitchen by myself. I have the tape on – listening to (I just had to stop writing because I couldn't concentrate while I was listening to the music; apparently, part of me was more interested in listening to that piece of music than writing). The music I'm referring to is the piece that relates to the unborn baby. The sound of the trumpet reminds me of angels. My thoughts then go to this sanctuary *Ta' Pinu* – where babies come from (this is what we were told as kids). There is calmness inside me, and tears have started coming down my cheeks. I really enjoy listening to that piece of music, and I play it over and over again.

Before I go to sleep, I want to give an account of a dream I had last night. In this dream, I was sitting down *fuq iċ-ċint tal-bejt* (on the low, stony fence on top of the roof of our house back home), and my mother was talking to me. However, she wasn't there. I could only hear her voice (as I'm writing this part, I have tears in my eyes). I can't remember the exact words, but roughly she asked me, 'Aren't you going to do the teaching course?' 'No, but I will be preaching psychology', I replied. My mother's voice struck me – it was such a gentle voice, and my mother was so understanding!

As I was sitting on the bed this morning, just after I got up, I remembered that dream, and as I was wondering about the voice, I realised that although it was my mother, it wasn't her voice at all. Sophie, my cousin's wife, came to mind. I wondered why I thought of her, but I couldn't figure it out. While I was having breakfast at about 10:30 a.m., I realised who was behind that voice – it was Sophie Garcia! That's why I thought of my cousin's wife. Her name is Sophie. What struck me also in the dream was why it took place *fuq iċ-ċint tal-bejt*. When we were kids, we used to pretend to talk to each other on a 'telephone' made of two tins or matchboxes attached on a string. One of us would sit on that *ċint* and the other would sit somewhere else. Apparently, the little girl fell in love with Mrs. Garcia's voice when she talked to her on the telephone when I rang up Dr. Garcia. She wants to identify with her as her mother. The interpretation of this dream really strikes me.

Friday, 15 January 1988
11:55 a.m.

I have just experienced a fit of repressed fear. *It must have been the baby that was frightened.* Michelle was sitting on the bed while I was lying down – I noticed the hair on her arms, then I became a bit obsessed by my facial hair above the lips. I kept imagining that bare, masculine arm that used to frighten me when I would go to the toilet at night. (For many years after I came to Australia, I had this fear that a masculine bare hand was going to grab my genital area while I'm sitting on the toilet seat.) That mental fear was only a thought that used to go through my mind; it wasn't exactly an emotional fear. However, the repressed emotional fear associated with this mental fear apparently is still there. *This is certainly repressed fear* – where was it stored? Is the unconscious mind subdivided again? I don't know why I wrote 'again'. Was I unconsciously thinking of the conscious mind instead of the unconscious mind?

When I'm expressing fits of fear, *there are no mental conflicts* – a sign of regression. This is a message to the future Victoria. The little girl, perhaps even the baby, is behind this message.

11:00 p.m.

By myself in the kitchen – Louie and the kids are asleep. I don't feel like writing because about ten minutes ago I had a conflict inside me and regressed to babyhood. I felt sleepy – I had no emotional or mental conflicts. Actually, I've noticed that every time the little girl is faced with a mental problem that is too much to handle, she regresses to babyhood. *Victoria is glad this technique helps the little girl get some relief from the work she is doing.*

The little girl is certainly working hard in helping Victoria discover not only what happened to her during the 'age of darkness' (amnesia) but also lots of other things regarding psychology. Through her, Victoria is learning so many things, which at the moment she wants to share with Dr. Garcia.

Lately I have been experiencing lots of panic attacks, which I have been able to handle pretty well. They don't last long because as soon as I analyse the situation, the panic subsides. I can see that Victoria is truly emerging now – it will be a while before she emerges completely. Apparently, she still needs to work with those negative emotions and mental conflicts – she is not ready to let them go yet.

This evening while Michelle was sitting next to me on the couch, she said jokingly, 'You're not my mother' – i.e. the same mother in the photo (the one in which I'm holding her with Mary, Louie, Freddie and baby Charles on her Christening Day). Then a few minutes later she said to me with a smile on her face, '*Will you help me find her*?' Touching her gently on her arm, I replied, 'I certainly will help you find her.' Yes, Michelle does need to find her mother, a mother who, due to her psychological problems, emotionally deprived her daughter. The little girl will be the one walking hand in hand with Michelle to help her find her mother. As I'm writing this sentence I'm emotionally moved – I now thought of Mrs. Garcia and experienced that sense of loss – the little girl needs to 'find' her own mother first before she helps Michelle find hers.

P.S. The burning pain on my right wrist is back.

Saturday, 16 January 1988
1:40 p.m.

The baby that is about to be born has just experienced that emotional trauma again – it certainly was the baby. While I was going through that emotional state – there was fear inside me *iferfer ġo fija* (stirred fear inside me), not the same fear the little girl experienced during the age of terror – it was a verse of a song on the radio: 'There is freedom within'. I mumbled, 'No there isn't', thinking of an unborn baby inside the womb. As soon as I realised what was happening, I dashed into the bedroom to get the diary because I wanted to record it straightaway. At that point the fear inside me subsided. *This is a very special moment for me because Victoria met the unborn baby.*

8:45 p.m.

As I was sitting in the lounge analysing myself, I realised that the baby is identifying with Victoria and is frightened of her. This is what happened.

When I came into the lounge, I was wondering what happened to Victoria, the analyst (she isn't there). There was stillness (silent anger) inside me, and mentally there were no conflicts. Then I decided to reflect upon something I said while thinking out loud. I can't remember the sentence, but it had to do with the baby. As soon as the baby realised that Victoria the analyst is back, she felt frightened. It's a pity I cannot remember the sentence that proves it was the baby. I have just remembered the key word: *realising*. That word changed the stillness into fear. The word 'realising' reminded me of the baby who, when she realised she was being sexually abused, began experiencing fear.

Sunday, 17 January 1988
10:21 a.m.

After I had a shower and made my bed, the baby wanted to lie down. As I was lying down, the little girl who can't wait to go to school started to cry. She wasn't given a chance by the authorities, just because she has a problem (I was thinking that I am not going to be accepted at the Western Institute). That same girl feels/felt rejected because of her weakness. Then there is that other little girl, who won't be going to school even if she is offered a place, because she will be studying at home. She won't need any books; all she needs is her negative emotions, mental conflicts, sexual sensations/drives, urges and intuition. She needs lots of time on her own; it seems she is not only in search of her real self but also in search of something else, which she can only find from her experiences.

Studying from experience is so different than studying what others have said. This is quite an experience for me. There are moments of despair – however, this is an experience I will never regret. It's not only teaching me so many things, it's also giving me the opportunity to be born again and relive my babyhood. I feel it is a privilege to be given this opportunity to relive my babyhood and find out what happened to me when I was so little. Babies *are* more clever than we believe them to be.

9:45 p.m.

There is so much I want to write about regarding my self-analysis! However, there are times when the little girl feels she doesn't have to do anything, not even write. At dinnertime she rebelled – she had a fit of rage because she 'had to' prepare dinner. During that fit she became angry at her father. She broke down crying when Mark and Louie reached out to console her, especially when Mark said, 'You don't have to do anything.' Prior to that she said, 'But I have to cook.' Yes, the little girl *had to* do lots of things – she had no choice – that's why she gets so angry. When she takes over, she repeatedly says, 'I don't have to do anything.' This morning for example, she felt she didn't *have to* write, analyse herself or even eat. 'I don't have to', she kept saying. That girl was still there this evening. When Louie asked me where a plate should go, the little girl felt panicky because she *had to* think about where it goes.

This reminds me of another part of my study, which I discovered today: *Panic is the disguise for another fear*. This morning, for example, when I was washing my hair, I noticed I was losing a lot of hair. Panic struck. Then a thought/image flashed in my mind – my driving instructor's bald head. Victoria then took over and started reflecting upon the underlying causes of panic. *Panic is an indirect fear*; in other words, it's a fear that, instead of being expressed emotionally as a fear, takes the form of a panic.

In this study I'm conducting, the sequence of the thoughts and emotions is important. I'm referring to the emotions and their effects on the mind and the other way around: the thoughts and their emotional impact.

Monday, 18 January 1988
11:15 a.m.

At 9:40 a.m. I went for the driving test. I passed. I still have to get a medical certificate. When I filled out the application, I told them I have a psychiatric condition, because I wanted to do the right thing. I'm afraid I'm not excited about passing. I just told Mark to tell Irene that I passed. I'm still suffering from anger depression. I said 'still' because that anger depression has been there since I met my testing officer – as soon as I realised it was a woman, I started identifying with her as a nun. The testing officer was understanding when I briefly explained that I'm not on medication because my problem is not cured by medication, and I believe in it. She replied, 'That's the main thing. So long as you believe in it.' As I pointed out, she was very understanding. To the little girl, she was so understanding that she (the little girl) felt she was not going to be *fairly* tested because she was going to be given 'special consideration'. I said with a smile on my face, 'You do your job and I'll do mine' when she told me to pretend she wasn't there. That's not what the little girl wants – she wants challenge.

The little girl is definitely looking for a challenge. Neither the word 'psychiatric' nor 'nervousness' suited her. I'm referring to the form the testing officer had to fill out. That added to the anger.

I have to give myself a lot of credit, even though the feeling is not there at the moment. There is stillness inside me. Mentally, however, I feel so exhausted – a lot of pressure on my forehead. It's just as well that I have mastered the ability to analyse myself. Once I understand what's going on, I feel better. However, I've noticed that with this anger depression I cannot get any relief, even though I seem to have analysed the situation.

I'm now thinking of my mother. I'm looking forward to her letter, but the way I feel at the moment, what she tells me in the letter won't be enough – I'm referring to the challenge, and with that in mind I'm thinking of the burning pain on my wrist.

10:45 p.m.

Just before I went for my session this afternoon, I received a letter from my mum. She didn't tell me anything new regarding my fears. All she said was that the fears I might have had were when I used to see a snake. *U inti qedtli biex neidlek fuq xi qtajja kont tieħu forsi meta kont tara xi serp jien ma nafx li kont tieħu qtajja* (You told me to tell you about any frights, maybe when you used to see a snake, I don't know if you had any frights). The word *serp* (snake) has triggered a lot of fear inside me.

When I was reading the letter, the word *serp* reminded me of incest. When I realised that, I imagined the big red door that I think I talked about in the diary being slammed in my face, and I felt I was being rejected. I asked for help and didn't get it. But with that rejection came inner strength, and I felt strong enough to continue fighting my own battles.

That little girl is crying again. She just touched those two spots on the wrist, which at the moment are burning a lot. She was punished by her father for dobbing him in.

Pause – I can hardly think – I'm experiencing silent anger. I wanted to elaborate more on what happened during my session today. I'm sure by now Dr. Garcia has realised that Victoria has a lot of potential regarding self-analysis, and she is serious about her *own* study.

A comment that I made during therapy was, 'Victoria is not there at the moment. How can she be when there is silent anger?' (However, she was mentally there.) This prompted me to reflect upon that comment, and I realised that Victoria is just there mentally and not emotionally. *She will become a whole person when she is there both mentally and emotionally.* That is an important sentence. I had problems expressing myself, even though I knew what I meant. I'm sure Victoria will understand when one day she comes back to that sentence. The little girl is trying her best to express herself (Victoria is realising that).

Today I also told Dr. Garcia that during his absence on long service leave, I was faced not with one but two emotional problems – one regarding my past and the other regarding the study I have now embarked on. I said, 'Now that I am on the right track, I don't seem to be troubled anymore.' (At that time – 23 Oct. 1987 – I was certainly troubled. I didn't know what was going on – something inside me was definitely guiding me.) And he replied, 'You said you are on the right track. Does that mean you were on the wrong track?' I replied pensively, 'No, I wasn't.' Reflecting upon it this afternoon, Victoria realised how right the little girl was when she said 'No, I wasn't' – that track wasn't there at all.

Tuesday, 19 January 1988
7:00 p.m.

These last couple of hours, I have been trying to figure out what's happening to me physically, mentally and emotionally. I was in an emotionally and mentally frozen state – the same state I experienced a couple of months ago. Victoria was puzzled – she tried to figure out which part of the 'I' is experiencing that frozen state. She thought it was the unborn baby; apparently, she was wrong. The psychosomatic symptoms were trying to tell her so. In addition to the pins and needles I initially had when I became mentally and emotionally frozen, both upper arms became sore, as if someone were holding them tight. I started feeling abdominal pain, and the vaginal thrush I've had these last three days (since the last time I had sexual intercourse) got worse – I was desperate to put on the cream. *Could the little girl be protesting against sex with Louie*?

During my last intercourse with Louie, a thought did go through my mind regarding a wish to avoid sex. Since I came up with that question just before I started writing, I have been identifying/associating Pupull ta' Sodor (a man who lived in the neighbourhood back home) with the man that served me at the Road Traffic Authority building – he was a bit chubby like Pupull. Was the little girl raped by him? If so, this must have been a frightening experience for her. I'm thinking of the fantasy I used to have about him playing the game 'Ring a Ring o' Rosie' in the nude with his own kids and the dream I had involving the wild horse that went tame after sex. This man had a reputation for promiscuity, and it was alleged that he raped my auntie.

Fear is definitely behind this mental and emotional freeze. This morning, as soon as I found out I have been offered a place (accepted) at the Western Institute, the little girl sat down in the front garden and cried a bit because she can't go to school, and after being overcome with *fear*, I started gradually freezing up both mentally and emotionally.

Wednesday, 20 January 1988
7:42 p.m.

The day is almost over, and I haven't written anything yet, not because I didn't have time but because part of me wanted to just sit and think. I'm finding it hard to describe the emotional and mental state I'm in. Besides the stillness inside me, there is some underlying apprehension. During these last two sessions, I have been self-conscious about the way I structure certain sentences, not because of a fear of speaking up but because the way I phrase the sentence makes a lot of difference in what I mean. There is part of me that wants to say *exactl*y what I mean by being as accurate as possible. Could this be the little girl who tried to explain to her ~~father~~ mother what was happening regarding incest? I had a slip of the tongue – the little girl apparently did try to explain or make her father aware that what he was doing was wrong. With this emotional state, there is that tingling feeling and even pressure on my head.

This afternoon, as I was in the waiting room, I related to this little boy about two years old and not to the five-year-old girl. I noticed him wanting to copy his sister in her drawing and in building up the blocks. I was impressed by his talking.

This little girl does not feel like giving an account of what has happened since last night, when I was about to continue with my diary. Apparently, she is so angry she doesn't even want to think out loud. In fact, the last word I said was 'diary'. This is the same girl who wouldn't talk for about five minutes, sometimes even longer at the beginning of the sessions with Dr. Garcia.

This little girl is the same girl who wanted a challenge last Monday when she went for her driving test. I'm now experiencing a great deal of anger tension.

Thursday, 21 January 1988
5:45 a.m.

I've been up in the kitchen since 4:30. When I woke up, I was still in the emotional state I was in last night – I also had an underlying fear inside me. As I felt a bit uneasy, I ended up coming into the kitchen. I kept thinking about the little girl I was still relating to emotionally, namely the one that is (or rather was – she is not there at the moment) angry at her father, who denied what she was trying to tell her mother. It was the same girl who said to Dr. Garcia in therapy a couple of sessions ago, 'Give me time and I'll challenge you. It's your word against mine.'

I was thinking of how that silent anger is going to dissipate. I was looking for something to 'break' that stillness, when all of a sudden I imagined myself sitting on the couch in Dr. Garcia's office. I imagined him sitting next to me. The little girl wanted to be touched by him from behind – she was too embarrassed to face him, but at the same time she *needed* to be touched. As he touched her, she experienced a beautiful sexual sensation that led to an orgasm. Victoria kept encouraging her not to suppress that sensation, and she kept getting orgasms one after the other. The little girl did not have to do anything – i.e. masturbate. All she did was allow herself to be gently touched on her shoulders by Dr. Garcia.

Apparently, she needed to be touched. With that sexual sensation, the silent anger vanished completely. While I've been writing all this, that sensation is still there – I was going to say that it's Victoria who is writing. But a thought went through my mind, 'Why Victoria and not the little girl? And the other way around?' It seems this sensation is one way to link Victoria and the little girl.

I'm going to get ready now – we're going to Mount Bulla for a couple of days. (I feel far away from Louie, as if I have cheated on him by having an affair.) That sensation is still there.

Friday, 22 January 1988
3:00 p.m.

Sitting by myself among the nature at Mount Bulla.

I have just been interrupted by Mark, who seemed quite upset. However, I didn't mind at all because my priority was to attend to Mark's needs. He was angry at his dad's attitude towards him.

I'm now sitting on my bed. I feel weak because I have a terrible gastro. It started a couple of nights ago at about 2:00 a.m., after I had a panic attack in the caravan at Mount Bulla and soiled myself. As I already pointed out, I feel weak. I'll continue with my writing when I get better.

Sunday, 24 January 1988
4:45 p.m.

I have just been packing the baby's clothes in the suitcase. I fell in love with this particular frock that belonged to Michelle when she was a baby – it's a silky pink frock with lace around the neck, short sleeves and bottom hem. I couldn't pack it away – I brought it with me in my bedroom, and I'm looking at it while I'm writing. The emotional state I was in when I fell in love with this frock related to the other little girl inside me, or rather, the other little girl who is still part of me. It was such a special moment that I wanted to record it in the diary.

7:15 p.m.

I have just been massaging my fingers (something I haven't done since I slipped back into depression few months ago), when a thought went through my mind: 'You only want to do your study to get attention from Dr. Garcia.' Who or what is behind that inner voice? Who is accusing me, or rather who is accusing the little girl? This could either be a false accusation (I'm thinking of the little girl who innocently was a victim of incest and frightened of the fire of hell by her mother, as if it was her fault) or a true one (I'm thinking of the little girl who enjoyed incest).

My inner voices so far have been based on accusations and remarks.

Monday, 25 January 1988
8:11 p.m.

It's Michelle's birthday. This morning, as soon as I realised it was her birthday, I felt excited, even emotionally close to Michelle. I wanted to ring her up and wish her a Happy Birthday (she slept over at her auntie's place).

There is anger inside me at the moment. I feel so angry that I'm careless about my handwriting. Part of me, at least, doesn't want to analyse myself. Is this the same girl that had a fit of rage about two and a half hours ago? *That rage was triggered by a fear of the devil.*

While I was lying down on the couch, I thought about the superego. Victoria seems to be interested in who or what lies behind the superego. When I asked myself that question, I wondered whether it's the devil. I thought of the inner voice I had a few months ago when I was embarking on this study. That voice felt threatened. Through inner peace, I found God. I thought that it's the devil who feels threatened. I was frightened – the fear turned into rage. I even turned against God and Our Lady. I ended up feeling a bit angry at my father. When my rage subsided a bit, I went into the lounge and as I was looking down, my eyes fell on the widest part of my toe, where there is no hair. I kept staring at it – it triggered something. It reminded me of a penis.

Could it be the baby that had a fit of rage? Was the fear of the devil a disguise for another fear? Was the baby identifying with the devil, who appeared to be *lying down* and trying to shield himself with his hands from the Archangel Michael, who was about to stab him with a pitchfork? (This is the holy picture on the wall in the bedroom back home.) I talked about this picture in therapy once, and Dr. Garcia asked me, 'What position did the devil have?' I replied, 'He didn't like that position at all.' When I said that, I had a smile on my face. Apparently, it didn't dawn on me that I was in the same position and situation as the devil.

This afternoon the baby rebelled against God just like the devil did (that's what we were told when we were little – that the devil was previously an angel who rebelled against God). That's probably why there were times when *I was afraid I was possessed by the devil*. The baby and the devil have something in common – they were both lying down at the mercy of Michael (my father's name was Michael).

All the rage that came out was in Maltese, except when that

rage was directed at my father, and I called him 'a rotten bastard'.

Tuesday, 26 January 1988
9:35 p.m.

Mark's Birthday! He is thirteen years old.

What a special day – 26 January 1975 – Mark was born. I have just shared an emotional moment with him. I told him what a special boy he is. I shall never forget those moments he sat beside me, comforting me and wiping my tears. Oh, Mark, I love you so much! You're such a special boy! I feel so close to you at the moment – it's certainly a special moment for me, so special that it is beyond description.

How I wish I could express myself better! I wanted to pay tribute to Mark. I don't know what to say. Anger is building up now because I couldn't describe that emotional moment as well as I wanted to.

I feel so angry now that I don't even want to continue with my writing.

Wednesday, 27 January 1988
6:45 p.m.

What's happening to Victoria? I haven't felt her presence these last couple of days. I can't afford to lose her – I feel helpless without her, just like I did during therapy today. I found it difficult to answer Dr. Garcia's questions, and when I did, I wasn't pleased with the way I expressed myself. I felt frustrated.

I can't keep writing. I feel sleepy.

10:27 p.m.

'Handle your emotions, and time will be in your favour.' This is my horoscope for today. It couldn't have been more appropriate.

Today I filled out the form to defer my studies for the Bachelor of Arts at the Western Institute. Part of me is sad about it. Another part of me, however, believes that my study, for the time being, is at home. 'So, your emotional problem is stopping you from studying', Dr. Garcia said today. Shaking my head I replied, 'No, you're wrong.' In other words, it's stopping me from studying in the classroom (that's what I said in therapy), but it's not stopping me from studying at home.

Thursday, 28 January 1988
10:00 p.m.

I'm shrouded in anger depression. Victoria wants to use this mental/emotional state constructively. Since I wrote my last sentence, I have started experiencing emotional anger.

These last twenty-four hours, I've noticed myself slipping back intellectually. I didn't have the urge to analyse myself. I asked myself many times, 'What is happening to me?'

Anger is so destructive, not only emotionally but also intellectually. It seems to freeze a big part of the brain. (That's the only way the little girl could express herself – Victoria just realised that.) I'm glad Victoria is back. At one point I thought I had lost her. I feel so safe with her, even though she makes me aware of my 'split personality'. However, this split personality doesn't frighten me at all.

(I was just interrupted. Irene came to pick up Marlene).

Friday, 29 January 1988
4:20 p.m.

At the moment, there is a conflict between Victoria, who wants to write in the diary, and this other little girl I have just discovered. She is apprehensive about writing in the diary, not because she is frightened of what happened to her, but rather, she is frightened of finding out the truth about herself. She seems to feel responsible for what happened to her, and therefore, she not only feels embarrassed but also guilty. She seems to be saying, 'Oh, no' to Victoria, who wants to find out more about her, and Victoria has been assuring her, 'It's all right. Whatever happened to you is not your fault.' She is the same girl who wanted male attention. These last couple of days, every time she tries new clothes on, she thinks of Dr. Garcia. Yesterday I tried on this black skirt and yellow shirt, and this morning I bought a khaki jumpsuit.

As I was lying down, before I discovered this little girl, I thought of this man on Channel 10 who reminds me very much of Marcell, and when Michelle and Mark came to tell me that they were going swimming over at Irene's, I thought of the *ġibja* (a small reservoir where the water pumped up by the windmill was collected in the fields back home) where we used to go swimming as kids. This little girl would be about seven years old. The thought went through my mind, 'What if I'm wrong?' – as if this little girl *wants* to be wrong.

Saturday, 30 January 1988
8:09 p.m.

Although the day is almost over and I haven't written anything, I still felt close to the diary – I did not avoid it deliberately. I just had a busy day, and I wanted to feel at ease before I wrote.

I'm glad I discovered that little girl yesterday – like the other little girls, this little girl took over, and she kept 'troubling' me until I discovered her. I couldn't analyse myself, and I wasn't interested in my study. Since I discovered her, she seems to have quieted down a bit emotionally. *It's amazing how powerful emotions are – they are really like a driving force.* That's why I used the word 'troubling' before.

Today I also discovered that part of me is vindictive and seems to be happy about what happened to me in the past. This morning, for example, the little girl felt angry at her father, and that part of me (I'm not sure if this is the little girl I discovered yesterday or part of an overall personality) was pleased to see me angry. They ended up having a clash – the former called the latter a rotten bitch. Even this afternoon, when the little girl was frightened because she felt she *has to* write a letter to my mother, that same vindictive part of me was pleased to see me frightened.

Could this vindictive part of me be an alternative to direct or channel my anger? I'm now thinking of silent anger, which apparently is another way to direct my anger at myself. *The difference between these two ways of directing my anger is that the former is more obvious, while the latter requires more skill to identify.*

Sunday, 31 January 1988
2:37 p.m.

I just had a mild fit of rage at Michelle, who wanted me to bake a cake. I wanted to come and write. No doubt I identified with Michelle and projected my rage towards her.

These last twenty-four hours I've been reflecting upon what I wrote on page 78 (20 Nov) regarding different ways of identifying. The more I think about it, the more I'm realising how right I was when I wrote that we are possessed by other personalities. It explains so many things.

It's now becoming so clear to me who is behind the inner voices and why I have so many conflicts (both emotional and mental). And what about the swearing in Maltese? This afternoon, for example, I realised that when I am identifying with my father, I get angry just like he used to and start swearing. Again, I feel I am so much like my father, as if he is the one who is swearing.

Pause – During the pause I've been thinking about the double identification, i.e. when we identify with people outwardly (when I identify with Michelle, for example) and inwardly (when one of the parts we possess takes over, just like when 'my father' gets angry, and I start swearing). When I get those fits of rage, it's one (or even more) of those parts/personalities that is angry. When it's more than one, they are *at war* with each other. I have already talked about this in my diary [8 Nov]. These last twenty-four hours, I have become more and more aware of it.

It's the fear of the devil I experienced a few days ago that prompted me to reflect upon the inner voices and possession by the different parts/personalities. During my last session I talked about that incident, and because of the emotional state (fear and anger) I was in, I didn't think about my discoveries [20 Nov]. When Dr. Garcia reflected back to me that I am possessed by the devil, it sounded strange to me – I suppose I was so frightened that unconsciously I didn't want to believe it.

Chapter 16
Self-Understanding, Past Trauma and Healing

He who does not know himself is lost.

—Mahatma Gandhi

I decided to stop here with the journal entries for practical reasons. Overall, I handled it well. However, there were times when I found it quite challenging and confronting to go over these experiences. The intensive work I put into this diary is acknowledged. The question now is, 'Where to from here?'

Besides the personal experiences, these diary entries focused also on Victoria and future study. Over the years, as I continued with my introspection, inner work and diary entries, I could see that the study I embarked on involved many theories, and I eventually felt I was dealing with a Weltanschauung (a world view of an individual or group) as an overarching construct. Whether or not this is the case remains to be seen. I do know that I came up with a model that helped me a lot in terms of understanding my inner world, including my relationship with the outer and inner worlds and the subsequent healing process. For the purpose of this memoir, I would like to focus on highlighting some elements that played a significant role in my power over darkness and the convoluted inner drama.

Unpacking the Self and the Inner Drama

When I started the inner journey of self-discovery, I identified a number of parts of my self – including the little girl, the real self, the old self, the emerging self, the future self, the father and mother in me, the devil and God. I remember having a dream that took place at the *setaħ* (a corridor outside the bedroom upstairs) back home. In the dream there was a projector, which was projecting a photo of myself taken with my mother and brother when I was about seven years old. The projected picture was made up of many pieces, which gradually formed together as that image of myself as a little girl.

Over the years, as I continued with this journey of self-discovery, I became familiar with the significance of myths, the inner drama, archetype characters, fables and fairy tales. I also became more open and receptive to various gods and goddesses. This certainly helped me take my self-understanding to another level and enriched my healing process. There is a lot to say about this. However, for the purpose of this memoir, I am limited in how much I can include.

One such character was Maleficent. When I related to that part of myself, it was horrible and terribly painful. I used to be ferocious (to myself), and I couldn't bear to look at myself in the mirror. It was emotionally draining. It usually manifested itself when I was close to a new insight. The rage that came with it was so strong that in hindsight, I am quite surprised I did not end up having a heart attack or stroke. What a painful process to get to the dark recesses of the soul and bring out my demons! However, as part of the healing process I needed to befriend and nurture this part of my self through a lot of inner work.

The identification of my *inner voices* and who was behind them was a significant part of the process of self-understanding, inner freedom and healing. I called them 'inner voices' because they were directed at me from the 'other' – the subject was 'you', as if someone else was speaking to me. These inner voices were quite complex. However, through my introspection I managed to unpack them and deal with them accordingly. This process eventually restored order in my chaotic inner world – both mentally and emotionally.

The need to attend to these voices became paramount from the beginning of my inner journey, as I was vulnerable to them. I could see they needed to be identified and heard. They also needed to be allocated to the subjects (parts of myself) behind them, as I was dealing with such a fragmented self, and handled accordingly. *The need to deal with them from the perspective of the inner child was imperative***.** I needed to allow her to experience the fear, shame, guilt and anger (including silent anger and rage), without trying to rationalise them as an adult. It also helped me empower my inner child and provide her with the opportunity to give the fear of the truth revealing itself, guilt and shame back to whom they belonged, thereby freeing myself from such heavy burdens.

These inner voices provided me with lots of insight into what had happened to me. One such inner voice accused me of lying. This was quite a tricky one, in the sense that it came indirectly to me. The inner voice was *not* in Maltese. However, the analysis of an experience I had during the time of writing the diary indirectly indicated that as a child I was accused of lying and *ma tafx x'qegħda tgħid* (not knowing what I was saying).

Another inner voice was the voice of the superego, which is

well-known in psychoanalytic theory. This voice is characterised by its imperative approach: 'You have to do this, and you have to do that.' It usually involves a fear of negative consequences. For me this voice was powerful, especially during vulnerable times. It came to the forefront when I used to go to confession and when I was experiencing neurosis and obsessive thoughts. It was when I took the family skeletons out of the cupboard and dealt with them that I eventually subdued this voice. What a relief!

The 'devil' and its inner voice is also quite an interesting one. I created a cultural character to represent evil. Another way of putting it is that I personalised evil as if a person were behind it. As a child and for many years as an adult, I really believed in the devil as an alien character. I still remember clearly the moment when I started rebelling against the Catholic Church and the priests who had instilled such debilitating fear in me over the years through the concept of the devil. In my rage during the journey of self-discovery, I wanted to chuck them to the smaller island of Comino and leave them there, without contact with the laypeople. At times I even wanted to tie a *mażra ma' għonqhom* (huge rock around their neck) and throw them into the sea, making sure they would not resurface. I cannot emphasise strongly enough the psychological damage done to me through the fear of the devil. During the course of my inner journey, I came to realise there is no such thing/alien as a devil. Indeed, it is the humans, including my parents, who are the 'devils'. *That realisation eventually led me to an inner war between good and evil in the year 2000*. And what a war it was, characterised by enormous rage! It is all recorded in my sketchbook – in addition to the written diary. And yes, the former won – at least on one level.

As part of the process, it was important for my inner child to *befriend the devil.* It is important to point out that the devil not only represented evil but was also considered an enemy. As time went on, this character started to fade away. So did my vulnerability to it. What a relief! No words can describe it. Since that war between good and evil, I have entered a new dimension where there is no division between good and evil. There is also no judgemental self; no laws are required, and yet there is no anarchy. This dimension is characterised by compassion and understanding.

Other voices were repressed and surfaced up from 'darkness', namely the unconscious mind. I'm referring to the voices in Maltese: *Tarraqlek qalbek, issa ġiek il- ħara* (Damn you, you had to have a shit now); that I was stupid and *ma tafx x'qegħda tgħid* (does not know what she is saying); and *ibki kemm tiflaħ* (cry as much as you can), with a tone suggesting no compassion whatsoever. Once they surfaced and provided me with insight into what happened to me as a child, these voices formed an elite choir that sang the symphony to which I danced and danced (and still do). They also added quite a richness to the landscape of my inner world as I travelled through my journey of self-discovery.

Another aspect of myself that was predominant throughout my life, including the time when I embarked on my journey of self-discovery, was the judgemental self. This highly judgemental self and the subsequent fear originated from the judgemental God I was brought up with – until I reached a highly significant moment in my life when I continued delving into my past in 1988. I remember standing in the kitchen, in the same place I had been when I had the insight regarding being a victim of incest. My inner voice said, 'Do not censor anything that goes through your mind, no matter how horrible it is.' That was a turning point for me. I was open and receptive, and I was determined to go down that path without fearing any negative consequences. This was quite a shock to the system, as censorship was deeply ingrained in me. Censorship with regard to 'bad thoughts' was one of the golden rules of Catholicism when I was growing up. It was my highly judgemental self, fear of God and the subsequent punishment that was the driving force behind such censorship.

Creating a Secure Base: Expressions of Anger and Fear

The abovementioned inner voice telling me not to censor anything in my mind was one of the highlights of my inner journey of self-discovery and the subsequent healing process. This required quite a leap of faith. For the first time I entered a new dimension of myself, where I experienced a sense of freedom to express my thoughts (and associated feelings) without fearing any negative consequences. There was unconditional love I had never experienced before – as a child or as an adult. I identified in myself a secure base. That was quite a milestone to reach. I soon realised those thoughts were there for a reason, and I needed to understand my inner drama. So were the emotions that surfaced as I regressed and relived my childhood. One such emotion was anger and rage.

It appears that as a baby, I was already able to express silent anger. This became evident during my regressions. As I grew older, the 'little girl' was behind the fits of rage I expressed. She was not in a position to express such anger, for fear of rejection and abandonment as well punishment by God. Getting angry at your parents was considered a sin. The little girl was also expected to be obedient to her parents and do what she was told without question.

Going back through my diary, I can see that back in 1987, when I was thirty-five years old, I was still not in a position to direct my anger at my parents, even though I consciously tried. There was quite a gap between my mind and my emotions – even a non-alignment between them. I displaced my anger towards God and Our Lady, who represented my father and my mother, respectively. I will never forget a psychotic state during which I expressed a fit of rage and directed it at Our Lady of *Ta' Pinu*. I had this holy picture in a frame in the kitchen. I broke it to pieces, squashed the picture and threw it in the rubbish bin. Not being satisfied with that, I got a paring knife, opened the bin and kept stabbing the squashed holy picture for several minutes. Then I got out of that state and felt close to God, as an image of the 'little girl' hugging Jesus came to my mind – she came up to his knees. I also felt that I did not need to apologise to God because he understood what I was going through, and I had every reason to be angry.

I kept displacing my anger at other people (besides God and Our Lady) for many years, even though at one level I was aware of it. To keep the alignment of my thoughts and emotions, I allowed it to happen. I wanted to give myself *freedom* to express my anger without fearing any consequences. This was quite confronting and challenging for me, as anger/rage was usually accompanied by vengeful thoughts. So, I decided to send an aura/light that was impenetrable and shrouded that person, to protect them from evil while cursing or wishing them evil as a result of my rage. Such urges were quite common, and this strategy was helpful to me not only to purge myself from rage but also to overcome my fear of the consequences.

From my experience, the inner child harnessed a lot of anger that needed to be expressed. That anger was expressed through fits of rage and silent anger beginning in 1987, and it continued for some years as I progressed on my journey and had further painful insights into my past. It was important for me to allow that expression of anger to take its course while I was in that state. It was an opportunity for me to walk the talk – I was showing and allowing my inner child to *experience my unconditional love*. I believe this was critical for me as part of the healing process. As I mentioned in my diary with regard to hostility, it also helped me purge myself by getting rid of those feelings (at least at one level) and replacing them with love, more specifically with compassion and understanding for the emerging self.

Speaking of understanding, the inner child, especially at a very young age, cannot reason. As mentioned above, it was imperative for me to view situations from *the inner child's perspective* without trying to reason with her. I therefore allowed her to express her feelings without being judgemental or fearing any repercussions. She needed to express her feelings from a secure base. And I provided her that base, which had not been available to her when she was growing up. At another level, I knew that although the sexual, emotional and physical abuse could not be justified, I gradually became aware that we are all victims of victims, and unless the abuse and other wrongdoings are identified and dealt with, the chain of such behaviours is likely to continue from one generation to another, as will the traumas that come with them.

I remember one particular experience at the beginning of my inner journey, when I had a realisation about my own negative attitude/hostility towards my daughter and how I was behaving the same way (up to a certain point) as my own mother. I was sitting on the couch where the kids were playing. Upon that realisation I stood up, went to Michelle and Mark and put my arms around them, saying 'I want to break this chain.' That was the first step towards changing my behaviour, especially towards Michelle. The realisation that I was identifying Michelle with my parents and projecting and displacing emotions was also helpful to me in breaking that chain. Indeed, all the intensive, hard and painful work I did over so many years, within the context of my inner child, has certainly paid off in more ways than one.

The same can be said about the expression of fear. From my experience, there are various types of fear – including repressed fear. The traumatised little girl who was subjected to many frightening experiences was still fully alive within. She surfaced from the depths of the abyss after she felt secure enough to do so, and I was open and receptive to her.

The fear about my daughter's fine facial hair growing out of control and making her look like a monster was another type of fear. What psychological torture accompanied that fear! It was the creation of a secure base that eventually led me to realise the 'monster' was my mother and father.

Depression: Loss, Grief and Anger

Within the first few months of my inner journey of self-discovery, I realised there was much unresolved loss and grief behind my depression. I could see I'd experienced significant loss from an early age, especially when I was tied up by my mother and made to witness her having sex with my father, to show me that my father was hers, not mine. What a horrendous trauma! Its psychological impact on me was enormous. In 1963 I suffered another loss when my sister Carmen died. She was thirteen years old, and I was eleven. I never grieved her death. I remember laughing at her funeral. I was not able to process such emotion because the environment was not conducive. Instead, I learned to use a defence mechanism to deal with it, thereby getting stuck in the grieving process. The same thing happened when both my grandmothers died during the '60s. When the caretakers came to take the body of my grandmother for the funeral service, I remember going upstairs and putting my hands over my ears because I did not want to hear my mother crying!

As years passed, I also discovered I had a twin sister who was murdered at birth by my mother and kept as a family secret. I have named my twin sister Angelique. There was grief over her loss. Through this memoir, I want to give Angelique a voice and make a public statement about her existence.

On Friday, 11 June 1999, I identified another significant loss. This loss was projected on Fr Daniel, who became a very significant person to me in my journey of self-discovery and healing. I had rung him a few days earlier, but he did not return my call. I also sent him an email, but he did not reply. I was not aware that he was away at camp for a few days. I felt I had lost him. The intensity of this pain was excruciating. I eventually could see there was something else going on behind this loss and started questioning it. I woke up at 2:20 a.m. doing intensive inner work, including questioning what was behind this loss, and I had an insight. This is what I wrote in the diary: 'It seems that the heartache behind this Significant Loss that entails such an intensity of pain is in relation to the *Loss of the Self/core of the Self – including the little repressed girl.*' What a painful process to get to the core of my being! I was and am so blessed to have such insights and bring to light what was behind my depression. As the saying goes, 'Knowledge is power.'

Anger was also behind my depression. As a child I did not feel safe to express my anger, especially when it involved my parents, mainly because it was a 'sin'. The environment was not conducive and did not feel safe. I could not even direct my anger at God, since I had been told God was responsible for whatever happened to me. Instead, I internalised my anger, and it turned into depression. And I continued doing this, not only as a child but also as an adult.

No one can fully understand the experience of depression and how it feels unless they have been down that path. It is characterised by complete darkness and helplessness. There is no sense of hope that you will eventually get out of it. *The flame within is extinguished.* I can quite confidently say that at one level, the state of depression is also characterised by the absence of the spirit, or driving force, of life. It takes great courage and strength to navigate your way through it and eventually come out of it.

Unresolved Trauma and the Truth

Throughout life, I experienced a lot of psychological pain and suffering without knowing what was behind it. As I embarked on my journey of self-discovery in 1987, I also started to experience a number of physical pains and other symptoms that had no medical or other apparent explanation. According to psychoanalytic theory, these are called psychosomatic symptoms. These included burning pain on my wrist, abnormal heat in my legs, pain in the groin, lack of sensation in my right arm and hand, a feeling of suffocation and abdominal pain.

Upon intensive self-analysis, these symptoms provided me with a window into the painful past experiences that had been blocked from my consciousness and trapped in the dark recesses of the unconscious mind. These symptoms provided another medium for my inner child to communicate with me and eventually show me what had happened in the past. In other words, this was a way of finding the truth. Indeed, once I had an insight into the underlying traumas, the symptoms disappeared. I may not remember what happened to me, and no recollections of the traumas have surfaced as a result of this journey of self-discovery. However, whereas recovered memories can be questionable or possibly false according to the literature, the symptoms and the resolutions of their underlying traumas are evidence of the truth. So are the insights I had.

These insights come from a space that goes beyond believing. It is a space where *you know*. It is important to point out that the inner journey was not linear. In spite of my insights, I still had to go through a challenging process of doubt, denial and fighting the dark inner forces that attacked me left, right and centre, until eventually I surrendered to the truth. The path to healing is still a work in progress, especially when I think of specific insights. However, I have come a long way in terms of healing.

Feelings of Affection and Connection

I don't think anyone can fully comprehend the feelings of affection and connectedness unless they experience their absence. This became evident to me when I experienced that state of elation in 1987, when I had so much inner freedom and inner peace. I fully experienced the feeling of affection towards Louie, Michelle and Mark like I never had before. This was very much intertwined with the sense of connectedness I also experienced with them and the environment around me and beyond. I remember saying to myself, 'I never knew what I was missing out on.' And then, as I plunged into the throes of depression, I lost those feelings again. I longed for those feelings so much!

As time went on, I started experiencing the feelings again from time to time, and I was more mindful of them when they happened. I am now in a much better position to experience emotional connection and affection, not only with my immediate family but also with other people. This is a real milestone for me, considering the lack of such deep emotional connection I had for so many years. What a beautiful, warm and energising feeling! Many times, for example, if I feel exhausted and happen to have a call from my children and granddaughter Monique, and I experience that emotional connection, all the exhaustion disappears. This is certainly an integral part of my holy grail.

The Self and the Integration of the Parts

As mentioned above, I identified a number of parts of myself that were highly distinctive and even had lives of their own. In spite of this fragmentation, I still managed to maintain a sense of who I was as a focal point of reference.

Two of the parts I want to focus on are the old self and the real self, and what the latter now means to me. Whereas the real self was distinct from the old self that was characterised by 'negative emotions' (fear, shame, guilt, jealousy, hostility, anger, anxiety, doubt, loss), I have now integrated it with the main self within the context of my self-discovery and the traumatised inner child, including the unborn baby and the baby who had something to tell me through the repressed fear that surfaced on 15 January 1988.

The old self was also the self that lived in darkness, not being consciously aware of the traumatised little girl, through amnesia in childhood and beyond. Over the years, this old self was highly disturbed and mentally and emotionally persecuted, especially when I had various psychological breakdowns. This is also the one that was deprived of enjoying my daughter's babyhood and childhood through the obsessive fear of her fine facial hair growing out of control and making her a 'monster'. Last but not least, this old self is also the one that was deprived of joie de vivre (joy of life) most of the time. In spite of all this, I soldiered on and continued with my life to the best of my ability.

The old self is also intertwined with the protective part of myself that kept my traumatised inner child hidden in a deep, dark dungeon until I was ready to discover her. In protecting myself, however, I also created another part of myself that felt like a prisoner tied up in chains, deprived of so many things, including its existence. The way she could express herself was mostly through *depression and panic attacks.*

The integration of the old self with the real self was a long and painful process. The new, real self did enormous inner work with the emerging self before I could finally bring the hidden self to light. The climax of this integration was reached in the year 2000, when a spiritual marriage took place between good and evil. This gave rise to the dance of love by the opposites (dark and light; male and female) and the subsequent birth of a renewed spirit and a new integrated self.

There is a lot to say about this self. However, all I want to say here is that this self is characterised by compassion and understanding. I have embraced the people who hurt me in the past, including my parents, and the subsequent pain and suffering – at least at one level. I say ‘at one level’ because the model I developed and have been working with has two levels. At the other level, the self that has been traumatised and hurt (as well as all other parts of the self) will always be there – imprinted in me. I now operate and function through the new integrated and renewed self – most of the time. I have gone beyond the critical and judgemental self. In everyday situations, I am more responsive than reactive. Compassion and understanding are at the forefront.

Dethroning and Re-Creating My Personal God/Goddess

During my inner journey, the notion of God was important to me. In addition to searching for my inner self, I was also dealing with 'God' and finding out who or what God is. I came to realise this perception of God was in fact a projection of my own self – that is, a higher self that is part of me. This became clearer to me during this journey, as I continued to question the existence of God. When I experienced inner peace during the time of elation, I believed I had found God. As time went on, my perception of God began to change. I started seeing God as both male and female. I identified and honoured the goddess in me. I also found other gaps in the teachings of the Catholic Church and became open and receptive to different gods and goddesses. This has certainly enriched my understanding of myself in many ways. I do believe in a higher self that exists in each and every one of us.

Having a Catholic background, I had lots of people, including a Maltese nun, try to comfort me by reminding me that Christ also suffered and died for us on the cross. For me that was not comforting at all – far from it. It even infuriated me, because 'Jesus was not betrayed and sexually abused by his own parents.' The subsequent psychological pain and suffering was (is) incomparable. That prompted me to ask the question, 'Where is God?' during such times.

I started to see God as being *magħffeġ* (intertwined/immersed/suffering/helpless) with me as I was in the abyss of depression, going through rings of fire, walking on hot ashes, finding my way through thick jungles and crossing deserts, fighting all elements unprotected – at times attacked from all directions. Through such perception, I came to realise that at one level, I needed to **re-create** my own god/goddess through my pain and suffering, within the context of my personal experiences. On another level, I needed to **dethrone** God and the goddess and make them experience the depths and heights of my psychological pain and suffering. I even made them accountable for what had happened to me. This process started by dethroning my own parents within the context of my insights.

As time went on during my journey of self-discovery and healing, I needed to turn my belief about God and forgiveness completely upside down! Whereas I had believed I needed to ask God for his forgiveness, as I had been taught via the Catholic Church, *I came to realise God also needed to ask for MY forgiveness for having put me through such pain and suffering*. I also realised that according to the model I was using, *I needed to ask for forgiveness to my own parents and other perpetrators for having to commit such abuse towards me for me to be WHO I AM!* This was quite a paradigm shift, but I did it. As part of the healing process, I wrote a number of love letters to my parents, asking for their forgiveness. Even mentally, I imagined being with other perpetrators and asked for *their* forgiveness.

I know this can be challenging and controversial to the reader. But I would like to point out that as part of the journey and the healing process, we need to deal with both – as victims as well as perpetrators of the same experience, including the higher self. We are both the master and the slave, male and female, dark and light – indeed, we are the opposite selves and have their respective characteristics. As part of the healing process, we need to deal with them to get to the highest dimension, where there is no division.

The State of Elation and Inner Freedom

Early in my inner journey of self-discovery, I experienced a period of what I called at the time 'a state of elation'. I did not know what else to call it. It was the complete opposite of depression. I was fully alive, highly energised and at the same time thoroughly grounded. This state was characterised by inner peace and inner freedom like I had never experienced before. I also felt emotionally connected to my loved ones and beyond, as well as to the environment. Creative writing came to the forefront, and I could not wait to sit down and write. This was a state of great flow during which my activities were effortless. There was also a lot of joie de vivre.

As I lost that state and experienced the throes of depression once again, I questioned the state of elation many times. I could see it was *not* the result of my inner work with regard to incest and other sexual and physical abuse, because it was quite premature. I could see that something special had happened, but I could not name it. I could also see that I related to another part of myself in relation to the future – the part of myself that related to the truth/Truth, had a good understanding of what had happened to me, felt healed and experienced inner freedom from the shackles and bondage that had enslaved me for so many years. That same self was also free of the dark forces that so resisted the truth coming to light.

A few years later, I happened to listen to an interview with Dr. Robert Johnson, a Jungian analyst, in which he spoke about the holy grail on the radio. According to him, at first it is given to us as *gratis* – a gift. Then it disappears, and after a lot of hard inner work we regain access to it. It may not be there all the time, but it is accessible. That made a lot of sense to me, and I started to look at it as my holy grail.

In 1999 I went to a retreat at St Paul's missionary residence at Wantirna for a few days. One night I woke up at about 2:00 a.m. and started doing inner work. Then I had an insight: it is the inner child that holds the key to the holy grail. Again, that made a lot of sense to me and consolidated what I already knew: namely, how central the inner child is to my inner freedom and subsequent joie de vivre.

The self that experienced that state of elation became both the end and the means of my inner journey. For many years I believed strongly that I *will* regain that state. As years went on and I did not regain it, I eventually lost that hope. But I continued with my life, especially my academic achievements. Once I finished my doctorate thesis and graduated, I tried to write for publications but without success – even though I tried different genres. Although I knew I wanted to write about my personal experiences and journey of self-discovery, somehow, I could not go down that path. I even made a pact with myself and said, 'If you want me to write, take me back to that state of elation when I had so much flow, and I will write.' I did not want to subject myself to all the pain and suffering I had gone through to write my doctoral thesis. No words can fully describe that part of my journey.

As years passed, I took detours in my inner journey of self-discovery. I stopped writing the diary and the love letters to my inner child and other parts of myself, as well as my parents. I even stopped introspecting, more specifically analysing myself. I became sick of it. I focused more on the healing process using the model I had developed, especially with regard to forgiveness.

Towards the end of the year 2020, although I was (and still am) quite pleased with my role as a re-elected Councillor in local government, I could see that I had come to another crossroads in my inner journey. I did a lot of soul-searching. It was clear to me that it was time to embark on this chapter of my life – to start writing my memoir. I needed to take the bull by the horns and do it – even though I did not experience the flow to write as I had during the state of elation. I could see that I needed to go through the ring of fire once again.

I am now close to finishing my memoir. I may not have regained my holy grail to the extent I experienced it in 1987. However, I have come quite a long way, and I am pleased to say that most of the time I am experiencing elements of it – including inner peace, a great sense of gratitude and appreciation, connectedness, compassion and understanding. I am also experiencing freedom from the chaotic inner world, shame, guilt, doubt, inhibition, jealousy, fear and the dark forces that tried to stop me from coming to the light for so many years. I am more responsive than reactive in my interactions with other people and certainly more connected to members of my family and beyond.

In the Introduction, I referred to the castle I am heading toward as I walk alongside my inner child. I/we have now entered the castle. However, there is still some trepidation in moving around and experiencing its richness. I cannot help thinking of Marianne Williamson's quote: 'Our deepest fear is that we are powerful beyond measure. It is our light, not our darkness, that most frightens us.' There is still some work to be done to prepare my inner child to present this memoir to the inner queen/goddess. The presentation will take place when I hold a hard copy of this published memoir. This will be a deeply spiritual experience for me and the greatest achievement of my life.

About the Author

Growing up in a staunch Catholic and traditional village on the island of Gozo, Malta, Victoria experienced what appeared to be a 'normal' childhood. At the age of thirty-five years, she found out that she had been carrying a highly traumatised inner child that she kept hidden from her own self.

The subsequent journey of self-discovery is unique and inspirational as manifested in the diary entries. These provide the reader with a window into the chaotic inner world of a highly mentally disturbed person. And at the same time, they portray a beautiful mind as well as a Spirit that proved to be victorious over the power of darkness – including acute depression, anxiety attacks, obsessive thoughts and psychosomatic symptoms. Many times, Victoria reached the point of not only losing the battle but also the war against mental illness. Although her case is unique, it resonates with many people one way or another. Feelings of loneliness, alienation, abandonment, betrayal, rejection, shame, loss and fear are common to the human experience.

Victoria's strong determination to find her real self as well as her passion to embark on an intensive study of herself gave her a strong purpose in life as she clawed her way through life as a wife, a mother of 2 children and an academic student while on the journey of self-discovery. The path to reconciliation and healing is also highly insightful.

Dr Victoria Borg was an academic for many years, specialising in mental health across cultures. Her academic journey as an under- and post-graduate student was highly challenging. It was compounded by acute episodes of depression and anxiety as it coincided with her journey of self-discovery. In spite of this, she forged her way through and won a number of awards along the way.

Currently, Victoria is serving her second term as an elected Councillor in Local government at the City of Brimbank, Melbourne, Australia.

www.ingramcontent.com/pod-product-compliance
Ingram Content Group UK Ltd.
Pitfield, Milton Keynes, MK11 3LW, UK
UKHW021052270726
13967UKWH00012B/591

9 781737 442523